MULTIDIMENSIONAL SCALING

VOLUME I
Theory

MULTIDIMENSIONAL SCALING.

THEORY AND APPLICATIONS IN THE BEHAVIORAL SCIENCES

EDITED BY

Roger N. Shepard

Department of Psychology
Stanford University
Stanford, California

A. Kimball Romney

School of Social Sciences
University of California
Irvine, California

Sara Beth Nerlove

School of Social Sciences
University of California
Irvine, California

VOLUME I
Theory

SEMINAR PRESS   1972
New York San Francisco London
A Subsidiary of Harcourt Brace Jovanovich, Publishers

SEMINAR PRESS, INC.
111 Fifth Avenue, New York, New York 10003

United Kingdom Edition published by
SEMINAR PRESS LIMITED
24/28 Oval Road, London NW1

LIBRARY OF CONGRESS CATALOG CARD NUMBER: 74-187260

PRINTED IN THE UNITED STATES OF AMERICA

CONTENTS

Introduction to Volume I

Roger N. Shepard

A Taxonomy of Some Principal Types of Data and of Multidimensional Methods for Their Analysis

Roger N. Shepard

A General Survey of the Guttman-Lingoes' Nonmetric Program Series

James C. Lingoes

A Model for Polynomial Conjoint Analysis Algorithms

Forrest W. Young

Individual Differences and Multidimensional Scaling

J. Douglas Carroll

Nonmetric Multidimensional Techniques for Summated Ratings

David Napior

Linear Transformation of Multivariate Data to Reveal Clustering

Joseph B. Kruskal

The Geometric Representation of Some Simple Structures

Richard L. Degerman

Information Distance for Discrete Structures

John Paul Boyd

Structural Measures and the Method of Sorting

Scott A. Boorman and Phipps Arabie

CONTRIBUTORS TO VOLUME I

Numbers in parentheses indicate the pages on which the authors' contributions begin.

PHIPPS ARABIE, Stanford University, Stanford, California (225)

SCOTT A. BOORMAN, Society of Fellows, Harvard University, Cambridge, Massachusetts (225)

JOHN PAUL BOYD, University of California, Irvine, California (213)

J. DOUGLAS CARROLL, Bell Telephone Laboratories, Inc., Murray Hill, New Jersey (105)

RICHARD L. DEGERMAN, University of California, Irvine, California (193)

JOSEPH B. KRUSKAL, Bell Telephone Laboratories, Inc. Murray Hill, New Jersey (179)

JAMES C. LINGOES, The University of Michigan, Ann Arbor, Michigan (49)

DAVID NAPIOR, University of California, Irvine, California (157)

ROGER N. SHEPARD, Stanford University, Stanford, California (1, 21)

FORREST W. YOUNG, Psychometric Laboratory, University of North Carolina, Chapel Hill, North Carolina (69)

OTHER PARTICIPANTS

JAMES S. COLEMAN, Department of Social Relations, Johns Hopkins University, Baltimore, Maryland

DAVID G. HAYS, Program in Linguistics, State University of New York, Buffalo, New York

STEPHEN C. JOHNSON, Bell Telephone Laboratories, Inc., Murray Hill, New Jersey

PAUL KAY, Department of Anthropology, University of California, Berkeley, California

ROBERT KOZELKA, Department of Statistics, Williams College, Williamstown, Massachusetts

KENNETH LUTTERMAN, Social Science Section, National Institutes of Health, Bethesda, Maryland

JOHN M. ROBERTS, Department of Anthropology, Cornell University, Ithaca, New York

WARREN S. TORGERSON, Department of Psychology, Johns Hopkins University, Baltimore, Maryland

PREFACE

Workers in an increasing variety of behavioral and biomedical sciences are using multidimensional scaling and related methods of clustering and factor analysis in their attempts to discover structures underlying the observed relations among stimuli, concepts, traits, persons, cultures, species, or nations. Indeed, developments have been so rapid since the introduction of the computer-based "nonmetric" methods just ten years ago that workers in one field are often unaware of the emergence of methods that, though developed in a quite different field, may be directly applicable to the very problem with which they are currently struggling.

In an effort to counteract this situation, two of us (Romney and Shepard) jointly organized an advance research seminar on recent theoretical and methodological developments and on substantively significant applications of these developments in a wide range of social and behavioral science fields. The present two volumes are the tangible output of that seminar. The first focuses on the primarily theoretical and methodological developments while the second presents a variety of applications in such diverse fields as anthropology, psychology, political science, and marketing research.

The seminar was sponsored through the auspices of the Mathematical Social Science Board. The Board is financed by a grant from the National Science Foundation (GS-547) through the Center for Advanced Study in the Behavioral Sciences, Stanford. We are grateful to the Mathematical Social Science Board and the National Science Foundation for their support.

David Hays, a member of the Board, who originated the idea for such a conference, had invited Roger Shepard to undertake its organization. Independently, A. Kimball Romney was planning a conference of the same sort specifically oriented toward applications in anthropology. When the two of us learned of each others' plans (by each inviting the other to his own conference!) we decided to integrate our very similar plans into a single Interdisciplinary Advanced Summer Research Seminar. The resulting combined seminar was held near the campus of the University of California, Irvine, in June, 1969.

Copies of the papers initially contributed by the participants were circulated to all participants in advance of the seminar. These papers then served as a basis for the discussions conducted at the seminar. Following the seminar each author revised his paper to take advantage of suggestions and criticisms that arose during the discussions. The final versions of these papers make up the two volumes. Sara Nerlove has taken the major responsibility in working with each author on editorial revisions and in writing the introduction to Volume II. Part of the work of Romney and Nerlove was supported by NIH Grant MH17468–02S1.

It is our impression, shared by all participants, that the seminar was unusually stimulating and productive. We believe that, despite their diversity, the papers form a coherent contribution to the current state of knowledge of multidimensional scaling. Students and researchers concerned with problems of discovering or interpreting patterns or structures in data from diverse fields of social, behavioral, or biomedical science may find them useful.

CONTENTS OF VOLUME II: Applications

INTRODUCTION TO VOLUME I

Roger N. Shepard

STANFORD UNIVERSITY
STANFORD, CALIFORNIA

The Purpose of Multidimensional Scaling

Increasingly varied and powerful techniques for the analysis of data of several of the types collected in the social and behavioral sciences are loosely subsumed under the term "multidimensional scaling." The unifying purpose that these techniques share, despite their diversity, is the double one (a) of somehow getting hold of whatever pattern or structure may otherwise lie hidden in a matrix of empirical data and (b) of representing that structure in a form that is much more accessible to the human eye— namely, as a geometrical model or picture. The objects under study (whether these be stimuli, persons, or nations) are represented by points in the spatial model in such a way that the significant features of the data about these objects are revealed in the geometrical relations among the points.

The resulting spatial representation or "scale" resembles more traditional scales such as those of mass, temperature, or intelligence in that it attempts to capture fundamental properties of the objects under study solely by setting them into correspondence with positions within a spatial continuum. It differs from these simple unidimensional scales however in that, in order to capture the full complexity of the data, the points may be allowed to assume positions within a two-dimensional plane or even within a three- four- or higher-dimensional space as well.

The Problem of Dimensionality

In most cases one seeks a representation of the lowest possible dimensionality consistent with the data. Clearly, a lower-dimensional representation is more parsimonious in that it represents the same data by means of a smaller number of numerical parameters (the spatial coordinates of the points). Moreover, to the extent that fewer parameters are estimated from the same data, each is generally based upon a larger subset of the data and, so, will have greater statistical reliability. Finally, and perhaps most significantly, a picture or model is much more accessible to human visualization if it is confined to two or, at most, three spatial dimensions.

On the other hand, one cannot reduce dimensionality arbitrarily without running the risk of doing some violence to the data. A representation of one or even two dimensions just may not be rich enough (in total degrees of freedom) to accommodate the full complexity of the relations in the given data. Still, it is a fact of decisive practical significance that most applications of multidimensional scaling have yielded interpretable and sometimes even enlightening representations in no more than three and, indeed quite often, in only two spatial dimensions.

Multidimensional Scaling and Factor Analysis

This matter of dimensionality and hence visualizability tends, in practice, to distinguish these relatively new methods of multidimensional scaling proper from the related methods that have long been used in the social sciences under such names as "factor analysis" and "principal components analysis." True, there is nothing inherent in the factor-analytic methods that requires that they always yield a representation of high dimensionality. Indeed, there are a number of cases—including analyses of data from sensory psychology and from Osgood's "semantic differential"—that have yielded readily interpretable results in as few as three dimensions. Nevertheless, in most social-science applications, the standard factor-analytic methods have in fact led to representations of as many as five, ten, or even more dimensions.

Such results cannot, of course, be cast into the form of a readily visualizable picture. In fact, they are usually presented in the very same form as the original data themselves—namely, as a large matrix of numbers (the coordinates for the points in the high-dimensional "factor space"). In some of these cases one may come to wonder whether the underlying structure that we seek is not almost as badly hidden in the final matrix of coordinates as it was in the original matrix of raw data. It is not surprising, then, that factor-analytic studies often place heavy reliance upon still further (and sometimes controversial) methods of analytic rotation to "simple structure," of "cluster analysis," or the like, in order to discover what interpretable patterns still remain hidden in the resulting factor matrix itself.

The high dimensionality characteristic of factor-analytic results is in part a consequence of the rigid assumptions of linearity upon which the standard factor-analytic methods have been based. To the extent that appreciably nonlinear relations exist among the underlying variables governing the phenomenon under study, there remains the possibility that a more flexible, nonlinear method of factor analysis would lead to a lower-dimensional, more visualizable representation.

Such a notion has been at least implicit, for some time, in Guttman's concepts of the "simplex" (Guttman, 1955) and, more generally, the "radex" (Guttman, 1954). However Guttman's novel ideas along these particular lines have not had an extensive practical impact as yet, owing perhaps to the unavailability of sufficiently general and workable nonlinear methods for actually recovering the low-dimensional spatial representation corresponding to any radex structure that may lie latent in a set of data. A promising aspect of some of the newer multidimensional scaling procedures is that they appear to provide, for the first time, a general way of implementing this quite different and potentially more visualizable approach to factor analysis (Shepard & Carroll, 1966).

The Problem of Interpretation

Generally, of course, a representation obtained by any of these multidimensional methods should not be regarded merely as and end in itself. The primary purpose of such a representation is to enable the investigator to gain a better understanding of the total underlying pattern of interrelations in his data and, hence, to decide what further observations, experiments, or modifications of theory will most advance the science as a whole.

Part of this desired gain in understanding may be achieved through the identification of (new) directions or axes through the spatial representation that can be given compelling substantive interpretations. Thus we may note that, as we move farther and farther in some particular direction through the space, the points that we successively encounter correspond to objects that possess more and more of some particular, identifiable property. We can then conclude that this property—unlike properties that do not have any discernible relation to the spatial representation—played an important role in whatever process gave rise to the data.

Again, this procedure of finding interpretable axes becomes considerably more difficult and uncertain when the number of dimensions exceeds what can be immediately apprehended in a picture or model. Still, if all of the potentially significant properties can be specified and quantified in advance, analytic procedures are available for finding directions through the space that correlate optimally with each such property. In any case, it has been customary to look for interpretable axes in the solutions obtained by multidimensional scaling and by factor analysis alike. And, certainly in the case of multidimensional scaling, the interpretations that have been made in this way have sometimes provided a useful insight concerning the number and nature of the basic processes, factors, or variables governing the phenomenon under study.

The discovery of interpretable axes is not, however, the only way in which a meaningful pattern can be found in a spatial representation. In many cases it has turned out that a quite different aspect of the spatial configuration—such as the way the points cluster into several homogeneous groups, or the way the points are ordered around the perimeter of a circle—constitutes the most interpretable aspect of that configuration (e.g., see Degerman, this book, Volume I). Often one may not even know in advance which of these possible structural features of the configuration will be most susceptible to meaningful interpretation. In such cases it is clearly hazardous to leave the analysis to any rigidly prespecified analytic method which, necessarily, must rest upon some specific, though perhaps implicit, assumptions about the features to be interpreted. Here again we see the clear advantages of a low-dimensional pictorial representation, in which the investigator can simply look for interpretable features without having to specify in advance exactly what form these must take.

The History of Multidimensional Scaling

Historically, the first of the two major phases in the development of multidimensional scaling proper culminated in the perfection of what has, by contrast with later developments, come to be referred to as the "classical" or "metric" approach to multidimensional scaling. It might also be called the "Princeton" or, more specifically, the "Torgerson" approach. For although some mathematical groundwork was laid by others (notably, Young & Householder, 1938), classical multidimensional scaling appears to owe its initial inspiration as well as its full development largely to people associated with Gulliksen's psychometric group at Princeton University—including Messick and Abelson (1956) and, principally, Torgerson (1952), who first achieved a generally workable method of multidimensional scaling proper. Torgerson's (1958) textbook, which has long been regarded among psychologists as the classical treatment of theory and methods of scaling in general, includes a comprehensive presentation of the results of this first phase of the developments in multidimensional scaling in particular.

The second phase began some ten years later and 30 miles to the northeast of Princeton, at the Bell Telephone Laboratories, with the development of what is often termed the "nonmetric" variety of multidimensional scaling. Sometimes it is also referred to as the "Shepard–Kruskal" variety, in recognition of the initial introduction of this approach (under the name "analysis of proximities") by Shepard (1962a, b), and the closely following conceptual and computational improvements added to this approach by his mathematical colleague Kruskal (1964a, b). Since then, and in order to deal with data of increasingly diverse types, numerous methods deriving in one way or another from this new approach have been devised not only by Shepard and Kruskal but also by many others—including J.-J. Chang, S. C. Johnson, E. T. Klemmer, L. Nakatani, M. Wish and, particularly, J. D. Carroll (all of the Bell Telephone Laboratories), as well as J. De Leeuw, T. Gleason, L. Guttman, J. C. Lingoes, V. McGee, E. I. Roskam, W. S. Torgerson, F. Young, and others (elsewhere).

Although it falls somewhere between rather than within either of these two phases, a third, independent development, which has had an appreciable influence on some aspects of the second phase, should also be noted. This is the conceptualization by C. H. Coombs and his students at the University of Michigan of a variety of models for the multidimensional representation of ordinal or "nonmetric" data (Coombs, 1964).

The specific methods devised by Coombs and his students have not been widely used for multidimensional analyses of actual data. One reason for this may be that the methods have lacked sufficient formalization to be converted into computer programs and, so, are not manageable except with a relatively small number of objects. Another, less remediable reason is that these methods fail to extract the very substantial metric information that is implicitly contained in the given "nonmetric" data and, so, do not provide the kind of highly constrained, uniquely picturable, and rigidly rotatable sorts of spatial representations now obtainable by the newer methods. Still, even if some of Coombs' *methods* have been superseded in this way, a number of his *models*—most notably his "ideal points" or "unfolding" models (including their multidimensional elaborations by his students, Bennett and Hays)—have served as a basis for some significant extensions of the newer methods (by Carroll, Kruskal, Guttman and Lingoes, and others).

Some Special Features of the New Approach

The methods and applications presented in this volume are mostly within the spirit of the newer, "second-phase" approach to multidimensional scaling. The now very rapidly spreading use of these methods throughout the social sciences, seems to be a consequence of several advantages inherent in this newer approach.

We have just noted that the newer methods, unlike the nonmetric ones described in Coombs (1964), are able to yield tightly constrained, metric representations. Nevertheless, even these newer methods are referred to as "nonmetric." This is to signalize the fact that they—in contrast to the still earlier, "metric" methods perfected by Torgerson—are able to do this without taking account of any more than the merely ordinal relations in the data (Shepard, 1962b, 1966). This seemingly paradoxical ability of these newer methods to extract quantitative, metric information from qualitative, nonmetric data is especially attractive to workers in the social sciences. For, their data so often come from human subjects, observers, or informants who can readily and reliably give only ordinal judgments (e.g., that one subjective magnitude exceeds or falls short of another—without being able to specify by how much); or who, if they do give actual numerical ratings of these subjective magnitudes, give ratings for which the only trustworthy properties are the merely ordinal ones (e.g., one can specify that one number is larger than another—without being able to attach any significance to the exact numerical difference between them).

A second important advantage of the newer methods derives from their emphasis upon a close coupling of the final result to the original data. In some of the earlier methods, one first estimated tentative interpoint distances on the basis of the data, and then computed spatial coordinates on the basis of those tentative distances—but without any reference back to the original data. Consequently, no assurance was provided that the final spatial representation achieved what one would most desire in the way of an optimum fit to the initially given data. By contrast, the newer methods, though interative, do provide this kind of assurance. In them, each successive iteration—far from simply adding another step of removal from the initial data—is specifically designed to provide a still closer fit to those same data (Shepard, 1962b, p. 243). This feature of the new approach first attained a fully satisfactory formalization with Kruskal's (1964a) clear statement that we should always seek to minimize an *explicitly defined* measure of departure from perfect fit.

A third, closely related feature of the new approach is the ease with which it can be generalized to new situations. Problems that seemed insurmountable within the framework of Torgerson's original approach could easily be overcome in the newer, iterative methods. These included— in addition to the very central problems of coping with merely ordinal data—such further problems as are posed by cases in which some data are either entirely missing or, at least, should be differently weighted, or cases for which some non-Euclidean metric is desired for the spatial representation (Shepard, 1962b, p. 243). Again, Kruskal's (1964a) formalization of this iterative approach which provides for optimization by standard, gradient methods has significantly facilitated the subsequent extension of this approach to a whole host of related multidimensional problems—such as those of nonmetric factor analysis, transformation to an additive structure (or "conjoint measurement"), "ideal points" analysis (or "multidimensional unfolding"), multidimensional representation of individual differences and of pair-comparison data, cluster analysis, and "parametric mapping." (See the overall taxonomy of types of data and methods for their analysis presented in the chapter by Shepard, this book, Volume I; and, also, the descriptions of other, recent methods in the chapters by Carroll, Kruskal, Lingoes, and Young, Volume I.)

The Basic Nature of the Shepard–Kruskal Development in Multidimensional Scaling

The conceptual basis of the new, nonmetric variety of multidimensional scaling is—in the elementary form originally formulated by Shepard and Kruskal—extremely simple. We are given, for every two "objects" (i and j) in some set of n, a datum s_{ij} representing the similarity, substitutability, affinity, association, interaction, correlation, or, in general, "proximity" between them. We seek, simply, that configuration of n points in the (Euclidean) space of smallest possible dimension such that, to an acceptable

degree of approximation, the resulting interpoint distances d_{ij} are monotonically related to the given proximity data in the sense that

$$d_{ij} < d_{kl} \quad \text{whenever} \quad s_{ij} > s_{kl}$$

In order to apply the gradient method and, hence, to find the optimum
configuration of points, the only further specification required is an explicit
function to measure the to-be-minimized departure from the desired
monotonic relation between the given proximity data s_{ij} and the distances
d_{ij} (which are computed among the points in the configuration reconstructed during each iteration). Then, one simply employs an algorithm
according to which the coordinates for the points are adjusted, during each
iteration, in the direction of the (negative) gradient of that function until
the "stationary" situation is reached in which the gradient vanishes
and—barring entrapment in a merely local minimum—any further adjustments could only make the fit worse.

Most of the functions that have been adopted as a measure of departure
from monotonicity resemble Kruskal's "stress" measure in that they are
based, in one way or another, upon the sum of squared discrepancies
between the actually reconstructed distances d_{ij} and corresponding numbers
$\hat{d}_{ij}$ that minimize this sum subject to the constraint that they are monotonic
with the corresponding s_{ij} in the sense that

$$\hat{d}_{ij} \leqslant \hat{d}_{kl} \quad \text{whenever} \quad s_{ij} < s_{kl}$$

However, Guttman's (1968) "rank-image principle" does something of this
sort by what amounts to an inverse of the procedure originally used by
Shepard (1962a). Most of the other variations in the measures used have
to do with relatively minor differences in such things as the normalizing
factor employed. (See Kruskal & Carroll, 1969; Young, this book, Volume
I.)

In any case, experience suggests that, when they are applied to the same
set of data, the various methods of this general type—whether they are
called "proximity analysis" (Shepard), "smallest space analysis" (Guttman
and Lingoes), or simply "nonmetric multidimensional scaling" (Kruskal
and others)—usually yield virtually indistinguishable results. After all,
monotonicity is a rather well-defined notion and any reasonable way of
evaluating it could be expected in practice to lead to similar results.

For any of these iterative methods, it is necessary to provide a starting
configuration of points in a space of some trial number of dimensions.
The starting configuration can be entirely arbitrarily or randomly generated, or it can be constructed in some rational way on the basis of the
given data—perhaps by using a variant of Torgerson's classical, metric

procedures. The rational starting configuration, since it is bound to be closer to the final, optimum configuration being sought, may have the advantages (a) of cutting down the total number of iterations required and, more importantly, (b) of avoiding entrapment in merely local minima. Except in special cases (e.g., of one-dimensional representations or "city-block" metrics), however, such local minima have not been a serious problem and, whenever they are suspected, one can usually circumvent them by repeating the process with several different, perhaps random starting configurations.

The Determination of Number of Dimensions and Orientation of Axes

If, as in the usual case, the appropriate number of dimensions is not already known in advance, a separate best-fitting configuration can be obtained in spaces of one, two, three, or even four dimensions. One can then choose among these alternative representations in order to achieve the desired balance between parsimony, stability, and visualizability, on the one hand, and overall goodness of fit to the data on the other. And there generally *is* a trading relation between these two since, as the number of dimensions increases, goodness of fit always improves but, necessarily, at the expense of the factors related to parsimony. Four considerations are relevant to the final choice of dimensionality:

1. The residual departure from monotonicity (i.e., "stress") should not be too large or, still more pertinently, should not drop too abruptly as further dimensions are added. (Ideally, if stress is plotted against number of dimensions, the number of dimensions chosen will correspond to an "elbow" where this curve first approaches zero and then declines only very slowly thereafter.)

2. The representation should be statistically reliable. In particular, if solutions are obtained separately for two independent sets of data (or for two independent subsets of the same set of data) and if these two solutions are rotated into optimum correspondence with each other, then the n points should project in essentially the same orders on corresponding axes of these two representations. (This kind of agreement will tend to break down if the representations are permitted to have more dimensions and, hence, degrees of freedom than the amount of data will reasonably support.)

3. The representation should be interpretable. If substantive inter-pretation can be given for the way the points are arranged in the space as

a whole (for example, but not necessarily, by interpreting a complete set of orthogonal axes in the space), it is reasonable to conclude that the dimensions are all real. If, however, the representation cannot be interpreted in its full dimensionality, it may be because the parameters of the representation are too numerous and therefore dominated by error in the data. In this case a representation of lower dimensionality should be tried.

4. Except in the case of special methods that do not require the rotation of axes for interpretation (such as Carroll's INDSCAL, see Carroll, this book, Volume I; Wish, Volume II), the representation should be readily visualizable and, so, confined, whenever possible, to two or, at most, three spatial dimensions.

In practice the last two of these four criteria—and particularly the very last—have often been decisive. Certainly it is contrary to the whole spirit and purpose of this approach to data analysis to focus exclusively on goodness of fit (the first criterion) and, so, to go for a representation of so many dimensions that the structure is no longer accessible to the human eye.

With regard to the problem of interpretation, it is essential to understand that (in the standard Euclidean case) the orientation of the configuration of points generated by the iterative process is often completely arbitrary with respect to the coordinate axes. (In fact it is determined primarily by the particular orientation arbitrarily chosen for the starting configuration.) For, clearly, the interpoint distances d_{ij} (which are being fitted to the data s_{ij}) are strictly invariant under rigid rotation of the entire configuration of points. This means that the axes will generally be properly interpretable, if at all, only after a suitable rotation. But, more than this, it means that it is entirely unjustifiable to try, as has been done in some published studies, to interpret (or to compute correlations with) the projections of the points on the initially obtained, unrotated axes. It is only in the cases of non-Euclidean metrics and certain other special cases—most notably, Carroll's new method for dealing with individual differences (Carroll, Volume I)—that the axes that come out of multidimensional scaling can be expected to be interpretable without further rotation.

Problems and Possible Limitations of Multidimensional Scaling

However great its potential, multidimensional scaling cannot—any more than any other single type of tool—meet every need of the investigator who is trying to interpret a set of data or to revise a theory. In particular, it may serve as a guide—but never as a substitute—for careful under-standing or creative thought. In this connection, we should perhaps take note of three rather specific ways in which multidimensional scaling may be limited or even limiting.

First, and most obviously, many kinds of data that are collected in the social or behavioral sciences just are not of a form suitable for analysis by the available methods. Some sets of data are too fragmentary or unstable to support the determination of a well-defined spatial representation; while other sets, even though essentially complete and reliable when considered in themselves, are of a basically incomplete or inappropriate form when considered as an input for multidimensional scaling. (For example, data that concern only the relation of one thing to each of n others are insufficient for this purpose; we must also have some information about the relations *among* those n others. See the taxonomy of usable types of data in the chapter by Shepard, Volume I.) Fortunately, this first kind of limitation is relatively innocuous in the sense that it does not entail any serious hazards for the investigator.

Somewhat more troublesome is the fact that, even when the data *are* of a superficially appropriate form to be used as input for a particular multidimensional scaling method, this is no guarantee that they should be so used. Indeed, that particular method may be quite unsuited to the job of asking—let alone of answering—the right questions for those particular data. Worse still, the fact that just certain types of methods are readily available, may lead an investigator to choose the kind of data he is going to collect solely on the basis that they be of the superficially correct format for one of those methods, without ever giving careful consideration to the question of what sort of data are most likely to provide a real insight into whatever phenomenon is under study. (Some of these kinds of limitations of multidimensional scaling are discussed, in the context of marketing research, in the chapters by Green and Carmone, and by Stefflre, Volume II.)

Finally, and most worrisome of all, it can happen that the availability of a certain kind of method for the analysis of data can subtly influence an investigator to accept the formal model underlying that method as a substantive model for the phenomenon under study—to the exclusion of other quite different and perhaps more fruitful substantive models. (A cautionary note of this kind is sounded, particularly, in the chapter by Boyd, Volume I.)

The nature of this last kind of hazard is rendered somewhat obscure in the cases of particular methods of multidimensional scaling by the fact that it is difficult to state precisely what properties an underlying phenomenon or process must have in order to be strictly consistent with the model assumed by such a method. (Consider, for example, that any symmetric matrix of proximity data can be fitted exactly by a monotonic function provided only that we go to a spatial representation with a sufficient number of dimensions. And, also, see the comments concerning "constraints" in the data, in the taxonomy presented in the chapter by Shepard, Volume I.) Some headway is nevertheless being made on the problem of making explicit the substantive implications of various multidimensional scaling models (e.g., see Beals, Krantz, & Tversky, 1968; Boorman & Arabie, this book, Volume I).

Perhaps the best we can say about these problems and limitations of multidimensional scaling at the present time is that the more fully these methods and their limitations are understood, the more useful and less hazardous will they become. It is the hope of the editors of this volume that the papers presented here will go some way toward achieving the desired understanding among researchers in the social and behavioral sciences.

Organization of Volume I: Theory

In this first volume we present a series of nine papers concerned with theoretical and methodological aspects of multidimensional scaling and related issues. Each of these does one or more of the three following things: (a) It demonstrates a specific new method (Kruskal) or set of methods (Carroll) for multidimensional scaling. (b) It surveys and interrelates a number of existing methods designed to deal either with a particular class of problems (Carroll) or to deal with a variety of problems from a particular point of view (Lingoes; Shepard; Young). (c) Or it examines some of the problems of measurement and representation of structure either within the framework of multidimensional scaling proper (Degerman; Napior) or from a somewhat different point of view (Boorman & Arabie; Boyd).

During the conference, for which these papers were originally prepared, the participants became increasingly aware of the difficulty of keeping track of the numerous methods and computer programs that were being bandied about under names that ranged from those as general as "multidimensional scaling" to those as specific as "M–D–SCAL IV." At the conclusion of the conference it was generally agreed that it might be quite helpful to include in any published proceedings of the conference an attempt to bring some order or structure into this bewildering profusion of terms, methods, and programs.

Accordingly an overall "taxonomy" of types of data and methods for their analysis was attempted by Shepard, and is included here as the first of the papers—together with the apologies of the author for those biases that his close identification with the developments that have grown out of the "group at Bell Labs" has undoubtedly occasioned.

Hopefully, such biases are at least in part offset by the inclusion, next, of the paper by Lingoes, which surveys the most extensive series of programs for multidimensional scaling that has originated entirely outside of the Bell Laboratories; namely, the series arising from the geographically distributed collaboration between Guttman, of the Israel Institute of Applied Social Research in Jerusalem, and Lingoes, of the University of Michigan in Ann Arbor. Although a number of the programs in this series appear to be essentially equivalent to ones developed by Kruskal, McGee, Shepard, Torgerson, and others, there are some differences in such things as generation of starting configuration or choice of the particular measure of departure from monotonicity to be minimized. In the long haul, even relatively minor differences of these sorts could prove to have practical advantages of hastening convergence or of avoiding merely local minima or "degenerate" solutions. Moreover, some of the methods in the Guttman–Lingoes series provide for new and potentially useful options of analysis, and still others—such as "multidimensional scalogram analysis"—represent distinct departures from existing methods. It will be particularly interesting to see during the coming years what happens as these latter, rather different methods are applied to data of real substantive interest.

In the next paper, Young is concerned not so much with computer programs per se as with a general, formal framework within which to generalize and to interrelate algorithms for a variety of methods for multidimensional analysis. He does this under the rubric "conjoint analysis." However, it should be kept in mind that his usage of this term represents a considerable extension beyond that usually accorded to "conjoint measurement" (as, for example, in the taxonomy presented by Shepard). In any case, Young succeeds in bringing into rather crisp focus a number of formal relations among a wide variety of algorithms that have been developed by other workers. He also provides quite explicit indications of how such methods can be generalized in several promising ways.

There is a point that might usefully be made here about all new methods of the general sort considered here—whether they have been cast only in the form of abstract mathematical algorithms (as in the paper by Young), or whether they also have been translated into concrete computer programs (as in the paper by Lingoes). This is that there is generally no way to be sure how useful a new method or program will be in practice until it has been put to an adequate test against real data. A number of nonmetric methods of these sorts that have looked quite promising on paper have subsequently been found to be attended by problems of slow or uncertain convergence, to be excessively susceptible to so-called "degenerate" solutions, or to yield results that are not appreciably different from those obtainable by the previously available and much less costly metric methods.

A reassuring feature of the paper by Carroll, from this standpoint, is that it does include a number of illustrative applications of the methods that he has developed (with the programming assistance of Mrs. J.-J. Chang). In part, this is a reflection of the ready access that Carroll and Chang, along with the other members of the group at the Bell Telephone Laboratories, have had to the comparatively powerful graphical output facilities that have been available there for some ten years now. In particular, the Stromberg–Carlson 4020 microfilm recorder and associated hardcopy printers have enormously facilitated the exploration and testing of new methods (by Carroll, Chang, Kruskal, Shepard) by making possible the rapid and accurate generation of numerous graphical plots which, in many cases, have had to contain several hundred points each.

Carroll's paper constitutes the only comprehensive and up-to-date survey of methods that are specifically designed to take account of the real and potentially informative differences that often arise between the judgments of two or more individuals with respect to the same set of objects or stimuli. Basically two different kinds of judgments are considered: similarity judgments—which in this case lead to a separate "proximity" matrix for each judge; and preference judgments—which can lead to a single matrix of "profile" data with a separate column, say, for each judge (or, in the case of pair-comparison judgments, to a separate "dominance" matrix for each judge). A number of important new developments are reported here, some for the first time. One of these which aroused particular interest, known (in its program form) as INDSCAL, is a method for dealing with individual differences in similarity judgments by assuming that different subjects have different patterns of weights (or "saliences") for a common set of perceptual dimensions. An especially significant characteristic of this method is that it results in a unique orientation of coordinate axes, often apparently corresponding to immediately interpretable psychological dimensions. Without the problem of rotation of axes, moreover, it becomes feasible to achieve meaningful representations in four or more dimensions. (See the applications of this method to some extensive data relating to political science by Carroll's colleague, Wish: Wish, Deutsch, & Biener, this book, Volume II.)

The succeeding paper, by Napior, also contains an illustrative application (this time to the field of education) and, indeed, could as well have been included in Volume II, on applications, as here. However, the principal concern of the paper appears to be more methodological than substantive. What Napior demonstrates is that multidimensional scaling and related methods can be used to separate the items of a large inventory of multiple-choice questions into subsets such that the items within each subset are adequately representable on a unidimensional scale (in a sense proposed by Likert in 1932). He compares three nonmetric methods (viz., multidimensional scaling proper, hierarchical clustering, and a variety of factor analysis) for this purpose and shows that they all yield the same subsets—though not in equally convenient forms. Once the items have been assigned to subsets, Napior argues for the use of a least-squares procedure devised by Guttman to construct the desired one-dimensional scale corresponding to each subset.

With the exception of a few clustering methods briefly mentioned by Shepard, by Lingoes, and now, by Napior, the papers up to this point of Volume I are almost exclusively concerned with methods for representing the objects under study by positions in a continuous underlying space. From this point on, we begin to shift toward a consideration of other types of representations designed to bring out clusters or other, relatively discrete types of structures.

As usually conceived (and as defined in the taxonomy proposed by Shepard), a clustering procedure as such is one that yields as output a partitioning of the objects under study into several subsets or "clusters." The resulting subsets may be mutually exclusive and exhaustive, or they may be hierarchically nested. In either case, though, the resulting representation is discrete or categorical. It is also nondimensional and even nonspatial in the ordinary sense, for the objects are not positioned in any underlying space that is continuous and, hence, of topologically definable dimensionality.

Kruskal describes some previously unreported explorations of a new type of multivariate analysis designed to yield representations that are in a sense intermediate between continuous spatial representations and discrete clustering representations. For this reason, it seemed appropriate to place his paper at just this turning point. Basically what he proposed is a method of transforming a spatial representation so that any tendency of the points to group or cluster together in the space will be revealed more clearly. Since any degree of clustering could be arbitrarily imposed by applying sufficiently complex transformations, it is necessary to place some strong, appropriate constraints on the kinds of transformations allowed. He restricts his discussion to the case of linear, or affine transformations, which are sufficient to bring long chainlike "clusters" into a much more compact and readily detected form. A procedure of this kind might, for example, prove to be quite useful as a way of finding interpretable clusters in the results of factor analysis—particularly since such results are in an important sense determined only up to an affine transformation anyway. However, it should be clear that, since Kruskal's procedure leaves us with an essentially spatial representation, the explicit assignment of points to clusters as such must be done after the transformation—whether by eye or by some other, objective method for identifying clusters as such. Moreover, as Kruskal points out, the general approach he outlines has not yet led to a completely practical computational method.

Degerman's paper, also, is concerned with an intermediate kind of case in which the objects under study are already represented by points in Euclidean space, but in which our interest is in just how these points are arranged in the space—e.g., whether in discrete clusters or in accordance with other "simple structures" such as circles, spherical surfaces, etc. He is not primarily concerned, as was Kruskal, with the practical problem of developing a method that will help us actually to discover clusters or other such simple structures. Rather, he is concerned with the more theoretical question of what the different *kinds* of structures are that one might reasonably hope to discover in a spatial configuration obtained, perhaps, by one of the standard methods of multidimensional scaling. He points out that most of the kinds of structures for which examples are already known can be generated by combining three basic types (simple clusterings, one-dimensional scales, and circular structures) according to two types of operations (Cartesian products and nestings). Degerman's basic idea about structure (which he shares with his former mentor, Torgerson) is that to say that there is structure is to say that certain possibilities are excluded and, hence, that certain regions of the space are necessarily unoccupied (such as the region between two clusters or within the circle, etc.). In trying to interpret a multidimensional scaling solution it may be as informative to look for where the points are not as to look for where they are.

The papers preceding Degerman's could be said to represent a kind of engineering approach to the problem of discovering structure in data. They are primarily concerned with developing methods that will do the job. In relation to these, Degerman's paper can be seen as a transition to the last two papers of Volume I, which represent a quite different, more axiomatic approach to the problem of structure.

The paper by Boyd goes far beyond the suggestion merely that some sets of data might best be *analyzed* by methods that yield representations that are discrete or categorical rather than continuous or spatial. He argues that the most significant phenomena in the social sciences are much more profitably *conceptualized* in terms of discrete algebraic models of the general sort that Chomsky has introduced into linguistics, rather than in terms of continuous spatial models of the sort that underlie most multidimensional scaling methods. From this standpoint, multidimensional scaling can be objected to on the grounds—not just that it may not be very useful—but that it is apt to predispose the investigator toward thinking about his substantive phenomena in entirely the wrong way. Boyd's paper thus amounts to the closest thing to a "minority report" that issued from the conference.

The dangers that Boyd points out are undoubtedly real and should not be ignored by one who is contemplating the use of multidimensional scaling methods or their spatial models. Nevertheless, two points could be made in defense of these methods and models: First, it is by no means clear that spatial models are always wholly inappropriate for the underlying substantive phenomena; certainly these models—not discrete models—seem most suited to the psychological representation of stimuli that can be varied continuously, such as colors or pure tones. Secondly, even though there may well be other phenomena (such as the human conceptualization of kinship terms) for which discrete models might indeed be more appropriate, general methods for extracting such discrete representations from real and therefore fallible data are still largely lacking. A very positive effect of Boyd's paper could be that it will inspire some harder thought about how such methods might yet be developed.

In the last paper in Volume I, Boorman and Arabie develop the mathematical apparatus necessary for a quite general approach to the problem of defining a measure of dissimilarity or "distance" between any two partitionings of the same n objects (or "elements") into mutually exclusive and exhaustive subsets (or "cells"). This is of course directly relevant to the problem of dealing with reliable differences among the clusterings produced under different conditions or by different individuals, say, and thus represents a recurrence to the problem of individual differences treated by Carroll—but, now, from the standpoint of representations of a discrete rather than continuous type.

In addition, however, the contribution of Boorman and Arabie is immediately applicable to the problem of multidimensional scaling proper. For, one kind of data that has increasingly been used as a basis for multidimensional scaling is *sorting data*. (See Burton, this book, Volume II; Rapoport & Fillenbaum, Volume II.) It seems to be a very natural task for people to sort objects or items into homogeneous groups, and a considerable amount of data can rather quickly be collected in this way concerning how people tend to perceive or conceptualize the items being sorted. As noted in the taxonomy of types of data prepared by Shepard, the simple relative frequency with which any two items are sorted into the same group by a number of people provides a relatively "direct" measure of overall proximity between those items. However, if we are interested in scaling the people rather than the items, a much more "derived" measure of proximity must be computed between entire sortings. The framework developed by Boorman and Arabie allows them to characterize, contrast, and evaluate most of the measures of this kind that have been proposed by others as well as some interesting new possibilities of their own. In addition to its mathematical elegance, an unusual aspect of this last paper is that, at the time of its preparation, its two authors were undergraduates at Harvard.

Owing to their more theoretical nature, some of the papers in this volume necessarily make considerably more use of mathematical concepts and notation than those in Volume II. This is true, particularly, of the paper by Boorman and Arabie and, to a lesser extent, of the papers by Boyd, Carroll, Kruskal, and Young. However, none of these presupposes an advanced knowledge of any particular mathematical discipline. It is hoped that concepts and notation are generally introduced in such a way that their meanings will be clear to most readers.

Relationship to Volume II: Applications

The second of these two volumes presents a wide variety of substantive applications in the behavioral sciences. A number of papers in the second volume are closely related to papers in this first volume (e.g., the paper by Wish, Deutsch, and Biener in Volume II makes extensive use of methods developed in the paper by Carroll in Volume I). Nevertheless, the two volumes are, in a logical sense, independent and either volume can be read first—or, indeed, without the other. Thus social scientists who are exclusively interested in the light that applications of these methods may throw on substantive issues may want to by-pass the more technical, methodological issues considered in this first volume, while those concerned only the development of new methods and techniques may be willing to skip some or all of the chapters of Volume II, which are oriented toward substantive problems in specific fields of social science. Still other readers may find it helpful to consult the taxonomically organized overview of types of existing methods, presented in the immediately following chapter of this volume, either before or during their progress through the applications in Volume II.

References

Beals, R., Krantz, D. H., & Tversky, A. Foundations of multidimensional scaling. *Psychological Review*, 1968, **75**, 127–142.

Boorman, S. A., & Arabie, P. Structured measures and the method of sorting. This book, Volume I.

Boyd, J. P. Information distance for discrete structures. This book, Volume I.

Carroll, J. D. Individual differences and multidimensional scaling. This book, Volume I.

Coombs, C. H. *A theory of data.* New York: Wiley, 1964.

Degerman, R. The geometric representation of some simple structures. This book, Volume I.

Green, P. E., & Carmone, Jr., F. J. Marketing research applications of nonmetric scaling methods. This book, Volume II.

Guttman, L. A new approach to factor analysis: The radex. In P. F. Lazarsfeld (Ed.), *Mathematical thinking in the social sciences.* Glencoe, Illinois: Free Press, 1954. Pp. 258–348.

Guttman, L. A generalized simplex for factor analysis. *Psychometrika*, 1955, **20**, 173–192.

Guttman, L. A general nonmetric technique for finding the smallest coordinate space for a configuration of points. *Psychometrika*, 1968, **33**, 469–506.

Kruskal, J. B. Multidimensional scaling by optimizing goodness of fit to a nonmetric hypothesis. *Psychometrika*, 1964, **29**, 1–27. (a)

Kruskal, J. B. Nonmetric multidimensional scaling: A numerical method. *Psychometrika*, 1964, **29**, 115–129. (b)

Kruskal, J. B. Linear transformation of multivariate data to reveal clustering. This book, Volume I.

Kruskal, J. B., & Carroll, J. D. Geometrical models and badness-of-fit functions. In P. R. Krishnaiah (Ed.), *International symposium of multivariate analysis: Dayton, Ohio, 1968, II.* New York: Academic Press, 1969. Pp. 639–670.

Lingoes, J. C. A general survey of the Guttman–Lingoes nonmetric program series. This book, Volume I.

Messick, S. J., & Abelson, R. P. The additive constant problem in multidimensional scaling. *Psychometrika*, 1956, **21**, 1–16.

Shepard, R. N. The analysis of proximities: Multidimensional scaling with an unknown distance function. I. *Psychometrika*, 1962, **27**, 125–140. (a)

Shepard, R. N. The analysis of proximities: Multidimensional scaling with an unknown distance function. II. *Psychometrika*, 1962, **27**, 219–246. (b)

Shepard, R. N. Metric structures in ordinal data. *Journal of Mathematical Psychology*, 1966, **3**, 287–315.

Shepard, R. N. A taxonomy of some principal types of data and of multidimensional methods for their analysis. This book, Volume I.

Shepard, R. N., & Carroll, J. D. Parametric representation of nonlinear data structures. In P. R. Krishnaiah (Ed.), *International symposium of multivariate analysis, Dayton, Ohio, 1965.* New York: Academic Press, 1966. Pp. 561–592.

Stefflre, V. J. Some applications of multidimensional scaling to social science problems. This book, Volume II.

Torgerson, W. S. Multidimensional scaling: I. Theory and method. *Psychometrika*, 1952, **17**, 401–419.

Torgerson, W. S. *Theory and methods of scaling*. New York: Wiley, 1958.

Wish, M., Deutsch, M., & Biener, L. Differences in perceived similarity of nations. This book, Volume II.

Young, F. W. A model for polynomial conjoint analysis algorithms. This book, Volume I.

Young, G., & Householder, A. S. Discussion of a set of points in terms of their mutual distances. *Psychometrika*, 1938, **3**, 19–22.

A TAXONOMY OF SOME PRINCIPAL
TYPES OF DATA AND OF MULTIDIMENSIONAL
METHODS FOR THEIR ANALYSIS

Roger N. Shepard

STANFORD UNIVERSITY
STANFORD, CALIFORNIA

Methods for the spatial representation of structures in data—including multidimensional scaling proper as well as such related methods as factor analysis, cluster analysis, and conjoint measurement—are continuing to appear in ever increasing number and variety. The situation can become extremely confusing for the social or behavioral scientist who does not have a satisfactory overall view of the relations among the various types of data, methods, and computer programs that are reported in the literature.

The confusion has not been lessened by the widespread introduction of completely different "trade names" for what turn out under close examination to be but slightly different variants of already existing methods and, especially, by the resulting tendency of users to specify their analyses in terms solely of such trade names without ever indicating the generic nature of each method that they use. And, to compound the confusion still further, some users seem to identify a method with a particular program

21

and, so, report only that they used so-and-so's method when, in fact, what they used was so-and-so's computer program. The method, often, was of the general sort developed some time earlier, by someone else. As a consequence of all this, readers understandably may remain innocent of such elementary facts as the following:

On the one hand, papers that report the use of "proximity analysis," "smallest space analysis," "elastic multidimensional scaling," "Kruskal's M-D-SCAL program," "Guttman–Lingoes SSAI," or "TORSCA" are all referring to basically the same kind of analysis—namely, the kind of nonmetric multidimensional scaling originally introduced and perfected by Shepard (1962a, 1962b) and Kruskal (1964a, 1964b). For all of these terms refer to specific methods or particular computer programs that share the following three properties: (a) They are based upon the same basic model (viz., one that assumes a monotonic relation between interpoint distances and the given data). (b) They use an iterative procedure of adjusting the coordinates for the points to achieve a closer and closer approximation to this desired monotonic relation. And (c) they yield spatial representations that are typically indistinguishable, for practical purposes, when applied to the same matrix of data. (Most of the differences of real practical interest among these methods and programs concern such theoretically secondary matters as their speed, flexibility, vulnerability to local minima, or data capacity; or whether they provide for cases in which some data are missing or in which a particular non-Euclidean metric or a particular monotonic function is to be assumed.)

On the other hand, papers that report the use of "multidimensional scalogram analysis," "parametric mapping," "Kruskal's MONANOVA," or "Carroll's INDSCAL," are all referring to quite different kinds of analyses—based upon fundamentally different models concerning the relation between the data and the spatial representation. (With respect to procedure, however, even *these* methods are mostly patterned after the methods of the preceding type in that they, also, use iterative adjustments of a spatial representation in order to achieve the best approximation to the desired relation—however specified—between that representation and the data.) Finally, to cap things off, the very same term, "nonmetric factor analysis," has been adopted as a name for three methods (developed by three different pairs of workers: Coombs–Kao, Kruskal–Shepard, and Guttman–Lingoes) that are entirely different with respect to the type of data for which they are intended, of the computational procedure used, and/or the nature of the underlying model.

It would be presumptuous of any one person to attempt to prescribe precisely what generic term should be used for each of the general types of methods now in use. Moreover, it is an undertaking far beyond the scope of this chapter to propose a hierarchical taxonomy that is sufficiently ramified to include and yet distinguish each and every one of the numerous (and still-proliferating) methods and individual computer programs that have been proposed to date. Nevertheless, it may be of some use to the readers of this volume to present at least a partial taxonomy of those methods and programs that figure prominently in applications reported in this volume and in the social sciences generally.

Admittedly, this taxonomy is likely to be "partial" in both senses of that word. Since the present author was for eight years associated with the group at the Bell Telephone Laboratories, the contributions of that group may be more heavily represented than the contributions of people working elsewhere. However, if there is to be a bias, this may be the least objectionable since computer-based nonmetric multidimensional scaling did originate at the Bell Laboratories and, indeed, methods of very great promise (such as Carroll's new method for treating individual differences in multidimensional scaling) continue to emerge from that same group. And, anyway, a number of the developments that have recently emerged elsewhere (and that may therefore not be as fully covered here) are surveyed in some of the subsequent chapters (e.g., by Lingoes and by Young, this book, Volume I).

From the standpoint of the potential user, the most convenient way to classify the various methods would seem to be on the basis of the type of data for which they are intended. Accordingly, before presenting a taxonomy of the methods, it is desirable first to propose a taxonomy of types of data. And to do this, it turns out, is half the battle.

A Partial Taxonomy of Some Basic Types of Data and Their Models

The way a particular matrix of data is classified may depend as much upon the underlying model that one wants to assume in analyzing those data as upon any identifiable property of the data themselves. Indeed, different aspects of the structure hidden in a matrix of data can sometimes be brought out most clearly, for example, by analyzing that very same matrix first as a matrix of "proximity" data and then as a matrix of "profile" data. On the other hand, there are certain minimum, identifiable properties that the data in a matrix should exhibit before the array could usefully be treated as, say, a "proximity" matrix or as a "dominance" matrix. Moreover, data collected by some of the standard methods typically exhibit one or another of these sets of minimum identifiable properties. Accordingly, the following taxonomy is intended to indicate something about some of the basically different ways of classifying a matrix of data, together with (a) examples of some sources of such data, (b) any properties or constraints apt to be evident in the data themselves, and (c) the underlying model that one is assuming when one classifies the data in the indicated way (and which provides, in turn, a kind of explanation for the properties or constraints evident in the data). The overall classification to be given here, in terms of "proximity" "dominance," "profile," and "conjoint measurement" data, parallels, in part, classifications suggested earlier by Coombs (1964; Coombs, Dawes, & Tversky, 1970) and by Shepard (1966). However, it also goes beyond those earlier classifications in its treatment of profile data and in its inclusion of conjoint measurement. In a later section, this same classification will be used as a framework within which to present some of the more salient methods for the multidimensional analysis of these various types of data.

Basic types of data and examples of their sources

Assumed underlying models, and the constraints they entail

I. Proximity Data

A. Square matrix, rows and columns correspond to the same n objects.

Each cell of an $n \times n$ matrix contains some measure of the similarity substitutability, affinity, confusion, association, correlation, or interaction between the two objects corresponding to that row and column of the matrix. The measure can be *direct* in the sense that it arises from the pair of objects immediately (rather than having to be calculated on the basis of other data).

Examples. A direct subjective judgment of the apparent similarity between two stimuli; the frequency with which two things co-occur or are sorted into the same category by a population of subjects; or the frequency of actually observed interaction between two persons, groups, or nations.

Alternatively, the measure can be *derived* in the sense that it is calculated on the basis of other, profile data.

Examples. A computed measure of

Model. The proximity data are monotonically related to distances among n points in some underlying coordinate space. (The monotonic function is assumed to be decreasing in the case of measures of similarity or closeness, and increasing in the case of measures of dissimilarity or distance.)

Constraints. In the more usual case, in which the function is assumed to be monotonically decreasing, the standard metric axioms for distances, viz.,

(a) $d_{ij} = 0$ if and only if $i = j$
(b) $d_{ij} = d_{ji}$
(c) $d_{ik} \leq d_{ij} + d_{jk}$

imply a somewhat related set of constraints for the proximity data, viz.,

(a') $s_{ij} \geq s_{ik}$ if $i = j$
(b') $s_{ij} = s_{ji}$
(c')   if s_{ij} and s_{jk} are both very large, then s_{ik} should be at least moderately large too.

profile similarity for two objects, such as some "metric" or "nonmetric" (e.g. Napior, Volume I) measure of the correlation or covariance between those objects with respect to some set of m measured variables.

(If the matrix from which such derived measures of proximity are computed is itself a proximity matrix for the same n objects, we speak of a "second-order" analysis of the original proximity data. For an example of such a second-order analysis, see Rosenberg & Sedlak, this book, Volume II.)

Further remarks: (a) The term proximity data is taken, quite generally, to subsume measures of dissimilarity or distance as well as measures of similarity or closeness. (b) In either case, the proximity measures may be given on a numerical or on a merely ordinal scale. (c) Some cells of the proximity matrix may be empty and, in particular, the diagonal or even the triangular above-diagonal half of the matrix is sometimes entirely missing. (d) The proximity data may also take the form of a set of square matrices, each of which gives the proximity measures among the same n objects—but obtained under a different condition or from a different person (see Carroll, this book, Volume I; McGee, 1968).

Owing to the weakness of the monotonicity condition, this last constraint is necessarily vague. Still, if a square matrix has its largest values in the diagonal (a'), is approximately symmetric (b'), and has few triplets that are clearly contrary to the spirit of the analog of the triangle inequality (c'), then the matrix would seem to be a good candidate for treatment as a proximity matrix.

(To the extent that the underlying space is of a special sort—e.g., Euclidean and of low dimensionality—the proximity data will be subject to still further constraints. In two dimensions, for example, three—but not four—points can be equally proximal to each other. Such constraints may not be evident from a mere inspection of the matrix but, nevertheless, are what make possible an adequate representation of the data in a low-dimensional space.)

B. Rectangular matrix, rows and columns correspond to different objects.

Each cell of an $n \times m$ matrix contains some measure of proximity between one object in a set of n objects and another object in a *different* set of m objects. (No measures are available for the proximity between any two objects in the same set.)

Examples. The preference expressed by each of n persons for each of m stimuli; or the frequency of heterosexual contact between each of n male and each of m female animals in a confined colony.

Note: The "rectangular" proximity matrix can of course be square and, in that special subcase, the rows and columns

Model. Two sets of (n and m) points are embedded in the same space in such a way that, for any object in one set, the given affinities between that object and all objects in the other set are monotonically related to the corresponding distances from that point to all points in the other set. This model is essentially the "ideal points" or "unfolding" model of Coombs. (As he pointed out, a rectangular "conditional" proximity matrix of this kind can be regarded as a corner submatrix of a complete $(n + m) \times (n + m)$ proximity matrix.)

Constraints. Since so much data are missing from the implied "complete"

can even correspond to the same n objects. The essential thing that distinguishes this case from the preceding is that the rows and columns are *treated* as if they correspond to different objects (i.e., they are represented by different points). A consequence is that, whereas in the preceding case comparisons could be made between any two entries, here they may legitimately be made only between entries within the same row (or possibly, within the same column) of the matrix.

C. Other forms of proximity data

Torgerson's (1952) complete method of triads and other methods for collecting data differ somewhat from the above in that the data arise from comparisons among only certain pairs of objects—e.g., those with one object in common.

Example. For every pair of stimuli in every possible triad, the relative frequency with which that pair was chosen as the most similar of the three possible pairs in the triad.

matrix, constraints are more difficult to formulate. In particular the conditions having to do with the diagonal (a') and symmetry (b') are no longer available. However, it is still possible to formulate some weaker condition relating to the analog of the triangle inequality (c').

Model. Basically the same kind of (monotone) model can be used, but the details of the correspondence between the spatial representation and the data will depend upon the particular case.

Constraints. To the extent that information concerning the complete rank order of all $n(n-1)/2$ pairs is not available, constraints will, again, be somewhat weaker.

II. DOMINANCE DATA

A. Single square matrix, rows and columns correspond to the same n objects

Each cell of the $n \times n$ matrix contains a measure of the extent to which the row object is preferred to, is chosen over, defeats, or otherwise dominates the column object.

Examples. The (positive or negative) degree of preference expressed by one individual for the first alternative in an ordered pair; the frequency of actual choice of that alternative (over the other) by some population of individuals; or the extent to which one individual in an ordered pair (of persons or animals, now) wins out over the other in some game, contest, or pecking-order confrontation.

(The simple statement "object i dominates object j," when it stands by itself, should be interpreted to mean "i dominates j to a greater extent than j dominates i." Of course these may amount to

Model. Each object is represented by a point positioned on a unidimensional scale in such a way that, for every ordered pair of objects (i and j), point i is higher on the scale than point j if object i dominates object j—or even if object i, to a greater extent than object j, dominates any third object k.

Constraints. For any three objects i, j, and k, if (to a sufficient degree) i dominates k to a greater extent than j dominates k, then i should dominate j.

This transitivity condition resembles the triangle condition (c') for proximity data. Nevertheless, a dominance matrix looks very different because the other two conditions (a' and b') are directly violated: the diagonal entries, instead of being the largest, have approximately the median value. And the matrix as a whole, instead of being symmetric, tends toward a kind of skew-symmetry in which, if one entry is

the same thing, anyway, when the dominance data take the purely dichotomous form of a simple choice or win of one object over another.)

B. Set of m square matrices, rows and columns of each correspond to the same n objects

Each matrix is of the same kind as was just described above, but each is obtained under a different condition—e.g., from a different person.

Examples. The pair-comparison judgments of the same n alternatives made by a different person; or the outcomes of encounters between the same n individuals in a different kind of contest.

(Note: As in the case of proximity matrices, dominance matrices could in principle be rectanuglar, with rows and columns corresponding to different sets of objects. However, this possibility has not received much attention and will not be separately considered here.)

Terminological notes: (a) What are here called dominance data have often been referred to as paired-comparison or, more justifiably, as pair-comparison data However, these terms do not adequately differentiate dominance data from proximity data (which also may arise from the comparison of objects in pairs). Partly for this reason the term dominance data, advocated by Coombs (1964), has been adopted here. (b) Similarly, what are called profile data in the following section have often been referred to simply as multivariate data. However, again, this latter term seems to be too broad to distinguish profile data from, say, those contained either in a rectangular proximity matrix or in a conjoint measurement matrix.

smaller than the diagonal entries, its symmetrically situated counterpart tends to be about as much *larger* than the diagonal entries.

Model. Each object is represented by a point in a space of two or more dimensions and each condition is represented by a direction in this space in such a way that, if object i dominates object j in a particular matrix, then point i falls beyond point j in the direction corresponding to that matrix.

(The relation between any one matrix and the order in which the points fall along the direction associated with that matrix is, thus, the same as indicated for the one-dimensional case, above. However, by arranging the points in a multidimensional space here, we provide for the possibility of different directions and, hence, are able to account, for example, for real differences in the preferences of different persons.)

Constraints. Again, the data must be suitably transitive within each matrix. Moreover, to the extent that the underlying space is of low dimensionality, only a few of the possible rank orders of the points can be generated merely by varying direction and, so, there must be some constraints *between* matrices as well.

Note: The dominance model described above can be regarded as a limiting case of a more general ideal points model of the sort mentioned in connection with rectangular proximity matrices. (See the discussion below concerning general relations among these models.)

III. Profile Data

A. Rectangular matrix, rows correspond to n objects and columns correspond to m variables (or vice versa).

Each entry gives the measured value of

Model. The objects are represented as n points (or vectors) in a space in such a way that the profile associated with each object varies according to some simple or

one object with respect to one of the variables. The row (or column) of m measured values for any object is considered to be a profile characterizing that object.

Examples. An individual's subjective rating of each of n stimuli with respect to each of m attributes; the objective scores on each of n tests of each of m individuals; or the measured values of each of n companies or nations with respect to each of m economic variables.

In any of these examples, whether the rows are regarded as the objects and the columns as the variables or vice versa will depend upon the interests of the investigator or upon the purposes of the investigation.

Further remarks: (a) A proximity or dominance matrix can also be treated as a matrix of profile data. (However, it then becomes necessary to decide whether the rows or columns of the matrix are to be regarded as containing the profiles.) (b) Conversely, a (derived) proximity matrix can always be obtained from a matrix of profile data simply by computing a measure of profile similarity (or dissimilarity) between every pair of rows (or columns).

orderly rule with the position of that point in the space. The precise nature of the assumed rule depends upon the particular model.

In the standard factor-analytic model the profile associated with a point is to be approximated as a linear combination of a set of basic profiles associated with the reference axes and weighted (in the combination) proportionally to the projection of that point on each of those axes. In parametric mapping, on the other hand, the only requirement is that the profile associated with a point vary sufficiently smoothly with its position (Shepard & Carroll, 1966).

Constraints. The constraints take a subtle form that is difficult to recognize by mere inspection of the data. However, to the extent that the underlying space is of low dimension, there will be strong limitations on the variety of different profiles that can exist. (Thus, if a two-dimensional factor-analytic model applied, all obtained profiles must be representable as purely linear combinations of just two basic profiles.)

IV. Conjoint Measurement Data

A. Rectangular matrix, rows correspond to n levels of one variable and columns correspond to m levels of another variable

Each entry is the magnitude of an effect that arises jointly when the two contributing variables take on the levels corresponding to the row and column of that entry.

Examples. The subjectively rated aversiveness of a loud noise that is characterized by the two variables of frequency and amplitude; or the amount that will actually be wagered in a gamble that is characterized by the two variables of intrinsic value of the prize and probability that it will be won. (For a psycholinguistic example, see the paper by Cliff, this book, Volume II.)

Model. The level (of one variable) corresponding to each row is to be represented by a point on one unidimensional scale, and the level (of the other variable) corresponding to each column is to be represented by a point on another unidimensional scale, in such a way that each entry becomes a simple (e.g., linear) combination of the scaled values associated with its row and column.

Constraints. Under the usual case in which the rule of combination has at least the natural monotonicity properties, the entries in any row should all tend to differ (if at all) in the same direction from the corresponding entries in any one other row—and the same should hold true for the columns. That is, the entries s_{ik}

The term conjoint measurement is taken, from Luce & Tukey (1964), to indicate that the purpose, here, is to find a one-dimensional scaling or measurement of the n levels of one variable and, conjointly, to find a one-dimensional scaling or measurement of the m levels of the other variable such that entries in the matrix are related to the resulting scaled values according to the simplest possible law. (Such a scaling or measurement may amount to a rescaling or remeasurement as, in the first example, when we rescale *physical* variables (e.g., the frequency and amplitude of a noise) to represent their *psychological* effects.)

Note: Unlike the cases of the inherently two-way matrices of proximity, dominance, or profile data, the case of the conjoint measurement matrix can immediately be extended to include N-way matrices as well. In this way one can deal with the way in which three or more variables jointly contribute to some effect.

should approximately satisfy the constraints that, for any two rows, i and j, and for any two columns, k and h,

$$s_{ik} > s_{ih} \quad \text{implies} \quad s_{jk} > s_{jh}$$

and

$$s_{ik} > s_{jk} \quad \text{implies} \quad s_{ih} > s_{jh}$$

(If linearity is assumed, still stronger constraints of proportionality will of course apply.)

Note: Although such a matrix may have the superficial appearance of a matrix of profile data, the model and, hence, the way of treating the matrix are different. Generally, in the case of a profile matrix, points are found to represent *only* the rows (or *only* the columns—whichever are taken to contain the profiles); and these points are arranged in a *multidimensional* space. In the case of conjoint measurement, on the other hand, points are found to represent *both* the rows and the columns; but (in the simple case considered here) the points in each of these two sets are arranged in a merely *one-dimensional* space. (In this case, conjoint measurement is multidimensional only in that the result consists of more than one scale.)

A Generalization of the Dominance Model, and Some Resulting Relations among the Four Basically Different Models

An important generalization of the dominance model is provided by the ideal points or unfolding model developed by Coombs and his students and partially outlined above in connection with rectangular matrices of proximity data. Instead of giving "i dominates j" the geometrical interpretation "i falls beyond j in a particular direction," one can give it the alternative geometrical interpretation "i falls closer than j to a particular 'ideal' point." These two interpretations become equivalent in the special case in which any ideal points move out sufficiently far beyond the periphery of the configuration of the remaining points. For then, clearly, the remaining points will fall in the same order both with respect to their closeness to that remote ideal point and also with respect to their projections on an axis suitably directed through that remote point. However, the ideal point model is the more general since it subsumes the other as a special case.

Here, then, we see a close connection between the basic notions behind the proximity model and the dominance model. The principal difference is that, whereas the proximity model concerns the distance between the two points within each pair considered by themselves, the dominance model concerns the relative distances of the two points in each such pair to some external, ideal point. With this, moreover, is associated the following further difference: Whereas in the case of a rectangular proximity matrix each ideal point corresponds to just one column of that matrix; in the case of a dominance matrix each ideal point corresponds to that particular dominance matrix as a whole.

Related connections can now also be pointed out between the model for proximity data and that for profile data—at least in its linear form. For, again, as the ideal points move farther and farther out beyond the periphery in the model for rectangular proximity matrices, the distances of the remaining points from any one ideal point must correspond more and more closely to some purely linear combination of the coordinates for those remaining points. And, even when the ideal points do not thus disperse toward infinity, the pattern of values in each row of the rectangular proximity matrix must still be a smooth—though no longer linear—function of the coordinates for the point corresponding to that row. Hence, this more general case is also compatible with the more general model for profile data.

The remaining link in this triad of models can also be closed by noting, first, that the dominance and profile models are basically equivalent in the special linear case, since both then concern the order in which points project onto axes or vectors passing in certain directions through the space. The only real difference concerns whether, for each such direction, it is the one complete order of all n points that is of interest (as in the case of profile data), or the $n(n - 1)/2$ separate pairwise orders within all individual pairs of points that is of interest (as in the case of dominance data). And, again, in the more general case corresponding to nondispersed ideal points, the dominance and profile models will have the same kind of compatibility that was noted above for the profile and proximity models.

The fourth, conjoint measurement model is basically different from these other three in that the points corresponding to the rows and the points corresponding to the columns are represented in what, in the general case, are conceived to be two *separate* spaces—each of which, moreover, is usually (though not necessarily) constrained to be purely one-dimensional. In part because the component scales can be multidimensional and because the analysis can be generalized to N-way matrices, the notion of conjoint measurement can be extended beyond this simple case to subsume more general cases (such as those of Eckart–Young decomposition or "canonical decomposition of N-way tables" used in some of the multidimensional scaling methods introduced by Carroll, this book, Volume I). Indeed Young (this book, Volume I) has suggested that conjoint measurement can even be sufficiently extended to subsume the other three cases of proximity, dominance, and profile data. However, it seems more useful, here, to maintain the distinctions among all four of these basically different ways of regarding a matrix of data.

A Brief, General Characterization of the Four Basically Different Ways of Classifying a Matrix of Data

At the most general level, for *any* of the four basic types of data considered here, we can say the following: (a) We are given either a single $n \times m$ matrix or a set of several $n \times m$ matrices (where, of course, it may be that $n = m$). (b) We seek a representation of the n rows as n points in some space and/or a representation of the m columns as m points in either the same or a different space (where, if $n = m$, the rows and columns may be represented by the *same* points). (c) We require of this spatial representation that the entries in the matrix be related in a simple and orderly way to certain geometrical relations among the points. The four basically different ways of interpreting a set of data can then be distinguished, very succinctly, in terms of the specific kind of simple and orderly relation that is conceived to hold between the data and the geometrical relations among the points. In particular if we agree to adopt the more general, ideal points model for dominance data, we have the following:

1. To interpret a matrix as a matrix of *proximity* data is to conceive that each entry is to be represented, geometrically, by the extent to which the point corresponding to its row falls *close* to the point corresponding to its column—within the same space.

2. To interpret a matrix as a matrix of *dominance* data is to conceive that each entry is to be represented, geometrically, by the extent to which the point corresponding to its row—more than the point corresponding to its column—falls close to (or in the direction of) some *third* (ideal) point corresponding to that particular matrix as a whole—all within the same space.

3. In the simplest case, to interpret a matrix as a matrix of *profile* data is

to conceive that the whole pattern or profile of entries in each row (or, alternatively, in each column) is to be represented, geometrically, by the absolute spatial position of the point corresponding to that row (or column) in such a way that the profiles depend upon their corresponding positions according to some simple rule (e.g., one that is linear or, at least, either properly monotonic or sufficiently smooth).

4. To interpret a matrix as a matrix of *conjoint measurement* data is to conceive that each entry is to be represented as a simple (e.g., additive, multiplicative, polynomial or, perhaps, only properly monotonic) function of two coordinates: the absolute position of a point corresponding to its row in one unidimensional space, and the absolute position of a point corresponding to its column in a separate unidimensional space.

In short, these four basically different ways of classifying a matrix of data may be very briefly characterized as in Table 1.

TABLE 1

If the data are interpreted as	then the points represent	and each entry is related to
proximity data,	rows and columns, in one multidimensional space,	the distance between its row and column points, within their common space.
dominance data,	rows and columns, in one multidimensional space,	the relative distances of its row and column points from (or toward) a third ("ideal") point, within their common space.
profile data,	rows (*or* columns), in one multidimensional space,	the absolute position of its row point (or column point), within the space.
conjoint measurement data,	rows and columns, in two separate unidimensional spaces,	some specified combination of the positions of its row and column points, within their separate spaces.

No claim is made that these four ways of interpreting a matrix of data are in any sense exhaustive. But they do appear to provide an adequate framework within which to classify the principal methods of multidimensional scaling considered in this volume, as well as in the social sciences generally. In particular, each of these ways of interpreting a matrix leads us to seek some sort of geometrical or spatial representation the purpose of which is to reveal to the eye the structure or pattern that might otherwise remain hidden in the array of numbers as a whole. A number of the methods that are now available for actually constructing such implied spatial representations on the basis of the models discussed above are organized according to the type of data for which they are intended in the following section.

A Partial Taxonomy of Some Frequently Cited Methods and Programs

Methods for multidimensional scaling and computer programs for these methods are continuing to increase in number and variety at a rate that defies any attempt at a comprehensive and systematic statement of all of their interrelations at this time. However, a more limited attempt to bring some order at least to the relations among some of the methods that have already been more or less widely used or discussed may serve some useful purpose in the context of this volume. Descriptions of some of the most recent methods, which will not be explicitly considered here, may be found in the later chapters by Carroll, Kruskal, Lingoes, and Young (this book, Volume I). For the convenience of potential users, the following taxonomy is organized, at the highest level, into the four principal classes of data for which the various methods are intended; viz., proximity, dominance, profile, and conjoint measurement.

Throughout, the terms "metric" and "nonmetric" are used to distinguish methods according to whether they yield results that are or are not invariant under monotonic transformations of the data or, equivalently, according to whether they are or are not appropriate for merely ordinal data. Such a usage, now widely adopted, is potentially confusing. In particular, it is essential to understand that most of these methods—including those classified as nonmetric—yield spatial representations that are themselves metric in the sense that they are uniquely determined up to some sort of linear transformation (Shepard, 1966).

Basic types of methods together with their models	Individual variants of these methods and/or particular computer programs

I. FOR PROXIMITY DATA

A. Classical metric multidimensional scaling (Torgerson, 1952)

Model. Proximity data are related to distances among points in a to-be-recovered coordinate space in a way that

1. Indirect (Thurstonian) methods. The proximity data are assumed to arise from comparisons of subjective magnitudes that vary according to a normal density function in the underlying scale of distance

depends upon a function of some particular, specified form.

Method. Two-phase: The specified form of the function is used to compute distance estimates from the proximity data (whether indirectly or directly—see right-hand column). Then characteristic roots and vectors of a scalar-product matrix derived from these distance estimates are computed in order to determine dimensionality and to obtain coordinates for the points in space.

B. Nonmetric multidimensional scaling (Shepard, 1962a, 1962b; Kruskal, 1964a)

Model. Proximity data are related to distances among points in a to-be-recovered coordinate space by a function that is merely monotonic.

Method. Iterative adjustment of coordinates of (initially perhaps arbitrary) points so as to minimize some measure of departure from monotonicity.

(Note: Some of these methods have been generalized (e.g., by Gleason, Kruskal, Lingoes, Torgerson, & Young) to deal with the case of rectangular matrices in which different points are used to represent the row and column objects. For an example of an actual analysis in which the rows and columns of a proximity matrix are taken to correspond to different objects, (using Kruskal's M-D-SCAL IV) see the chapter by D'Andrade, Quinn, Nerlove, and Romney, this book, Volume II.)

C. Multidimensional scaling for individual differences (Carroll, this book, Volume I)

Model. Similar to A and B, but with the important difference that the configurations of points for different subjects are permitted to be differentially elongated along unique underlying axes. (See Note in column to the right).

Method. Iterative adjustment of coordinates of points and, simultaneously,

(or, alternatively, in the underlying space itself). The distance estimates are then calculated so as to be optimally consistent with this assumption of normality (Messick, 1956; Torgerson, 1952).

2. Direct methods. The proximity data are assumed to be directly related to the to-be-estimated distances by a monotonic function of some particular, specified form. (Abelson, 1954; Indow & Uchizono, 1960; Shepard, 1958, in press).

1. Analysis of proximities (Shepard, 1962a, 1964)

2. M-D-SCAL (Versions I–IV) (Kruskal, 1964a, 1964b, 1968)

3. Smallest space analysis (SSA and SSAR) (Guttman, 1968; Lingoes, 1966, this book, Volume I)

4. TORSCA (Young & Torgerson, 1967)

5. Elastic multidimensional scaling (McGee, 1966, 1968)

(Note: Two approaches have been taken to the computer implementation of various generalizations and extensions of multidimensional scaling. Kruskal has worked toward a single comprehensive program (currently M-D-SCAL IV) that incorporates more and more control options to cover the various cases (e.g., of non-Euclidean metrics, rectangular or nonsymmetric matrices, etc.). Lingoes, on the other hand, has preferred to develop a separate program in the Guttman–Lingoes series (SSA I, SSA II, SSA III, SSAR I, etc.) for each particular case of interest.)

1. INDSCAL (Carroll & Chang, 1970)

(Note: A special aspect of this general type of method is that it is capable of yielding unique axes that are interpretable without rotation. However, although a quasi-nonmetric version of INDSCAL is now available, the version that is illustrated in this volume is not strictly non-metric in the sense of those of type B, just above.)

(For examples of applications of this

of stretch factors for each subject on each axis so as to minimize a measure of departure from overall good fit. (For other, earlier approaches to the representation of individual differences, see the reports by Bloxom, 1968; Horan, 1969; Kruskal, 1968; McGee, 1968; Tucker & Messick, 1963; or the discussion of these in Carroll & Chang, 1970.)

very promising new method, see the chapters by Carroll, this book, Volume I, and by Wish, Deutsch, & Biener, Volume II.)

D. Hierarchical clustering
1. Metric (Ward, 1963)
2. Nonmetric (Johnson, 1967; Sneath, 1957; Sørensen, 1948)
Model. Proximity data are related to "ultrametric" distances among the terminal nodes of a graph-theoretic tree by a monotonic function (in the "nonmetric" case).
Method. The tree is reconstructed from the proximity data by an algorithm that requires only a predetermined, finite number of steps.

1. Hierarchical grouping (Ward, 1963)
2. HICLUS (Johnson, 1967, 1968)
(Note: These methods differ from others included in this taxonomy in that they do not yield a spatial representation in the usual sense. However, their results can be embedded in a spatial representation in a way that has been found quite useful in practice. This is done by constructing a closed curve around all points in a spatial representation that are grouped together at each level of the hierarchical clustering (Shepard, in press).

II. FOR DOMINANCE DATA

A. Unidimensional analysis of a single dominance matrix
1. Metric (Thurstone, 1927)
2. Nonmetric (e.g., Klemmer & Shrimpton, 1963)
Model. Dominance data are related to the *signed* differences between positions of points on a one-dimensional scale by some function (that is derived from the normal density function in the metric case, and that is merely monotonic in the particular nonmetric case considered by Klemmer and Shrimpton).
Method. Iterative adjustment of points to minimize departure from monotonicity, in the nonmetric case.

1. Classical "indirect" methods based upon an assumption of normality (as in Thurstone's Case V)
2. Preference scaling via proximity analysis (Klemmer & Shrimpton, 1963)
(Note: Other possible variations of unidimensional scaling of dominance data could be mentioned. However, since the survey is primarily concerned with scaling in more than one dimension, the method of Klemmer and Shrimpton is mentioned only as one possible example of a unidimensional method. Also, for a thorough treatment of the derivation of unidimensional scales from pair-comparison data, see Bock & Jones, 1968; David, 1963; Kendall, 1955, 1962.)

B. Multidimensional analysis of multiple dominance matrices
1. Metric (e.g., Slater, 1960)
2. Nonmetric (Carroll & Chang, 1964b)
Model. Dominance data in each matrix

1. Analysis of personal preferences (Slater, 1960)
2. Nonparametric analysis of pair-comparison data (Carroll & Chang, 1964b)
(Notes: (a) The Carroll–Chang program

are related to the way in which the points project onto an axis corresponding to that matrix in the space. (In the nonmetric case only the order in which the points project is taken into account.)

Method. Computation of characteristic roots and vectors of a certain matrix (in the metric case), followed by iterative adjustment of the positions of points and directions of the axes to optimize overall goodness of fit, (in the nonmetric case).

(Note: For a number of other models and methods for the analysis of dominance data, including those based upon the concept of ideal points, see the chapter by Carroll (this book, Volume I).)

will find the best-fitting representation for either Slater's metric case or for the nonmetric case. However, experience has indicated that data often are not sufficiently constraining to support a fully nondegenerate solution in the nonmetric case. (b) Carroll has contributed to the metric case as well as to the nonmetric by showing what measure of goodness of fit is optimized in that case. (c) It can be shown that, if each dominance matrix is strictly transitive, then the nonmetric case becomes equivalent in a certain sense to nonmetric factor analysis as developed earlier by Kruskal and Shepard.)

III. FOR PROFILE DATA

A. Classical metric factor analysis (e.g., Thurstone, 1947)

Model. Each of the m observed values in each profile is a linear combination of the same smaller set of values giving the position of that profile as a point in a to-be-recovered coordinate space.

Method. Two-phase: First compute correlations, covariances, or scalar products between every two observed profiles, then estimate coordinates for points representing these profiles in a vector space of minimum dimensionality such that the correlations, covariances, or scalar products computed in the first phase are adequately reproduced as the (geometrical) scalar products among the resulting points (i.e., vectors) in this vector space.

(Note: Classically, the second phase was accomplished simply by computing (or, earlier, by in some way approximating) the characteristic roots and vectors of the correlation matrix computed in the first phase and, then, by discarding all but the vectors associated with sufficiently large characteristic roots. Geometrically, this amounted essentially to a rotation of m orthogonal axes—which initially correspond to the m original variables—so as to concentrate the

Numerous methods and programs for factor analysis are available. (See, e.g., Harman, 1967)

(Note: The approaches and particular methods advocated by various factor analysts differ in many subtle respects including (a) the handling of the "communality" problem (roughly, the problem of the diagonal of the correlation matrix), (b) the particular thing chosen for optimization in estimating the coordinates or "factor loadings" (e.g., whether maximization of coordinate variance on first few axes, minimization of residuals in correlation matrix, maximization of likelihood, etc.), (c) the criteria for determining number of dimensions, and (d) the method of further rotation, if any, to be used to facilitate interpretation of the resulting configuration in the final, reduced space. Disagreements center, particularly, around the problem of rotation. However recent methods of factor analysis in which something about the to-be-recovered structure can be specified in advance (Jöreskog, 1969) may help to avoid the problem of rotation in some cases. And, in any case, most of the other kinds of methods of multidimensional scaling considered in this volume usually lead either to representations of sufficiently low dimen-

variance of the projections of the points on the first few axes, which were then retained as a basis for the reduced-dimension representation. More recently, however, somewhat different, maximum-likelihood methods have become increasingly popular. Although they generally require more costly iterative numerical methods, they have the advantage that part or all of the pattern of to-be-recovered coordinates (the factor loadings) can be specified a priori (Jöreskog, 1969), and that statistical tests of significance can be performed (provided, of course, one is willing to accept the required assumptions of normality).)

sionality that one does not have to rely, for interpretation of the results, upon such "objective" methods of rotation, or else to representations (as in the case of Carroll's INDSCAL, this book, Volume I) in which the axes can be interpreted without rotation. For a variety of approaches to factor analysis see, in addition to Harman's (1967) revision of his comprehensive book and the already cited recent paper by Jöreskog, the various earlier papers, e.g., by Guttman (1953), Harman and Jones (1966), Lawley (1940), and Rao (1941).

B. Nonmetric factor analysis (Kruskal & Shepard, in preparation; see Shepard, 1966; Shepard & Kruskal, 1964)

Model. Each of the m observed values in each profile is a merely monotonic function of a linear combination of the coordinates giving the position of that profile in a to-be-recovered space (see, Bennett, 1956).

Method. Iterative adjustment of coordinates of points (for the objects) and vectors (for the variables) to minimize departures from a monotonic relation between the measured values of all objects on each variable and the projections of all points on each corresponding vector.

(Note: Some varieties of Guttman–Lingoes multidimensional scalogram analysis (Lingoes, this book, Volume I), which are intended for purely dichotomous profile data, might be regarded as representing a different kind of nonmetric factor analysis—or of cluster analyses (see D, below).)

C. Parametric representation (Shepard & Carroll, 1966)

Model. Profiles correspond to points in a coordinate space in such a way that nearby points are always associated with similar profiles or, more-or-less equivalently, a profile changes only smoothly or continuously with changes in the position

Nonmetric variety of linear factor analysis (Kruskal & Shepard, in preparation)

(Note: Although a program for this kind of analysis, written by Kruskal, has been running since 1963, it has never been widely used. Two reasons for this may be the following: (a) The method is somewhat susceptible to "degenerate" solutions. (b) Otherwise, the method tends—except in the case of extremely nonlinear data—to yield representations that differ but little from those obtained by classical (linear) factor analysis. Although it is of considerable theoretical interest that the same, metric solution can be obtained from a nonmetric analysis, there is little practical motivation to use the more costly iterative process to obtain essentially the same results. It is only when there is reason to suspect extreme nonlinearities in the data that the nonmetric method might prove helpful—e.g., by providing a better estimate of the true number of underlying dimensions.)

1. A program for finding intrinsic dimensionality (Bennett, 1965)

2. Locally monotone analysis of profile similarities (Shepard, in Shepard & Carroll, 1966)

3. Conformal reduction of nonlinear data structures (Shepard & Chang, in preparation)

of its corresponding point. (The co-ordinates of the space are considered to provide a parameterization of the profiles.)

Method. Iterative adjustment of points in a coordinate space so as (a) to minimize departures from a locally monotonic relation between interpoint distance and some measure of profile similarity or (b) to optimize an index of smoothness or continuity.

(In the former case an additional device of differentially stretching large distances may be used to flatten out curved structure and, thus, to reduce dimensionality.)

(Note: Between these methods and classical linear factor analysis, fall certain nonlinear extensions of the more classical approach (by Carroll, 1969a; Gnanadesikan & Wilk, 1969; McDonald, 1962).)

4. Parametric mapping to optimize an index of continuity, PARAMAP (Carroll, in Shepard & Carroll, 1966)

When there are strongly nonlinear and, especially, nonmonotonic relations among the measured variables, these methods are capable of reducing dimensionality well below what would be possible with linear methods of factor analysis. (They thus provide a general approach to the problem of finding a spatial representation for a very general form of Guttman's radex.) And even if there are no clearly nonlinear relations, these methods enable one to force the representation down into two or three dimensions with as little violence as possible to local structures (such as clusters) that may be of interest. (However, as a general class, these methods have seemed to be particularly vulnerable to practical problems of slow or unstable convergence of the iterative process.)

D. Cluster analysis

Model. Profiles are assigned to mutually exclusive and exhaustive categories or clusters in such a way that any two profiles belong to the same or different clusters depending upon whether they are sufficiently similar or dissimilar, respectively. (The clustering can also be hierarchical, as in the case of the clustering methods described for proximity data.)

Method. Basically two approaches have been taken: (a) The profile matrix can be, first, transformed into a proximity matrix (by computing some measure of profile similarity for every pair of profiles) and, then, analyzed by some clustering method of the sort already described for proximity data. (b) Or some method can be used to construct clusters in the m-dimensional coordinate space defined by the original variables of the profiles themselves.

An enormous and still increasing variety of clustering methods have been proposed for profile or multivariate data. (See, e.g., Ball & Hall, 1965; Cole, 1969; Friedman & Rubin, 1967; Sokal & Sneath, 1963; Wallace, 1968.)

Unfortunately, many of the methods are somewhat *ad hoc* in nature and, so, do not lend themselves to any very elegant general characterizations. Moreover, the results are not spatial or even multidimensional in the usual sense. And, finally, applications of cluster analyses *per se* are not much represented in this volume. Accordingly, no attempt will be made to describe the various procecures that have been preposed. Again, however, clustering results can be embedded in a spatial representation and may facilitate the interpretation of such a representation.

[For some recent approaches to clustering that are more closely related to multidimensional scaling in the usual sense, see the chapters by Kruskal and by Degerman (this book, Volume I)].

IV. For Conjoint Measurement Data

A. Construction of a simple (e.g., additive) representation

Model. Each entry is to be represented as a simple (e.g., additive) combination of its to-be-recovered row and column values.

Method. In most cases, iterative adjustment of a value for each of the rows and a value for each of the columns to minimize some measure of overall departure from the specified rule of combination.

Note: The method (and its model) may be nonmetric in that the entries are required to be related to the values generated by the specified rule of combination by a function that is merely monotonic (Kruskal, 1965; Tversky, 1967). This considerably increases the generality of the method since, for example, an additive rule of combination becomes equivalent to a multiplicative one under a pair of inverse monotonic transformations of the appropriate forms (viz., logarithmic–exponential).

1. Nonlinear additive analysis (Morey & Yntema, 1965; Yntema, 1968)

2. Monotone analysis of variance (MONANOVA) (Kruskal, 1965; Kruskal & Carmone, 1969)

3. Additivity analysis (Tversky & Zivian, 1966)

4. Guttman–Lingoes conjoint measurement (CM-I, CM-II, etc.) (Lingoes, 1967a, this book, Volume I)

5. Categorical conjoint measurement (Carroll, 1969a)

Note: Methods of this general sort can be used to find representations with other than a merely additive or linear structure. Not only multiplicative but also quite general polynomial rules of combination have been treated (e.g., Young, this book, Volume I). (However, if the method is to achieve a significant reduction of the data, it cannot be so general as to be able to fit any arbitrary set of data whatever. Some constraints must be imposed, e.g., on the degree of the polynomial.)

Methods for Facilitating the Interpretation of Spatial Representations

In addition to methods designed to find a spatial representation on the basis of a given matrix of data, methods of a variety of different kinds are being developed to assist in interpreting the resulting spatial representation or in relating it to other spatial representations or to other sets of data. The following is a list of some of the methods (and computer programs) of this sort that have already proved to be useful or that are referred to in this volume. They are classified into three general types, depending upon whether they are designed to discover structure within a spatial representation (1) by performing a purely internal analysis of that representation itself, (2) by relating that representation to other, "external" data, or (3) by relating it to one or more other spatial representations. In the first case, "purely internal analysis" is intended to include the possibilities either (or both) of an analysis of the spatial configuration alone or—as in the kind of "internal analysis" considered by Carroll (this volume)—of an analysis of the data from which that configuration was derived.

METHODS FOR FACILITATING INTERPRETATION BY A PURELY INTERNAL ANALYSIS

a. CLUSTER ANALYSIS TO DISCOVER NATURAL GROUPINGS OF POINTS IN THE SPATIAL REPRESENTATION. The clustering can be done on the points themselves by methods of the sort described under "Cluster Analysis for Profile Data" (Part III.D in the taxonomy of methods, above), or it can be done on the basis of the original data for that spatial representation by methods of the sort described under "Hierarchical Clustering for Proximity Data" (Part I.D in the taxonomy).

The discovery of natural clusters can greatly facilitate the interpretation of representations in more than three dimensions, where the geometrical structure is not immediately evident to the eye. And, even in two-dimensional representations, it has been found very useful to embed a hierarchical clustering (based upon the original data) by constructing closed curves around points that belong to the same cluster (Shepard, in press; also see Napior, this book, Volume I). In this way the natural clusters are brought out in a more explicit and objective way for purposes of interpretation, labeling, or comparison with independently obtained clusterings of the same objects. Finally, since the clustering method is nondimensional, the embedded clustering provides information as to whether there is structure in the data that is not being captured in the two-dimensional spatial representation and, if so, something about its nature.

b. ROTATION OF AXES TO COINCIDE WITH CLUSTERS OR TO LINE UP WITH OTHER "SIMPLE STRUCTURES." Included here are the numerous methods that have been developed in conjunction with factor analysis for rotating axes so that, to the extent possible, each axis passes through a prominent cluster, so that coordinates are either large or close to zero, or so that some other such simple pattern emerges in the coordinates (e.g., see Harman, 1967; Napior, this book, Volume I; Tryon & Bailey, 1966). Such methods are needed, particularly, when—as is common in the case of factor analysis—the spatial representation has too many dimensions for direct visualization.

Also included here are the related kinds of methods proposed by Degerman (1970; this book, Volume I) for rotating axes to separate dimensions of continuous or quantitative variation from dimensions of discrete or qualitative variation.

c. LINEAR TRANSFORMATION TO EMPHASIZE CLUSTERING. This is the case treated in the paper by Kruskal (this book, Volume I).

METHODS FOR FACILITATING INTERPRETATION BY DETERMINING RELATIONS WITH EXTERNAL VARIABLES

a. DETERMINATION OF NEW AXES SUCH THAT THE POINTS PROJECT ONTO EACH AXIS IN A WAY THAT CORRELATES OPTIMALLY WITH THE MEASURED VALUES OF THE CORRESPONDING OBJECTS ON SOME EXTERNAL VARIABLE. These new axes need not be orthogonal and, indeed, can be either fewer or more numerous than the dimensions of the space itself. The correlation that is optimized can be a linear correlation (e.g., Miller, Shepard, & Chang, 1964), a nonlinear correlation (Carroll & Chang, 1964a) or, of course, a purely "nonmetric" rank-order correlation such as that described by Carroll (this book, Volume I) under nonmetric external analysis in terms of the vector model. Provided that the correlation is sufficiently high, the external variable with which it is thus correlated provides a ready interpretation for the direction through the space indicated by that axis. Finally, an external variable used for this purpose can be a value determined for each object by an empirical measurement or assigned to it on the basis solely of rational considerations.

b. DETERMINATION OF IDEAL POINTS SUCH THAT DISTANCES OF THE POINTS FROM EACH IDEAL POINT CORRELATE OPTIMALLY WITH THE MEASURED VALUES OF THE CORRESPONDING OBJECTS ON SOME EXTERNAL VARIABLE. The situation here is similar to that described just above with the exception that the ideal points model rather than the vector model is used. As has already been noted, this second approach is more general in that it subsumes the first as a special case when the ideal points move out beyond the periphery of the points corresponding to the objects. A number of specific methods are possible within the framework of this general model (e.g., see Carroll, this book, Volume I).

c. DETERMINATION OF LEVEL CONTOURS CORRESPONDING TO AN EXTERNAL VARIABLE. In the special but not infrequent case of a two-dimensional spatial representation, it can be illuminating to interpolate constant-level curves between the points in the space so as to correspond to a given external variable. Abelson (1954) once proposed an ingenious way of doing this in an objective and potentially computerizable way.

Methods for Facilitating Interpretation by Relating Different Spatial Representations to Each Other

a. Transformation of two or more spatial representations into a mutual best fit. Sometimes different spatial representations have been obtained by different procedures for the same set of objects. In such cases it is often desirable to determine the extent to which the different representations agree with each other. Since, however, the results are generally determined only to within a similarity transformation (multidimensional scaling) or an affine transformation (factor analysis), the representations must be transformed into mutual congruence before their agreement can be assessed. A number of methods have been developed for purposes of this sort (e.g., see Carroll, 1968b; Cliff, 1966; Lingoes, 1967b; Schönemann, 1966; Schönemann & Carroll, 1970).

b. Determination of agreement between clustering structures of two or more spatial representations. As has been noted, an advantage of embedding a clustering in a spatial representation is that it provides a more objective way of determining whether the same clusters emerge from different sets of data concerning the same objects. Measures of the similarity or "distance" between different clusterings of the kind discussed by Boorman and Arabie (Volume I) provide a still more objective way of doing this—particularly in the usual sort of case in which the agreement is not perfect.

All of the above-mentioned methods for finding relationships within or between spatial representations or sets of data can be (or actually have been) programed as procedures that are "objective" in the sense that, once they are supplied with the required spatial representations or sets of data as input, they will proceed to yield a uniquely determined result without further human intervention. (Of course such methods furnish only an aid to final interpretation—not that final interpretation itself. Accordingly, the final interpretation, which is then based upon such unique objective results, will itself generally involve subjective considerations.) There are, however, other computer-based aids to interpretation for which no such sharp line can be drawn between a purely objective computation and an ensuing purely subjective interpretation. Sometimes the most efficient way to reach a final interpretation seems to be to let the objective and subjective components interact with each other.

An example that seems particularly promising is the use of on-line graphical interaction facilities to enable a researcher to transform a high-dimensional spatial representation according to objective constraints (e.g., of rigid rotation) in order to optimize some wholly implicit, subjective criterion. Noll and others at the Bell Telephone Laboratories have perfected an interactive stereographic display in which an investigator can, at the same time, (a) view a three-dimensional configuration or even a three-dimensional projection of a four-dimensional configuration in three-dimensional space, and (b) manipulate a kind of multidimensional control stick so as to rotate the configuration into any desired orientation in real time. (For a description of the generation of three-dimensional movies in somewhat this way, see Noll, 1965). This device has already been found helpful in discovering meaningful orientations (and, hence, axes) of complex representations in more than two dimensions, and it could presumably be used as an aid to discovering relationships of any of the general types (1–3) considered above.

Indeed one can now envisage an approach to the discovery of underlying structures in data in which the researcher sits down to an interactive console with various electronically driven graphical displays and multi-dimensional controls of this sort and, after reading in his set or sets of data, proceeds to apply various methods and transformations (perhaps in a largely intuitive and somewhat trial-and-error fashion) until he is able to elicit a sufficiently meaningful picture of the underlying structure through the graphical displays. In part, such a system would presumably consist of an internally stored library of programs of the sort listed in this taxonomy that, however, have been made mutually coherent (Stowe, Wiesen, Yntema, & Forgie, 1966) in the sense that they can be applied in any order to any representation or set of data—subject only to the constraints imposed by the inherent form of the data (e.g., whether a rectangular or necessarily square matrix) without any concern for the particular arbitrary format in which those data happen to be represented within the machine (e.g., whether columnwise or rowwise, fixed-point or floating-point, and the like). In contrast to the more traditional concern in data analysis with merely the testing of already formulated notions, it is not impossible that the analysis of data by the kind of machine-aided exploration proposed here might sometimes be accompanied—indeed even carried forward—by the inherent excitement of genuine search and discovery.

Acknowledgments

The preparation of this taxonomy was supported by a grant from the National Science Foundation (GS-2283). The author wishes to express his appreciation to J. Douglas Carroll and to Joseph B. Kruskal for their helpful suggestions concerning both this chapter and the preceding introductory chapter.

References

Abelson, R. P. A technique and a model for multidimensional attitude scaling. *Public Opinion Quarterly*, 1954, **18**, 405–418.

Ball, G., & Hall, D. ISODATA: A novel method of data analysis and pattern recognition. Menlo Park, California: Stanford Research Institute, Technical Report, May, 1965. (mimeographed)

Bennett, J. F. Determination of the number of independent parameters of a score matrix from the examination of rank orders. *Psychometrika*, 1956, **21**, 383–393.

Bennett, R. S. The intrinsic dimensionality of signal collections. Baltimore, Maryland: John Hopkins University, Department of Electrical Engineering, December, 1965. (mimeographed)

Bloxom, B. Individual differences in multidimensional scaling. Research Bulletin 68–45, Princeton, New Jersey: Educational Testing Service, 1968.

Bock, R. D., & Jones, L. V. The measurement and prediction of judgment and choice. San Francisco, California: 1968. Holden–Day,

Boorman, S. A., & Arabie, P. Structural measures and the method of sorting. Present volume.

Carroll, J. D. A general method for preference mapping of perceptual space. *Bulletin of the Operations Research Society of America*, 1968, **16**, 282. (a)

Carroll, J. D. Generalization of canonical correlation analysis to three or more sets of variables. *Proceedings of the 76th Annual Convention of the American Psychological Association*, 1968, 227–228. (b)

Carroll, J. D. Polynomial factor analysis. *Proceedings of the 77th Annual Convention of the American Psychological Association*, 1969a, **4**, 103–104. (a)

Carroll, J. D. Categorical conjoint measurement. *Mathematical Psychology Meetings, Ann Arbor, Michigan, August* 1969. (b)

Carroll, J. D. Individual differences and multidimensional scaling. Present volume.

Carroll, J. D., & Chang, J.-J. A general index of nonlinear correlation and its application to the interpretation of multidimensional scaling solutions. *American Psychologist*, 1964, **19**, 540. (Abstract) (a)

Carroll, J. D., & Chang, J.-J. Non-parametric multidimensional analysis of paired-comparisons data. Paper presented at the joint meeting of the Psychometric and Psychonomic Societies, Niagra Falls, October, 1964. (b)

Carroll, J. D., and Chang, J.-J. Analysis of individual differences in multidimensional scaling via an N-way generalization of "Eckart–Young" decomposition. *Psychometrika*, 1970, **35**, 283–319.

Cliff, N. Orthogonal rotation to congruence. *Psychometrika*, 1966, **31**, 33–42.

Cliff, N. Consistencies among judgments of adjective combinations. This book, Volume II.

Cole, A. J. (Ed.) *Numerical taxonomy*. New York: Academic Press, 1969.

Coombs, C. H. *A theory of data*. New York: Wiley, 1964.

Coombs, C. H., Dawes, R. M., & Tversky, A. *Mathematical psychology: An elementary introduction*. Englewood Cliffs, New Jersey: Prentice–Hall, 1970.

D'Andrade, R. G., Quinn, N. R., Nerlove, S. B., & Romney, A. K. Categories of disease in American–English and Mexican–Spanish. This book, Volume II.

David, H. A. The method of paired comparisons. In M. G. Kendall (Ed.), *The advanced theory of statistics*. Vol. 1. New York: Hafner, 1963.

Degerman, R. L. Multidimensional analysis of complex structure: Mixtures of class and quantitative variation. *Psychometrika*, 1970, **35**, 475–491.

Degerman, R. The geometric representation of some simple structures. Present volume.

Friedman, H., and Rubin, J. On some invariant criteria for grouping data. *Journal of American Statistical Association*, 1967, **62**, 1159–1177.

Gnanadesikan, R., & Wilk, M. B. Data analytic methods in multivariate statistical analysis. In P. R. Krishnaiah (Ed.), *International symposium of multivariate analysis: Dayton, Ohio*, 1968. *II*. New York: Academic Press, 1969.

Guttman, L. Image theory for the structure of quantitative variates. *Psychometrika*, 1953, **18**, 277–296.

Guttman, L. A general nonmetric technique for finding the smallest coordinate space for a configuration of points. *Psychometrika*, 1968, **33**, 469–506.

Harman, H. H. *Modern factor analysis*. (2nd ed.) Chicago, Illinois: University of Chicago Press, 1967.

Harman, H. H., & Jones, W. H. Factor analysis by minimizing residuals (Minres.). *Psychometrika*, 1966, **31**, 351–368.

Horan, C. B. Multidimensional scaling: Combining observations when individuals have different perceptual structures, *Psychometrika*, 1969, **34**, 139–165.

Indow, T., & Uchizono, T. Multidimensional mapping of Munsell colors varying in hue and chroma. *Journal of Experimental Psychology*, 1960, **59**, 321–329.

Johnson, S. C. Hierarchical clustering schemes. *Psychometrika*, 1967, **32**, 241–254.

Johnson, S. C. How to use HICLUS—A hierarchical cluster analysis program. Murray Hill, New Jersey: Bell Telephone Laboratories, November, 1968. (mimeographed)

Jöreskog, K. G. A general approach to confirmatory maximum likelihood factor analysis, *Psychometrika*, 1969, **34**, 2, 183–202.

Kendall, M. G. Further contributions to the theory of paired comparisons, *Biometrics*, 1955, **11**, 43–62.

Kendall, M. G. *Rank correlation methods*. (3rd ed.) London: Griffin, 1962.

Klemmer, E. T., & Shrimpton, N. W. Preference scaling via a modification of Shepard's proximity analysis method. *Human Factors*, 1963, **5**, 163–168.

Kruskal, J. B. Multidimensional scaling by optimizing goodness of fit to a nonmetric hypothesis. *Psychometrika*, 1964, **29**, 1–27. (a)

Kruskal, J. B. Nonmetric multidimensional scaling: A numerical method. *Psychometrika*, 1964, **29**, 115–129. (b)

Kruskal, J. B. Analysis of factorial experiments by estimating monotone transformations of the data. *The Journal of the Royal Statistical Society*, 1965 (Series B, methodological), **27**, 251–263.

Kruskal, J. B. How to use M-D-SCAL, a program to do multidimensional scaling and multidimensional unfolding, (Version 4 and 4M of M-D-SCAL, all in FORTRAN IV). Murray Hill, New Jersey: Bell Telephone Laboratories, 1968. (mimeographed)

Kruskal, J. B. Linear transformation of multivariate data to reveal clustering. Present volume.

Kruskal, J. B., & Carmone, F. J. MONANOVA: A FORTRAN-IV program for monotone analysis of variance. *Behavioral Science*, 1969, **14**, 165–166.

Kruskal, J. B., & Shepard, R. N. A nonmetric variety of linear factor analysis. In preparation.

Lawley, D. N. The estimation of factor loadings by the method of maximum likelihood. *Proceedings of the Royal Society of Edinburgh, A*, 1940, **60**, 64–82.

Lingoes, J. C. New computer developments in pattern analysis and nonmetric techniques. In *Proceedings IBM Symposium: Computers in Psychological Research*. Paris: Gauthier–Villars, 1966.

Lingoes, J. C. An IBM 7090 program for Guttman–Lingoes conjoint measurement—I. *Behavioral Science,* 1967, **12,** 501–502. (a)

Lingoes, J. C. An IBM 7090 program for Guttman–Lingoes configurational similarity—I. *Behavioral Science,* 1967, **12,** 502–503. (b)

Lingoes, J. C. A general survey of the Guttman–Lingoes nonmetric program series. Present volume.

Luce, R. D., & Tukey, J. W. Simultaneous conjoint measurement: A new type of fundamental measurement. *Journal of Mathematical Psychology,* 1964, **1,** 1–27.

McDonald, R. P. A general approach to nonlinear factor analysis. *Psychometrika,* 1962, **27,** 397–415.

McGee, V. The multidimensional analysis of 'elastic' distances. *The British Journal of Mathematical and Statistical Psychology,* 1966, **19,** 181–196.

McGee, V. Multidimensional scaling of N sets of similarity measures: A nonmetric individual differences approach. *Multivariate Behavioral Research,* 1968, **3,** 233–248.

Messick, S. J. An empirical evaluation of multidimensional successive intervals. *Psychometrika,* 1956, **21,** 367–376.

Miller, J. E., Shepard, R. N., & Chang, J.-J. An analytical approach to the interpretation of multidimensional scaling solutions. *American Psychologist,* 1964, **19,** 579–580. (Abstact)

Morey, J. L., & Yntema, D. B. Experiments on systems. *Information system sciences: Proceedings of the second congress.* Baltimore, Maryland: Spartan, 1965.

Napior, D. Nonmetric multidimensional techniques for summated ratings. Present volume.

Noll, A. M. Computer generation of three-dimensional movies. *Computers and Automation,* 1965, **14,** 20–23.

Rao, C. R. Estimation and tests of significance in factor analysis, *Psychometrika,* 1941, **6,** 49–53.

Rosenberg, S., & Sedlak, A. Structural representations of perceived personality trait relationships. This book, Volume II.

Schönemann, P. A generalized solution of the orthogonal procrustes problem. *Psychometrika,* 1966, **31,** 1–10.

Schönemann, P. H., & Carroll, R. M. Fitting one matrix to another under choice of a similarity transformation and a rigid motion. *Psychometrika,* 1970, **35,** 245–255.

Shepard, R. N. Stimulus and response generalization: Tests of a model relating generalization to distance in psychological space. *Journal of Experimental Psychology,* 1958, **55,** 509–523.

Shepard, R. N. The analysis of proximities: Multidimensional scaling with an unknown distance function. I. *Psychometrika,* 1962, **27,** 125–140. (a)

Shepard, R. N. The analysis of proximities: Multidimensional scaling with an unknown distance function. II. *Psychometrika,* 1962, **27,** 219–246. (b)

Shepard, R. N. Polynomial fitting in the analysis of proximities. *Proceedings of the XVIIth international congress of psychology.* Amsterdam: North-Holland Publ., 1964. Pp. 345–346. (abstract)

Shepard, R. N. Metric structures in ordinal data. *Journal of Mathematical Psychology,* 1966, **3,** 287–315.

Shepard, R. N. Psychological representation of speech sounds. In E. E. David and P. B. Denes (Eds.), *Human communication: A unified view.* New York: McGraw-Hill, 1972, in press.

Shepard, R. N., & Carroll, J. D. Parametric representation of nonlinear data structures. In P. R. Krishnaiah (Ed.), *International symposium on multivariate analysis, Dayton, Ohio,* 1965. New York: Academic Press, 1966. Pp. 561–592.

Shepard, R. N., & Chang, J.-J. Conformal reduction of nonlinear data structures. In preparation.

Shepard, R. N., & Kruskal, J. B. Nonmetric methods for scaling and factor analysis. *American Psychologist*, 1964, **19**, 557–558. (Abstract)

Slater, P. The analysis of personal preference. *British Journal of Statistical Psychology*, 1960, **13**, 119–135.

Sneath, P. H. A. The application of computers to taxonomy. *Journal of General Microbiology*, 1957, **17**, 201–226.

Sokal, R., and Sneath, P. H. A. *Principles of numerical taxonomy.* San Francisco, California and London: Freeman, 1963.

Sørensen, T. A method of establishing groups of equal amplitude in plant sociology based on similarity of species content and its application to analyses of the vegetation on Danish Commons. *Biological Skr.*, 1948, **5**, 1–34.

Stowe, A. N., Wiesen, R. A., Yntema, D. B., & Forgie, J. W. The Lincoln Reckoner: An operation-oriented, on-line facility with distributed control. *Proceedings of the Fall Joint Computer Conference*, 1966, 433–444.

Thurstone, L. A law of comparative judgment. *Psychological Review*, 1927, **34**, 273–286.

Thurstone, L. *Multiple factor analysis.* Chicago, Illinois: University of Chicago Press, 1947.

Torgerson, W. S. Multidimensional scaling: I. Theory and method. *Psychometrika*, 1952, **17**, 401–419.

Tryon, R. C., and Bailey, D. E. The BC Try computer system of cluster and factor analysis. *Multivariate Behavioral Research*, 1966, **1**, 95–111.

Tucker, L. R., and Messick, S. An individual difference model for multidimensional scaling. *Psychometrika*, 1963, **28**, 333–367.

Tversky, A. A general theory of polynomial conjoint measurement. *Journal of Mathematical Psychology*, 1967, **4**, 1–20.

Tversky, A., and Zivian, A. An IBM 7090 program for additivity analysis. *Behavioral Science*, 1966, **11**, 78–79.

Wallace, D. Cluster analysis. *International encyclopedia of the social sciences.* New York: Crowell Collier, 1968. Pp. 519–524.

Ward, J. H., Jr. Hierarchical groupings to optimize an objective function. *Journal of the American Statistical Association*, 1963, **58**, 236–244.

Wish, M., Deutsch, M., and Biener, L. Differences in perceived similarity of nations. This book, Volume II.

Yntema, D. B. Choosing an inverse polynomial transformation to achieve additivity. Presented at the Mathematical Psychology Meetings, Stanford, California, August 1968.

Young, F. W. A model for polynomial conjoint analysis algorithms. Present volume.

Young, F. W., & Torgerson, W. S. TORSCA: A FORTRAN IV program for Shepard–Kruskal multidimensional scaling analysis. *Behavioral Science*, 1967, **12**, 498.

A GENERAL SURVEY OF THE GUTTMAN-LINGOES NONMETRIC PROGRAM SERIES

James C. Lingoes

THE UNIVERSITY OF MICHIGAN
ANN ARBOR, MICHIGAN

If we broadly conceive of data as a relational system whose components are a set of objects or events and a set of attributes or variables (having at least two possible values), three basic facets emerge. First, there are the objects which we wish to differentiate one from the other (P); secondly, the variables which are relevant to the differences of interest (I); and, finally the category values or labels which distinguish one instance of an event from another (C, if the labels are common to all variables under consideration at any given instant of observation, e.g., the set of real numbers, and C_i, if the values are specific to a particular variable, e.g., the set of color labels). We do not wish to be restrictive in the meaning of "objects"— they may be palpable or impalpable, real or imaginary, in fact, anything that can be conceived. Events or objects as components of the relational system assume the role of subject in the *data proposition*, while the attributes and their modifiers describe and delimit the observation as predicate.

49

A data relational system typically takes on the form of an array of numbers or labels, where the rows are objects; the columns, items or variables; and the elements denote the observed differences. The data matrix is merely a shorthand way of communicating a series of propositions, whose essence consists of relations and interrelations. The fact that numbers might be used instead of words or some other convenient nonnumeric symbols is to a large extent irrelevant to the mathematico-logical nature of the information. Depending upon what assumptions we make about the values (be they quantitative or classificatory) in our multivariable matrix, we are free to manipulate the elements of this array in a multitude of ways (Lingoes, 1970b), e.g., arithmetically or by physically rearranging rows and columns—all to the purpose of revealing an order (if it can be found) and deriving some generalizations and conclusions from the observed order.

Our manipulations of the elements of the *data space* are subsumed, of course, under the rubric of data analysis (a high-level psychological activity of perception, integration, organization, abstraction, and conceptualization). These manipulations eventuate in some form of depiction or summary in, what we choose to call, the *representation space*, which serves as the basis for interpretation and action. To the extent that there is an isomorphism between the elements and interrelations of the data and representation spaces via the intermediary of an appropriate set of transformations in data analysis, then the task of interpretation both is made easier and is less risky. All of the above is quite elementary to be sure, but is spelled out here to underline some of the distinctions we wish to make. Essentially we view data analysis as transformational in character and the assumption base as a model or theory of measurement, both of which are intimately related, if not, indeed, inseparable.

The *form* that our transformations assume and their *range* of application provide two main guidelines for developing methods of analysis. If we are concerned with preserving metric information, then such data permit but a narrow set of transformations which are metrically invariant for mapping the data into the representation space (an isometric mapping). On the other hand, if we only wish to preserve order on the basis of our measurement model, then a much wider set of transformations is available for an isotonic mapping. Or, if only class membership is to be maintained, then an even greater set of transformations are permissible for an isomenic invariance, etc. Since the numbers or labels in our data matrix *qua* symbols tell us absolutely nothing about their meaning, we must surmise their import from our knowledge about the circumstances under which the data had been collected and reported and, even then, the context might be deficient to reveal what we need to know. In any event, we make assumptions about their meaning and accordingly apply those transformations which are consonant therewith. For whatever class of transformations chosen, however, we must be clear in our minds (as part of our measurement model) about its applicability to various parts of the data, e.g., all elements, within subsets, and, if the latter, how are these defined (within rows, columns, or partitions of the whole matrix), etc.? Expanding on these two principles provides a means of comparison among and within the three families of programs in the Guttman–Lingoes (G–L) series. Under the *form of transformation* we deal with the topics of monotonicity, reproducibility, communality, and functional forms, while in respect to *range of transformation* we address ourselves to the issues of comparability and identifiability of sets.

Three families of programs comprise the present G–L series: (1) the smallest space series or SSA, (2) the multidimensional scalogram series or MSA, and (3) the conjoint measurement series or CM. To date there are 15 programs (available upon request; Lingoes, 1968d) in the above three families. A sixteenth program is in the nature of an auxiliary procedure for determining the extent to which two configurations are isomorphic in respect to order over all elements of the matrix (Lingoes, 1967a). A brief description of each family and member will be given here as well as an outline of the rationale behind the various methods and indications as to their possible uses. Before delving into such descriptive details, however, a word or two on interfamilial similarities and differences would be appropriate.

The MSA series is distinguished from the SSA series on the basis of completeness of design. Each of the three basic facets (P, I, and C or C_i) are explicitly considered in the MSA series of programs (the analysis of the relation of *belongingness*) and appear as identifiable components of the representation space. Objects map into *points*, categories into *regions* or sets of points, and items map into *partitions* or sets of regions. SSA, on the other hand, collapses a pair of facets (e.g., in computing correlations among variables, objects and the categories into which they fall are considered a unity) in the data space and, as a consequence, there is no distinct element in the representation space for one of the data facets. Preservation of *order* characterizes the SSA family and the basic models are either that of distance or scalar products based on monotonic transformations. Invariance of *identity* is the hallmark of MSA even though a distance model may be employed for evaluating goodness of fit. The CM series contrasts with both SSA and MSA in that the coefficients or values generated are from a *polynomial form* which is *adimensional* in character (although the resulting scale can be represented linearly). CM, as SSA, is order preserving and employs monotonic transformations. The above interfamilial difference will become clearer in the following presentation (see Guttman, 1966a, 1967; Lingoes, 1968e, for further details on these comparisons).

The Smallest Space Series

Given a matrix of coefficients which are interpreted as measures of similarity/dissimilarity and which are assumed to be informative of order only, determine a Euclidean or city-block space for which either the distances among the points or the scalar products among the vectors have the same rank order (or are minimally discrepant from that order) in as few dimensions as possible. In general, fewer (and, at times, substantially fewer) dimensions will be needed to reproduce order information than to reproduce metric information. To reproduce order information, then, requires a simpler and more direct representation of one's data, which facilitates the interpretative process. If our interest is in patterns or configurations, the most natural concept for revealing them is order and the appropriate method for analysis is one which focuses on monotonic transformations.

Three sets of programs in the SSA series have been developed: four in the *square* matrix set (abbreviated simply as SSA, but more properly designated SSAS), four in the *rectangular* matrix set (SSAR), and one in the *partitioned* matrix set (SSAP)—all of which are designed to handle either different mathematical models or different contingencies of data collection. The term smallest space analysis is not a particularly apt name for this series (having been adopted by me to emphasize minimum dimensionality), since it fails to focus on the crucial feature of these procedures, viz., the use of monotone transformations. Similarly, the term nonmetric is quite ambiguous. Perhaps it is not too late to suggest a change in terminology for the SSA series, e.g., *monotone distance analysis* or MDA for those techniques concerned with a distance model and *monotone vector analysis* (MVA) for those methods using a vector model. As a transitional aid we shall use both nomenclatures.

SSA for Square Matrices

The basic aspect differentiating this set of programs from the remaining ones in the SSA series is the fact that the elements which are compared are drawn from *one set of things* resulting in a set of coefficients arrayed in a *square* matrix, e.g., the ijth element of the matrix represents the relationship between the objects or variables i and j. The entries are on relations among I or P or C, but *not* between data facets.

SSA-I (MDA-U). This program deals with the off-diagonal elements of a square, symmetric matrix of coefficients, where order is assumed to hold over all elements (e.g., a matrix of correlation coefficients)—the order is unconditional (hence the U following our alternative designation). The underlying model maps similarities/dissimilarities into Euclidean or city-block distances such as to satisfy the criterion of strong monotonicity (if there are no ties in the data) and semistrong monotonicity (if there are ties), i.e., $d_{ij} < d_{kl}$ whenever $r_{ij} > r_{kl}$ (for all pairs, excluding self-coefficients). Any matrix of real numbers may be analyzed by this technique provided that the formal requirements are met regarding symmetry and comparability among all pairs of indices *and* the substantive requirement that the values make sense as measures of similarity or dissimilarity.

The intent of this method is similar to that of Shepard (1962a, b) and identical to that of Kruskal (1964a, b), McGee (1966), and Young & Torgerson (1967). MDA-U differs from Kruskal's M-D-SCAL in terms of rationale of algorithm construction and is unlike any of the procedures developed to date for the same purpose (e.g., Torgerson–Young's TORSCA or McGee's HYBRID programs). Its main advantages over other algorithms lies in its robustness and rational step-size (Lingoes & Roskam, 1973). The method has been generalized to minimize Kruskal's *stress* coefficient (semiweak monotonicity) in addition to the G–L *coefficient of alienation* (semistrong monotonicity) and is capable of analyzing an indefinite number of variables. The refinements built into MDA-U reduce the local minimum problem (Roskam & Lingoes, 1970). Other references pertinent to MDA-U (SSA-I) are Guttman (1968), Lingoes (1965a, 1966a, d, 1969), and Roskam (1969).

SSA-II (MDA-C). This program analyzes the off-diagonal elements of a square, nonsymmetric matrix of similarity/dissimilarity coefficients whose order is conditional upon each of the points in turn. In contrast to MDA-U, the present method yields two solutions in general, i.e., a column solution and a row solution. Whenever one has a nonsymmetric matrix or can not justify the assumption of comparability among coefficients from different rows (columns), MDA-C is the method to choose. Although one might symmetrize a nonsymmetric matrix if one believes that the differences between the ijth and jith elements are minor and arise on a chance basis and then apply MDA-U or use Kruskal's approach for nonsymmetric matrices based on all the relationships in the matrix rather than within rows (columns) only, these tactics can at times give rise to distortions (depending on the degree of asymmetry in the matrix) and essentially ignore the psychology of the situation if the asymmetry is substantive in nature (see Coombs, 1964, for a discussion of unfolding theory).

Since the MDA-C model is weaker than MDA-U (since $n/2$ fewer constraints are imposed on the solution), an attempt is made to require a solution having tied distances whenever there are ties in the data (strong monotonicity). Sitting on any column or row endpoint the remaining $n - 1$ points will be properly ordered from it in terms of distance (Lingoes, 1965b, 1966d). Examples of matrices analyzable by MDA-C would be an import–export matrix of tonnage exchanged between countries, a sociometric choice matrix of friendship, or a matrix of transitional probabilities, etc. Again, the numbers can be purely arbitrary indicative of order merely, so long as one is willing to assume that distance in a Euclidean space is monotonely related to the indicants of similarity, the resulting solution will reflect that order insofar as possible and in as few dimensions as necessary. There are, however, certain matrices (e.g., an antisymmetric matrix where the row orders are the reverse of the column orders) which cannot be embedded in any space whatsoever. A MDA-C approach to such matrices will yield a solution which is essentially degenerate (all distances will be equal). If antisymmetry holds, it is recommended that each half of the matrix be analyzed by MDA-U or perhaps by the following routine (either half).

SSA-III (MVA-U). Whereas both previous programs have specifications for a point representation, map the ranks of distances into the ranks of a set of starting coefficients, and neither deal with the diagonal entries: MVA-U in contrast, has a vector representation, maps the ranks of scalar products into the ranks of the indices of similarity, and indirectly solves for communalities. By abandoning Thurstone's requirement that $R = FF'$ (as stated either in its strong form of exact minimum rank or in its weak form of residuals "small enough to be ignored"), another matrix θ can be determined such that: (1) $\theta = XX'$, where X is a rectangular coordinate set; (2) $\theta \underline{m} R$, i.e., the elements of θ are a weakly monotonic increasing function of the elements of the input coefficients, R $(i \neq j)$; and, (3) m, the number of dimensions, is less than or equal to the minimum rank of R. Thus, MVA-U is a nonmetric factor-analytic method whose algorithm consists of a sequence of linear and orthogonal transformations of values monotone with R, i.e., Guttman's *rank images*. The typical use of this technique is in those applications where one would do a standard linear factor analysis but could not justify the linear assumptions of the model (the general situation confronting the social scientist). Other possible applications arise when MDA-U, the distance model, yields too many dimensions (in general, $m > 3$), which poses awkward problems for interpreting the resulting space. MVA-U, on the other hand, can make use of Thurstone's simple structure concept to provide some purchase on higher-dimensional solutions.

While one may analyze any real symmetric matrix of similarity coefficients by the present technique, it is optimally employed when the indices are either correlations or covariances (Lingoes, 1966b, d, 1969d; Lingoes & Guttman, 1967). Because of the familarity of factor analysis as a model for data reduction, MVA-U serves as an excellent introduction to the field of nonmetric methods and what they can accomplish in terms of parsimony.

SSA-IV (MDA-UD). Given a matrix of correlations or covariances, determine a set of communalities for the diagonal (hence the D on the mnemonic device), such that the set of corrected correlations (see below) or covariances shall be isotonic with the set of squared Euclidean distances. In some respects MDA-UD is like MDA-U, while in others it is more like MVA-U. The present routine is like the unconditional distance model in that both have a point representation; and it is similar to MVA-U in that communalities are solved simultaneously with the determination of the coordinate system. SSA-IV (MDA-UD) is unlike both MDA-U and MVA-U in that the final coefficients are not mapped into the starting values, but are carried into a set of corrected coefficients. Of all the programs in the G–L series, MDA-UD is the most metric. Its areas of application are as broad as those of MDA-U and MVA-U as well as those of linear factor analysis; indeed, it can be shown that the latter is but a special case of the more general solution of MDA-UD.

An intuitive grasp of what is involved in mapping the corrected correlations or covariances into the set of squared distances can be obtained from the following artificial example. Let us suppose R to be an order-three matrix of correlations with off-diagonal elements of .3, .2, and .1 for r_{21}, r_{31}, and r_{32}, respectively. And further, let the corresponding elements of D (the matrix of squared distances) be 7, 3, and 6. It is obvious that the elements of R are not monotonic with those of D. If, however, we solve for a diagonal matrix W with elements: $3/7^{1/2}$, $7^{1/2}$, and $7^{1/2}$ and solve for R_c, the corrected correlations: $R_c = WRW'$ (or in scalar notation: $r_{c_{ij}} = w_{ii}r_{ij}w_{jj}$) we obtain .9, .6, and .7, which are in the proper order in respect to D, i.e., $R_c \underset{\sim}{m} D$, the solution desired. By solving for the diagonal elements we are able to achieve the smallest possible dimensionality by eliminating unique variance.

Now as to the point that linear factor analysis can be seen to be but a special case of MDA-UD, we quote Guttman (1967):

> This should have been "obvious" to all of us long ago; that it has not been is a tribute to the blinders certain habits have placed on us. We have been thinking of the correlation matrix in terms of *uncorrected* off-diagonal coefficients, with communalities in the main diagonal. But now *correct* all the coefficients for communality. This does not change the rank of the "reduced" matrix, but all the main diagonal elements become equal to unity. The corrected variables are now representable as vectors of *unit* length, emanating from a common origin; the dimensionality of the space is the number of common factors, namely the rank of the reduced matrix. The *termini* of the vectors are then *points all equidistant from the origin*. For the Spearman, or rank one case, the termini are at most at two points on a straight line, at opposite sides of the origin. For rank two, the termini must all lie on a circle or represent part of a *circumplex*. For rank three, we must have a spherex, etc. More generally, we have the theorem: all Gramian matrices of rank two and with constant diagonal elements must be circumplexes, all of rank three must be spherexes, etc. Bringing in the general radex concept enables more far reaching theorems on Gramian matrices in general, and the communality problem in particular, ...
> SSA-IV differs from SSA-I in that it seeks the corrections for communality which will yield the smallest space maintaining the *corrected* monotonicity among the correlation coefficients. If a two-space emerges that is *not* from a circumplex (the whole plane can be filled with points), the smallest possible reduced rank for the correlation matrix must *exceed* two, and indeed be much more than two in general (my theorems will tell by how much). And so for the one-dimensional and the higher dimensional cases of SSA. (p. 78f)

Despite the theoretical import of this procedure, there are practical limitations in its implementation and it by no means is intended to supplant either MDA-U or MVA-U. One difficulty, perhaps of transient importance, is computational in nature. With present computer facilities (less than four CPU's), the analysis of large matrices (i.e., those with more than 30 variables) is impractical because of the number of computations involved. A second difficulty arises at the level of interpretation. One of the chief merits of a nonmetric approach to one's data is the fact that there is a fairly simple correspondence between the data and representation spaces. In MDA-UD, however, the relationship between these two spaces is complicated by the issue of communalities, whose psychological meaning has not as yet been made explicit. It is one thing to attain a mathematically satisfying solution and yet another to obtain a psychologically meaningful one, particularly if the communalities solved for are not proper (e.g., greater than unity). Since one is theoretically restricted to either correlations or covariances and since the rank of most empirical matrices is large (if not equal to $n - 1$), for all practical purposes MDA-UD will probably not prove to be a widely used method. Only time and use will determine the fruitfulness of this approach to substantive issues, although there is no gainsaying its theoretical importance (Lingoes, 1966c, d).

SSA for Rectangular Matrices

The following four programs (in contrast to the preceding four) are concerned with the analysis of a set of relations between *two sets of entities* resulting in a *rectangular* array whose row captions refer to the elements of one set (e.g., persons) and whose column captions refer to elements of the other set (e.g., variables or stimuli). Given only the interset information, the goal is to determine a representation where distances are a monotone function of the interset relationships (a vector model has not yet been programmed). As a useful by-product one obtains intraset relationships without having to assume the appropriate coefficient to reflect them.

SSAR-I (MDA-RU). The algorithm used in MDA-RU is a modification of that used for MDA-U, but the specifications are somewhat different. MDA-RU is designed for the analysis of rectangular and informationally complete matrices where all elements are in a comparable metric, e.g., a matrix of standardized scores for N individuals on n tests or a set of correlations between two sets of variables. The relationships among individuals or tests are assumed to be either unknown or irrelevant to the monotonicity constraints, i.e., rank-order information is maintained only within the rectangular matrix. One can view this rectangular matrix as an off-diagonal matrix of a supermatrix which is symmetric, but whose diagonal submatrices are null. Viewed in this manner, MDA-RU reduces to an MDA-U analysis and gives rise to a *joint space* (Coombs, 1964), where the constraints are on interset relations only (Lingoes & Vandenberg, 1966).

Since there are only Nn constraints coming from the data, it is quite important that: (1) a good initial configuration is at hand, (2) strong monotonicity is used as a criterion, and (3) a solution to the problem is not attempted in too few dimensions. If these precautions are not met, then degenerate solutions are possible, although not as likely as in the following procedure for the conditional case. The user need not worry about the first two contingencies, but the third one relating to dimensionality is of concern. MDA-RU can be viewed in terms of a nonmetric factor-analytic model or as an example of multidimensional unfolding (Lingoes, 1966d, e).

SSAR-II (MDA-RC). The second program in the rectangular series, like MDA-C, imposes restrictions on monotonicity only within rows or only within columns and thus requires comparability among the coefficients within the rows or columns, respectively. As in the case of MDA-C, two solutions are possible such that sitting on any row (column) point all the column (row) points will be properly ordered from it. If the rows are persons and the columns stimuli, then MDA-RC performs Coombs' multidimensional unfolding analysis. On the other hand, if the columns are tests and one does a column analysis, then MDA-RC is a form of nonmetric factor analysis. Of all the programs in the G–L series, the present method represents the weakest model (there are only N or n constraints) and degeneracy may result even when one uses a good initial configuration and imposes strong monotonicity. At most $(N, n)_{min} - 1$ dimensions are required for reflecting all the order relationships of such a matrix when restrictions are placed on rows (columns) only. If one can justify some measure of relationship among both the row and column points, then SSAP-I below would be a more appropriate procedure. Barring such justification, however, one should not seek to solve a problem in too few dimensions using the present technique. In addition to those uses mentioned above, MDA-RC has applications in the study of oscillatory regression problems, where, as in scale analysis, conditional distributions are to be compared in one direction (Lingoes, 1966d, f).

SSAR-III (MDA-RSU). This program maintains rank orders within rows and columns separately (semiunconditional comparability), but achieves a single solution by averaging the row and column results at each iteration. Whereas MDA-RU requires comparability over the entire rectangular submatrix and MDA-RC assumes comparability within rows or columns only, MDA-RSU presupposes comparability of values within a row and within a column (but not between rows and columns). MDA-RSU, as such, is a stronger model than MDA-RC, but has fewer constraints than MDA-RU. In most instances, however, similar results can be expected from MDA-RU and MDA-RSU, the differences arising primarily from the weighting that is used. One is in effect doing a MDA-C on the symmetric supermatrix referred to under MDA-RU. The present approach offers an alternative to MDA-RC when degeneracy occurs (Lingoes, 1966d, g).

SSAR-IV (MDA-RCD). Given a square, nonsymmetric matrix where the points have all been drawn from the same set as in MDA-C and the diagonal elements are unknown but are to be estimated, determine the smallest space in which both the row and column points are embedded in a joint space, such that sitting on any row (column) point, the column (row) points will be properly ordered from it and the distance between that row point and its corresponding column point shall be an estimate of its communality. This program will also yield two solutions if both are considered meaningful by the investigator (sometimes only one, a row or a column solution has substantive meaning). MDA-RCD represents the first successful attempt to solve the communality problem for distances in a nonmetric fashion (Lingoes, 1967c). An example where the present approach would be applicable is a sociometric choice or ranking situation where self-liking is either unknown or not elicited. If an individual likes others to the extent that the others like him, his two points will be near one another; but if he chooses differently than he is chosen, then he will have a self-representation with a relatively large distance. The existence of several large self-distances might be interpreted as indicative of group conflict or misperception. Or, as another example, in communication networks or trade relations, the degree of nonsymmetry reflected by the self-distances could be interpreted as an imbalance in the system. Other applications and interpretations will no doubt occur to the reader.

SSA FOR PARTITIONED MATRICES

Although only one program has been written for this series to date, the general need for being able to specify that comparability apply to entire blocks of a matrix is apparent. We have a number of possibilities open to us for specifying the range over which monotonicity is to be maintained (e.g., within all elements of a partition or unconditionally, within rows of a partition or columns, or unconditionally within some blocks and conditionally within others, etc.). The central idea behind this series is that each partition is in essence treated independently from other partitions because of either different metrics being involved or the substantive requirements of the problem so dictate.

SSAP-I (MDA-PU). Given a rectangular score matrix (representing the relationships between two sets of entities, e.g., persons and variables), a symmetric matrix of coefficients that measure the relationships among the row elements, and a symmetric matrix of coefficients that relate the column elements of the score matrix (e.g., intervariable correlations), conjoin these matrices to form a supermatrix where the rectangular matrix is located off diagonally and the two symmetric matrices are diagonally placed. By restricting one's comparisons unconditionally within each of these three matrices separately, one obtains a joint-space representation where the order within each partition is isotonic with the values in the three matrices individually. This model is much stronger than MDA-RU, since we are prejudging the issue of the appropriate coefficient for the within-set relations of persons and variables. We achieve a solution which allows us to relate the configuration derived from an MDA-U of persons to a similar analysis of variables—the nonmetric analog of obtaining factor scores in linear factor analysis. Since the values in the score matrix must be in a comparable metric, a normalization of the scores is required prior to computation of the spatial representation. One may input any index of relationship (the same or different) for the diagonally placed matrices or let the program compute one of the several available. Purely qualitative as well as quantitative data can be analyzed by this procedure by the simple expedient of expanding the score matrix to its basic binary form (Lingoes, 1968a), where a 1 indicates that a person falls in a category of an item and a 0 denotes nonmembership. Coefficients of association congenial to categorical data are available (Lingoes, 1970a, c).

MDA-PU has applications in the area of nonmetric factor analysis, unfolding analysis, and multidimensional scalogram analysis and is similar to MDA-U in its ability to analyze an indefinite number of objects or variables.

The Multidimensional Scalogram Series

In this set of programs we are concerned with all three data facets: P, I, and C or C_i, where our mapping is isomenic (reproducing class membership), rather than isotonic as in the SSA series. This series, therefore, is particularly applicable to qualitative or categorical data. Again, our goal, as in SSA, is to determine the smallest space in which to represent data facets so as to reveal whatever order may be implicit in our data. To date, there are three programs in this series differing in respect to the nature of the boundaries (a function of one's assumptions regarding both comparability and scalability of the data) separating the regions of the space within each partition or set of regions. As we impose more and more restrictions on the form of the boundaries, the method becomes less general in application but permits stronger inferences about patterns vis-à-vis the three facets of data.

MSA-I (MSA-L). This method is the most general (and least metric of the G–L series) of the three presently programmed in that the regional boundaries can assume any shape whatsoever so long as it is always the case that for a given individual and fixed category, the individual will be closer to points defining the boundary limits (hence the L in the revised nomenclature) of that category than to a point delimiting boundaries of other categories for the same item. Such a region for class membership is characterized as being contiguous when satisfied. The solution is such that one can reproduce the relationship of each person to every category of each item (when a perfect fit is obtained) or assess the degree of fit for less than perfect reproduction (i.e., the failure to satisfy contiguity throughout). Not only do the number of errors or violations determine how well we have done, but their importance or weight is also considered in the *coefficient of contiguity*. This procedure is ideally suited to the analysis of qualitative or nominal data where we wish to make the minimum number of assumptions. One can analyze and obtain a geometric representation for the most general kinds of data, e.g., a set of theories where the variables are conceptual facets having elements (categories) as broad or as fine as we choose. The theories (or objects) can then be assessed for their degree of similarity with one another in respect to the variables we deem relevant to their characterization.

To apply MSA-L to one's data, one need but start with a purely qualitative characteristic function, denoting presence or absence, i.e., either the individual has an attribute or he does not (see above, the binary matrix for MDA-PU). No assumptions whatsoever are required about the nature of the underlying distributions, the scaling properties of the items, or what kinds of relationships are involved among individuals, among items, or between the categories of any item with respect to order. All that is required is that the categories of each item be mutually exclusive and exhaustive. The category rubrics themselves can be numbers or names or mixtures thereof (so long as identity is preserved)—they are immaterial for other than nominal purposes since they do not enter into any of the computations.

The task set for MSA-L is one of mapping types (individuals having the same profile over the set of variables or items) into a Euclidean space with minimal dimensionality. Types are represented as points in this space, each item is a partition of the space into nonoverlapping regions, and each category is depicted as a region. Commensurate with this technique's generality, of course, is its weakness as a model for drawing conclusions about item and category relationships. The dimensions themselves (or any rotation of them) do not, in general, have psychological or substantive significance. Interpretations must flow directly from the configuration of points and any uniformities that emerge with respect to regional forms or to partitionings despite the looseness of specification of boundary form. As a consequence, more than three dimensions present difficulties in interpretation that are virtually insuperable at this stage, while, generally, only a one- or two-dimensional solution is practicable, suggesting the appropriateness of other techniques having stronger assumptions when dimensionality is greater than three (see below). The value of MSA-L resides in its wide applicability to many kinds of problems which often occur in the initial stages of investigation or which are not amenable to other techniques (Guttman, 1966a; Lingoes, 1966d, h, 1968a).

MSA-II (MSA-S). By changing the specifications of the representation space of MSA-L (where points are objects, regions are categories, and partitions are items) to points for objects and points for categories, we can define a *radius of inclusion*, such that sitting on any person point all those properties that characterize him will have points falling within the radius (similarly, by sitting on any category point we can determine all those persons who fall in that category). Both sets of points are embedded in a Euclidean space of the smallest possible dimensionality, such that class membership can be reproduced with a minimum of error. Such an analysis permits inferences regarding intercategory and interobject similarity, without having to invoke a specified measure of similarity (see MDA-PU above). The boundaries of MSA-S are circular (or, more generally, spherical and accordingly abbreviated S), which implies that belongingness is comparable over the entire score or attribute matrix.

The present model is more restrictive than MSA-L, but permits stronger inferences (e.g., something about intercategory relationships). By using interset information (the relation between an object and a category) we obtain, as in MDA-RU, information about intraset relations. The dimensions resulting from MSA-S may be meaningful, permitting interpretations of more than three dimensions. Interitem relationships, on the other hand, can be surmised only when very special configurations obtain, since the method lacks a specification to reveal them automatically (Lingoes, 1967b, 1968a). MSA-S reduces to a MDA-RU of an adjacency matrix of a partial graph (Guttman, 1965) when a data matrix has been expanded into its most basic form and ties are optimally broken to reduce dimensionality.

MSA-III (MSA-B and MSA-BP). In contrast to MSA-S, the present method restricts comparisons within each item (our distinction between C and C_i, respectively), which results in sets of rectilinear boundaries. As in MSA-S there are two sets of points—one for objects and another for categories. By determining the perpendicular bisectors for pairs of category points (within but not between items), an object's relation to the categories of each item can be reproduced. One can either allow the bisectors to intersect (MSA-B) or restrict them to be parallel (MSA-BP). By using the former option one has the weakest possible multidimensional scalogram model, which may prove less robust than even MDA-RC. Care must be exercised in the use of MSA-B to avoid degenerate solutions (e.g., by not setting dimensionality too low). Interpretations comparable to those elicited from MSA-S can be obtained from MSA-B, e.g., interperson and intercategory groupings and patterns.

MSA-BP, on the other hand, is the strongest multidimensional scalogram model for nominal variables. Not only does one have purchase on interobject and intercategory relationships, but by constraining the straight-line boundaries to be parallel one is able to say something about category ordering within items and, perhaps more importantly, item ordering or scalability. As one would suspect, this additional information is usually bought at the expense of increased dimensionality, but may well be worth the coin in those instances where the qualitative variables have been well studied and preselected (e.g., after weeding out "noisy" variables by MSA-L). In general it is not recommended that MSA-BP be used in a "fishing expedition" approach to data. Here, as in MSA-B, there are no interobject or intercategory coefficients—the intraset relations are not predetermined in any direct fashion. As a consequence, one should not attempt a solution in too few dimensions, for otherwise points will fall upon points and the patterns will be destroyed. A stronger version of MSA-BP is planned which will compute interperson and intercategory indices of similarity, thus going a long way toward a remedy of possible degeneracy. Although it would be nice if one did not have to assume which coefficient would be appropriate for intraset relations—letting it fall out, as it were—experience to date would suggest that such permissiveness, all too often, results in a model much too weak to be both parsimonious and informative of patterns.

A final program in the MSA series (MSA-IV or MSA-BPO) is planned (Lingoes, 1968a, b), which will impose parallel straight-line boundaries like MSA-BP, but will further require a predetermined order among the categories within items. As such, MSA-BPO applies to quantitative variables, thus completing the MSA series for analyzing the relation of belongingness.

The Conjoint Measurement Series

In the conjoint measurement series we are concerned with deriving a set of values from a specified polynomial of lowest degree, such that the values map into a set of ranks. There are three programs in this series to date which have specific applications in the areas of analysis of variance, regression analysis, and factor or correlational analysis. The latter two programs permit one to scale the raw data score matrix preparatory to the use of either standard linear techniques or some of the nonmetric methods discussed previously. By imposing linearity of regressions (insofar as possible, subject to the monotonicity constraints) one obtains rescaled values lying on an interval scale.

CM-I (CM-V). Given an n-way rectangular matrix of numbers denoting the outcome of a set of conjoint events, determine n sets of values, say x_i and y_j, such that $z_{ij} = x_i + y_j$ (for all i and j), where z_{ij} has the same rank order value as w_{ij}, the original cell entry. More generally, for a two-way table $z_{ij} = \sum_{k=0}^{n} a_{n-k} x_i^{n-k} y_j^{k}$, determine a solution with n as small as possible. We are attempting to obtain the best possible fit to a simple linear model via a monotonic transformation of the original values. To the extent that we are successful we have eliminated certain interaction terms (Kruskal, 1965) without having to presuppose the optimal transformation (e.g., a log or reciprocal transform) in so doing. We, thus, are able to analyze a conjoint event into its simple components in an additive fashion. The additive model in CM-V is equivalent to an analysis of variance model for factorial designs with main effects only and no interactions (Guttman, 1966, 1967; Lingoes, 1967d). The program not only yields the best set of values satisfying monotonicity, but also that set which is least discrepant from the input values in a least-squares sense. Other applications of this additive model can be found in scaling and psychophysical measurement.

CM-II (CM-R). Given a set of independent variables X whose elements are orderable and a dependent variable Y which is also orderable, determine the best monotone transformation of both sets such that the average product-moment correlation of the dependent variable with the independent variables will be maximized. To the extent that it is possible to achieve a perfect solution, the dependent variable will be an additive function of the independent variables and monotone with the original dependent variable, i.e., $w_i = z_{ij} + z_{ij+1} + \cdots + z_{in}$ and whenever $y_i > y_k$ then $w_i > w_k$. Thus, as in CM-V, we are explaining a particular event in terms of its additive components, both sets of which are monotone transformations of the original variables. The set of rescaled variables (now lying on an interval scale) can be used as input to a standard linear regression program to determine if a more parsimonious equation will result in predicting the dependent variable. If mild nonlinearities exist in one's original data, CM-R tends to "iron" these out so that the product-moment correlation coefficient will more adequately reflect the dependencies that are present. This program is particularly useful when one has rank-order values only (Lingoes, 1968c).

CM-III (CM-C). When one has a set of orderable scores and wishes to take into account the full extent of the relationships that exist among these variables introductory to performing some multivariate analysis (either from the metric or nonmetric repertoire), then CM-C will accomplish a scaling of these variables, such that the average intercorrelation among them will be maximized subject to the restriction that rank order will be preserved. By linearizing the regressions in this fashion it is possible to reduce dimensionality even in the case of a standard linear factor analysis and a fortiori with nonmetric factor analysis (MVA-U or SSA-III and MDA-UD or SSA-IV). As in the case of CM-R, mild nonlinearities will either be obviated or minimized, giving rise to greater stability in one's results (e.g., upon replication) and making the product-moment correlation a better indicator of the relationships that exist but which are attenuated.

If the set of variables is factorially complex (the general situation), it may be necessary to apply the following strategy for getting the most out of CM-C: (1) scale the entire set and apply MVA-U to the set of product moments; (2) partition the set of variables into homogeneous subsets on the basis of the factor results; (3) rescale each of the subsets separately with an attempt to achieve either a one or a two (at most) dimensional MVA-U solution for each subset; and, finally, (4) using the best scaling from each subset, compute all intercorrelations and then factor analyze them nonmetrically. Such a procedure should yield a fairly "clean" set of factors with minimal overlap (a unifactorial assignment for each variable). CM-C represents a direct solution to Cattell's (1962) formulation of the *relational simplex* problem as outlined in my 1964 address at Blaricum (Lingoes, 1966a) and is similar to the MAC (multivariate analysis of contingencies) approach for linearizing relationships (Guttman, 1941, 1959; Lingoes, 1963a, b, 1968d).

With CM-C we conclude our brief introduction to the G–L nonmetric program series. Space limitations precluded a comparable discussion or review of the many applications to substantive problems that these methods have had for a wide variety of social science disciplines. We hope to supply actual examples in a forthcoming book entitled: *Nonparametric transformation analysis: A geometric mapping of data structures for the behavioral sciences*. A number of new methods presently in the planning stage will expand the G–L series to encompass further analogs of metric methods, the analysis of partial orders, time and space series, etc., making it possible for the social scientist to select that procedure specifically tailored to his problem and the set of assumptions that are justified for his data.

Acknowledgments

This research in nonmetric methods is supported in part by a grant from the National Science Foundation (GS-929).

References

Cattell, R. B. The relational simplex theory of equal interval and absolute scaling. *Acta Psychologica*, 1962, **20**, 139–158.

Coombs, C. H. *A theory of data.* New York: Wiley, 1964.

Guttman, L. The quantification of a class of attributes. In P. Horst (Ed.), with collaboration of P. Wallin and L. Guttman, *The prediction of personal adjustment.* New York: Social Science Research Council, 1941. Pp. 319–348.

Guttman, L. Metricizing rank-ordered or unordered data for a linear factor analysis. *Sankhya: Indian Journal of Statistics*, 1959, **21**, 257–268.

Guttman, L. A definition of dimensionality and distance for graphs. Unpublished mimeograph, 1965.

Guttman, L. The nonmetric breakthrough for the behavioral sciences. *Proceedings of the Second National Conference on Data Processing.* Rehovot: Information Processing Association of Israel, 1966. Pp. 495–510. (a)

Guttman, L. Order analysis of correlation matrices. In R. B. Cattel (Ed.), *Handbook of Multivariate experimental psychology.* New York, Rand McNally, 1966, Pp. 438–458. (b)

Guttman, L. The development of nonmetric space analysis: A letter to John Ross. *Multivariate Behavioral Research*, 1967, **2**, 71–82.

Guttman, L. A general nonmetric technique for finding the smallest coordinate space for a configuration of points. *Psychometrika*, 1968, **33**, 469–506.

Kruskal, J. B. Multidimensional scaling by optimizing goodness of fit to a nonmetric hypothesis. *Psychometrika*, 1964, **29**, 1–27. (a)

Kruskal, J. B. Multidimensional scaling: A numerical method. *Psychometrika*, 1964, **29**, 115–129. (b)

Kruskal, J. B. Analysis of factorial experiments by estimating monotone transformations of the data. *Journal of the Royal Statistical Society*, 1965, (Series B, methodological) **27**, 251–263.

Lingoes, J. C. Sequential dependency analysis—An IBM 7090 program for factoring nonlinear or nonmetric data. *Behavioral Science*, 1963, **8**, 370. (a)

Lingoes, J. C. Multivariate analysis of contingencies—An IBM 7090 program for analyzing metric/nonmetric or linear/nonlinear data. *Computer Report*, 1963, **2**, 1–24. (b)

Lingoes, J. C. An IBM 7090 program for Guttman–Lingoes smallest space analysis—I. *Behavioral Science*, 1965, **10**, 183–184. (a)

Lingoes, J. C. An IBM 7090 program for Guttman–Lingoes smallest space analysis—II. *Behavioral Science*, 1965, **10**, 487. (b)

Lingoes, J. C. New computer developments in pattern analysis and nonmetric techniques. In *Uses of Computers in Psychological Research—The* 1964 *IBM Symposium of Statistics*. Paris: Gauthier–Villars, 1966. Pp. 1–22. (a)

Lingoes, J. C. An IBM 7090 program for Guttman–Lingoes smallest space analysis—III. *Behavioral Science*, 1966, **11**, 75–76. (b)

Lingoes, J. C. An IBM 7090 program for Guttman–Lingoes smallest space analysis—IV. *Behavioral Science*, 1966, **11**, 407. (c)

Lingoes, J. C. Recent computational advances in nonmetric methodology for the behavioral sciences. *Proceedings of the International Symposium: Mathematical and Computational Methods in Social Sciences*. Rome: International Computation Centre, 1966. Pp. 1–38. (d)

Lingoes, J. C. An IBM 7090 program for Guttman–Lingoes smallest space analysis—RI. *Behavioral Science*, 1966, **11**, 322. (e)

Lingoes, J. C. An IBM 7090 program for Guttman–Lingoes smallest space analysis—RII. *Behavioral Science*, 1966, **11**, 322. (f)

Lingoes, J. C. An IBM 7090 program for Guttman–Lingoes smallest space analysis—RIII. *Behavioral Science*, 1966, **11**, 323. (g)

Lingoes, J. C. An IBM 7090 program for Guttman–Lingoes multidimensional scalogram analysis—I. *Behavioral Science*, 1966, **11**, 76–78. (h)

Lingoes, J. C. An IBM 7090 program for Guttman–Lingoes configurational similarity—I. *Behavioral Science*, 1967, **12**, 502–503. (a)

Lingoes, J. C. An IBM 7090 program for Guttman–Lingoes multidimensional scalogram analysis—II. *Behavioral Science*, 1967, **12**, 268–270. (b)

Lingoes, J. C. An IBM 7090 program for Guttman–Lingoes smallest space analysis—RIV. *Behavioral Science*, 1967, **12**, 74–75. (c)

Lingoes, J. C. An IBM 7090 program for Guttman–Lingoes conjoint measurement—I. *Behavioral Science*, 1967, **12**, 501–502. (d)

Lingoes, J. C. The multivariate analysis of qualitative data. *Multivariate Behavioral Research*, 1968, **3**, 61–94. (a)

Lingoes, J. C. An IBM 360/67 program for Guttman–Lingoes multidimensional scalogram analysis—III. *Behavioral Science*, 1968, **13**, 512–513. (b)

Lingoes, J. C. An IBM 7090 program for Guttman–Lingoes conjoint measurement—II. *Behavioral Science*, 1968, **13**, 85–87. (c)

Lingoes, J. C. An IBM 360/67 program for Guttman–Lingoes conjoint measurement—III. *Behavioral Science*, 1968, **13**, 421–422. (d)

Lingoes, J. C. The rationale of the Guttman–Lingoes nonmetric series: A letter to Doctor Philip Runkel. *Multivariate Behavioral Research*, 1968, **3**, 495–508. (e)

Lingoes, J. C. Some boundary conditions for a monotone analysis of symmetric matrices. *Michigan Mathematical Psychology Program Technical Report*, 1969, **9**, 1–10. Also in: *Psychometrika*, 1971, **36**, 195–203. (d)

Lingoes, J. C. An IBM 360/67 program for Guttman–Lingoes smallest space analysis—PI. *Behavioral Science*, 1970, **15**, 536–540. (a)

Lingoes, J. C. Measurement. In A. Z. Guiora, & Brandwin, M. (Eds.), *The basic science of psychology*. New York: Norton, 1970, in press. (b)

Lingoes, J. C. A general nonparametric model for representing objects and attributes in a joint metric space. In J. C. Gardin (Ed.), *Les Compte-rendus de Colloque International sur L'emploi des Calculateurs en Archeologie: Problèmes Sémiologiques et Mathématiques*. Marseille: Centre National de la Recherche Scientifique, 1970, 277–298. (c)

Lingoes, J. C. & Guttman, L. Nonmetric factor analysis: A rank reducing alternative to linear factor analysis. *Multivariate Behavioral Research*, 1967, **2**, 485–505.

Lingoes, J. C. & Roskam, E. A mathematical and empirical analysis of two multidimensional scaling algorithms. *Psychometric Monographs*, 1973, in press.

Lingoes, J. C., & Vandenberg, S. G. A nonmetric analysis of twin data based on a multifaceted design. *Louisville Twin Study Research Report*, 1966, **17**, 1–17.

McGee, V. E. The multidimensional analysis of "elastic" distances. *British Journal of Mathematical Psychology*, 1966, **19**, 181–196.

Roskam, E. A comparison of principles for algorithm construction in nonmetric scaling. *Michigan Mathematical Psychology Program Technical Report*, 1969, **2**, 1–58.

Roskam, E., & Lingoes, J. C. MINISSA—I: A Fortran IV (G) program for the smallest space analysis of square symmetric matrices. *Behavioral Science*, 1970, **15**, 204–205.

Shepard, R. N. The analysis of proximities: Multidimensional scaling with an unknown distance function. I. *Psychometrika*, 1962, **27**, 125–140. (a)

Shepard, R. N. The analysis of proximities: Multidimensional scaling with an unknown distance function. II. *Psychometrika*, 1962, **27**, 219–246. (b)

Young, F. W., & Torgerson, W. S. TORSCA: A Fortran IV program for Shepard–Kruskal multidimensional scaling analysis. *Behavioral Science*, 1967, **12**, 498.

A MODEL FOR POLYNOMIAL
CONJOINT ANALYSIS ALGORITHMS

Forrest W. Young

PSYCHOMETRIC LABORATORY
UNIVERSITY OF NORTH CAROLINA
CHAPEL HILL, NORTH CAROLINA

General Definitions

POLYNOMIAL CONJOINT MEASUREMENT

Tversky (1967) noted that one of the goals of scientific investigation may be regarded as the *decomposition of complex phenomena into sets of basic factors according to some specified rules of combination.* When the factors can be measured independently one desires to account for their joint effects by the appropriate combination rule. It is often the case, however, that the factors cannot be measured independently, and that only the order of their joint effects is known. In this case it is desirable to be able simultaneously to reduce the complex phenomena to its basic factors and to obtain a measurement of these basic factors such that the combination of the factors accounts for the order of the observations. This

69

is the conjoint measurement problem, and the combination rule is known as the conjoint measurement model.

In particular, a data matrix meets the requirements for polynomial conjoint measurement if some monotonic transformation of the data matrix can be decomposed into several factors. The decomposition rule must be some specified series of sums, differences, and products of the factors themselves. Such a decomposition rule is called a polynomial function.

In his paper, Tversky investigated the necessary and sufficient conditions under which a data matrix can be represented by a polynomial conjoint measurement model. It is not the purpose of this paper to delve into these conditions, but rather to present a model of a method for measuring the factors and their effects, conditions permitting. If the conditions do not permit such measurement, then the method to be presented obtains a least-squares estimate of the measurements and their effects, as well as providing information concerning the accuracy of the estimates.

Tversky (1967) presents several examples of polynomial conjoint combination rules. These rules include the Hullian and Spencian performance models cited in Hilgard (1956), the Bradley–Terry–Luce choice model (Luce, 1959), the subjective expected utility model (Savage, 1954), and the nonmetric multidimensional scaling models (Coombs, 1964; Shepard, 1962). For one of these models, the nonmetric multidimensional scaling model, the computation problem has been thoroughly investigated (Guttman, 1968) and several computer programs exist (Kruskal, 1964a, 1964b; Lingoes, 1965; McGee, 1966; Young, 1968a, 1968b).

It is the hypothesis of this paper that the general approach to construction of algorithms for nonmetric multidimensional scaling may also serve as an approach for constructing algorithms for polynomial conjoint analysis. In fact, the former is a special case of the latter. When the method for constructing algorithms for nonmetric scaling is understood, and when the relation between nonmetric scaling and polynomial conjoint analysis is understood, then it becomes clearer what steps must be taken to generalize nonmetric scaling algorithms to obtain polynomial conjoint analysis algorithms.

Nonmetric Scaling Algorithms

In 1962 Shepard introduced the first algorithm for nonmetric multidimensional scaling. He stated that the goal of this analytic method was to derive the metric structure of an unknown configuration of points in a Euclidean space of unknown dimensionality on the basis of nonmetric information about the proximity of the points. That is, Shepard's method attempted to simultaneously convert the proximity measures into Euclidean distances, and to obtain the coordinates underlying the distances. In polynomial conjoint measurement terms, the Shepard method, by applying a Euclidean combination rule, obtained the factors (coordinates) whose effects (Euclidean distances) were monotonic with the proximity measures. In matrix notation, Shepard's developments can be expressed as

$$S \overset{m}{\cong} D = f(X) \qquad (1)$$

where S is the symmetric matrix of proximities between p points, D is the p-order symmetric matrix of Euclidean distances, and X is the rectangular matrix of r-dimensional coordinates with p rows and r columns. The symbol $\overset{m}{\cong}$ is used to indicate that the matrix D is approximately monotonic with the matrix S. Shepard did not precisely define the notion of approximate monotonicity, but it involves, in the ideal case, defining $d_{ij} = d_{kl}$ whenever $s_{ij} = s_{kl}$ and $d_{ij} \leq d_{kl}$ when $s_{ij} > s_{kl}$. As indicated in the equation, matrix D is related to the matrix X through the function f. The function is the Euclidean distance function, and is performed on corresponding elements in all pairs of rows of X. The function is defined by

$$f(X) = \left[\sum_{a=1}^{r} (x_{ia} - x_{ja})^2 \right]^{1/2} \qquad \text{for} \quad i, j = 1, \ldots, p \qquad (2)$$

Notice that for Shepard's developments the approximate monotonicity requirement is actually a weak decreasing monotonicity requirement. That is, his requirement is weak in the sense that two distances may equal each other even though the two corresponding proximities do not, and his requirement is decreasing in the sense that smaller distances correspond with larger proximities.

The analysis of proximities, as represented by Equations (1) and (2), served as the basis for the development of a method by Kruskal (1964a, 1964b) which became known as nonmetric multidimensional scaling. Perhaps the most important difference between the two methods is that Kruskal desired to obtain a matrix of distances that was a least-squares fit to a matrix representing a monotonic transformation of the similarities. Notice that this differs from the Shepard approach in that it introduces an objective definition of the best solution and a precise definition of monotonicity. As a by-product of objectifying the definitions of best solution and monotonicity, Kruskal found it necessary to introduce a new matrix. This matrix, called the matrix of disparities by the current author (Young,

1968b), allowed Kruskal to perform computations on numbers which were precisely monotonic with the similarities without actually violating the ordinal assumptions about the similarities.

A second important difference between the Shepard and Kruskal methods is that Kruskal generalized his definition of the distance function to include all Minkowski spaces. The familiar Euclidean space is a special case of the more general Minkowski space, as is the "city-block" space used by Attneave (1950).

In matrix notation, Kruskal's developments can be expressed as

$$S = \overset{m}{\tilde{D}} \cong D = g(X) \tag{3}$$

where $\tilde{D}$ is the matrix of disparities (symmetric with p rows and columns);

where the symbol $\overset{m}{=}$ indicates that if $s_{ij} > s_{kl}$, then $d_{ij} \leq d_{kl}$; and if $s_{ij} = s_{kl}$, then $d_{ij} = d_{kl}$; and where the symbol $\cong$ indicates a least-squares approximation. The matrix D is related to the coordinates X by the function g. This is the Minkowski distance function and is defined as

$$g(X) = \left[\sum_{a=1}^{r} | x_{ia} - x_{ja} |^c \right]^{1/c} \qquad \text{for} \quad i, j = 1, 2, \ldots, p \tag{4}$$

where the function is defined for corresponding elements in all pairs of rows of X, and where c is the Minkowski constant such that $c \geq 1$.

In summary, nonmetric scaling, as represented by Kruskal's developments, allowed the analysis of similarities in any Minkowski space, such that the best possible monotonic transformation was obtained. In polynomial conjoint measurement terms, Kruskal's nonmetric scaling, using a combination rule defined by the Minkowski distance function in Equation (4), was able to obtain simultaneously the factors (coordinates) and their effects (Minkowski distances) such that the effects were monotonic with the data matrix (similarities).

Following Kruskal's developments, several investigators have introduced analogous methods of analysis (Lingoes, 1965; McGee, 1966; Young & Torgerson, 1967). An extremely thorough discussion of the general considerations for constructing nonmetric scaling algorithms has been presented by Guttman (1968). The relations among several of the methods have been discussed by Young & Appelbaum (1968) and by Roskam (1969).

In the next section of this paper it is shown how Equations (3) and (4) can be generalized in order to apply the methods of nonmetric scaling algorithms to polynomial conjoint measurement.

POLYNOMIAL CONJOINT ANALYSIS OF SIMILARITIES

The model for constructing algorithms for polynomial conjoint analysis of similarities involves two fundamental generalizations of the nonmetric scaling model. One of these generalizations involves modifying the function relating the matrix X to the matrix D, and the other generalization involves removing the restriction that the matrix S be a symmetric matrix.

ANALYSIS OF RECTANGULAR MATRICES. The key to understanding the generalization of the method to include rectangular matrices is the concept of a supermatrix. It will prove useful to rewrite Equation (3) in supermatrix notation as

$$\frac{S_{11} \mid S_{12}}{S_{21} \mid S_{22}} \overset{m}{=} \frac{\tilde{D}_{11} \mid \tilde{D}_{12}}{\tilde{D}_{21} \mid \tilde{D}_{22}} \cong \frac{D_{11} \mid D_{12}}{D_{21} \mid D_{22}} = g\left(\frac{X_1}{X_2}\right) \tag{5}$$

That is, we are redefining the matrix S of similarities as a supermatrix, and in a parallel manner are redefining the matrices $\tilde{D}$, D, and X as supermatrices.

Consider each submatrix in Equation (5). The matrix S_{11} contains the similarities of one set of stimuli, let us say set 1. Notice that the similarities are of the stimuli *within* set 1. The matrix S_{22} contains parallel information for the stimuli *within* set 2. Both these matrices are necessarily symmetric. We will denote the number of rows and columns in S_{11} as p_1, and the number of rows and columns in S_{22} as p_2. Turning our attention to the matrix S_{12}, we notice that it contains similarities *between* stimuli in sets 1 and 2. This matrix is rectangular with p_1 rows and p_2 columns. We note that S_{21} is simply the transpose of S_{12}. The same relationships hold for the matrices of disparities and distances. In a corresponding manner, the matrix X_1 contains coordinates for the stimuli in set 1 and X_2 for the stimuli in set 2. X_1, therefore, has p_1 rows and r columns, and X_2 has p_2 rows and r columns.

The final step in generalizing the Kruskal model to include the analysis of rectangular matrices as well as symmetric matrices is to assume that there is no information concerning the similarities *within* sets 1 and 2. On the basis of this assumption we write

$$S_{12} \overset{m}{=} \tilde{D}_{12} \cong D_{12} = g'\left(\frac{X_1}{X_2}\right), \tag{6}$$

where S_{12} is a rectangular matrix of similarities which is monotonic with $\tilde{D}_{12}$, the rectangular matrix of disparities. The matrix $\tilde{D}_{12}$ is, in turn, a least-squares approximation to D_{12}, the rectangular matrix distances. The distances in D_{12}, in turn, are between the points in set 1 (whose coordinates are represented by X_1) and those in set 2 (whose coordinates are represented by X_2). The definition of the function g is slightly modified so that each row in X_1 is compared with each row in X_2. We denote the new function g' and it is defined as

$$g'(X) = \left[\sum_{a=1}^{r} | x_{ia} - x_{ja} |^{c} \right]^{1/c} \quad \text{for} \quad i = 1, 2, \ldots, p_1; \; j = 1, 2, \ldots, p_2$$

(7)

It should be noted that by applying function g as defined by Equation (4) to the submatrix X_1 we obtain

$$D_{11} = g(X_1)$$

(8)

and applying it to X_2 we obtain

$$D_{22} = g(X_2)$$

(9)

Let us look at matrices X_1 and X_2 for a moment. Both matrices have r columns corresponding to the dimensionality of the space in which the analysis is being performed. The number of rows in X_1 corresponds to the number of rows in S_{12}, whereas the rows of X_2 correspond to the columns of S_{12}. That is, the matrix X_1 may be thought of as representing the row effects of data matrix S_{12}, and X_2 represents the column effects of the data. Note that X_1 and X_2 must be of the same dimensionality and are determined up to a joint unit and rotation.

In summary, the matrices X_1 and X_2 are combined, through the operation g', to produce the matrix D_{12}. D_{12}, in turn, is a least-squares fit to $\tilde{D}_{12}$, given that $\tilde{D}_{12}$ is perfectly monotonic with the data S_{12}. The monotonicity restraint may be either increasing or decreasing and is weak. The matrix D_{11} is related to X_1 by the operation g, and D_{22} is related to X_2 by the same operation g.

Developments conceptually similar to those proposed in this section have been set forth by Guttman and Lingoes (Lingoes, 1966), McGee (1968), and Kruskal (1965). The details of each of these developments differ in important ways from the one proposed here.

GENERALIZED FUNCTION. The second generalization of the nonmetric model is to relax the function relating the matrix D of distances and the matrix X of coordinates. The revised function is denoted h for symmetric cases, and is defined as

$$h(X) = h_1(h_2(x_{i.}, x_{j.})) \quad \text{for} \quad i, j = 1, 2, \ldots, p \tag{10}$$

and for rectangular cases is denoted h' and is defined as

$$h'(X) = h_1'(h_2'(x_{i.}, x_{j.})) \quad \text{for} \quad i = 1, 2, \ldots, p_1; \quad j = 1, 2, \ldots, p_2 \tag{11}$$

where the notation $x_{i.}$ is used to indicate the entire ith row of X.

The entire model for the polynomial conjoint analysis of similarities can be represented, for the symmetric case, by the equation

$$S \overset{m}{=} \tilde{D} \cong D = h(X) \tag{12}$$

where h is defined by Equation (10). For the nonsymmetric case, the model is represented by the equation

$$S_{12} \overset{m}{=} \tilde{D}_{12} \cong D_{12} = h'\left(\frac{X_1}{X_2}\right) \tag{13}$$

where h' is defined by Equation (11). It should be noted that the function h can also be applied to X_1 and X_2 in the rectangular case, giving us

$$D_{11} = h(X_1) \quad \text{and} \quad D_{22} = h(X_2) \tag{14}$$

In summary, for symmetric analyses the matrix X contains the coordinates (or factors or dimensions, etc.) whose distances in the space defined by the function h best reproduce the order (or the inverse of the order) of the entries in the data matrix S. For rectangular analyses the matrix X_1 contains the row coordinates (or row effects or row factors, etc.) and the matrix X_2 contains the column coordinates (or column effects, or column factors, etc.) whose between-set distances in the space defined by the function h' best reproduce the order (or the inverse of the order) of the entries in the rectangular data matrix S_{12}.

SPECIFIC SUBMODELS OF THE GENERAL MODEL

The function h relating the matrices D and X is too general to be of immediate interest. It is possible, however, to make specific assumptions concerning the functions h_1 and h_2, generating what will be called specific submodels of the general model. Some examples of a few familiar submodels are presented below.

EUCLIDEAN SCALING. The submodel for standard Euclidean nonmetric multidimensional scaling is obtained by assuming

$$h_1(h_2) = [h_2]^{1/2} \quad \text{and} \quad h_2(x_{i.}, x_{j.}) = \sum_{a=1}^{r} (x_{ia} - x_{ja})^2$$

With these assumptions Equation (10) becomes the familiar Euclidean distance function presented earlier as Equation (2). This submodel corresponds directly with one of the programs of Guttman and Lingoes (Lingoes, 1965), and with the program presented by McGee (1966).

MINKOWSKI SCALING. The submodel for nonmetric multidimensional scaling in any Minkowski space is provided by assuming

$$h_1(h_2) = [h_2]^{1/c} \quad \text{and} \quad h_2(x_{i.}, x_{j.}) = \sum_{a=1}^{r} | x_{ia} - x_{ja} |^c$$

where c is, as before, the Minkowski constant. With these assumptions Equation (10) becomes the Minkowski distance function presented as Equation (7). This submodel corresponds directly with the model proposed by Kruskal, and with the program prepared by Young and Torgerson (1967). One of the important Minkowski spaces which has been used in psychological research is the city-block space corresponding to a Minkowski constant of 1. Attneave (1950) has reported some analyses using this space.

MULTIDIMENSIONAL UNFOLDING. The rectangular version of the Euclidean nonmetric multidimensional scaling submodel corresponds to the multidimensional unfolding model proposed by Coombs (1964). The submodel is obtained by assuming

$$h_1'(h_2') = [h_2']^{1/2} \quad \text{and} \quad h_2'(x_{i.}, x_{j.}) = \sum_{a=1}^{r} (x_{ia} - x_{ja})^2$$

With these assumptions Equation (11) becomes a Euclidean distance function between two sets of coordinates. This function is the one proposed by Coombs, and corresponds to the programs prepared by Lingoes (1966) and McGee (1968), and options of programs written by Kruskal (1965) and Young (1968a, 1968b).

MINKOWSKI UNFOLDING. The rectangular version of the Minkowski nonmetric multidimensional scaling submodel generates a model which would logically be called a Minkowski unfolding model. This submodel is obtained by assuming

$$h_1'(h_2') = [h_2']^{1/c} \quad \text{and} \quad h_2'(x_{i\cdot}, x_{j\cdot}) = \sum_{a=1}^{r} | x_{ia} - x_{ja} |^c$$

The author is unaware of anyone having proposed this model, but the program by Young (1968a, 1968b) is capable of performing analyses based on this model.

DOMINANCE METRIC. In the area of discrimination and generalization several different models have been presented to account for response generalization when the stimuli are multidimensional. Some of these models are discussed by Cross (1965) and, as he has pointed out, they correspond to differing Minkowski spaces. One of the models corresponds to the Euclidean scaling model, and another corresponds with the city-block model discussed earlier. A third model, which Cross calls the dominance model, corresponds to a Minkowski space with an infinite Minkowski constant. In a dominance space the distance between two points is defined as being equal to the largest of the absolute differences between the co-ordinates. In the terminology being used here, we would define the dominance submodel as

$$h_1(h_2) = h_2 \quad \text{and} \quad h_2(x_{i\cdot}, x_{j\cdot}) = \max_{a=1,\ldots,r} (| x_{ia} - x_{ja} |)$$

To the author's knowledge, no computational method has been proposed for this model. However, with the Kruskal model, several available programs will provide essentially equivalent results by using a very large number as the Minkowski constant.

MONOTONE ANALYSIS OF VARIANCE. Luce and Tukey (1964) have presented a model which they refer to as the conjoint measurement model. This is basically an additive model and it can be represented as the specific submodel

$$h_1'(h_2') = h_2' \quad \text{and} \quad h_2'(x_{i\cdot}, x_{j\cdot}) = x_{i1} + x_{j1}$$

Programs exist which can perform analyses according to this model. (See Kruskal & Carmone, 1969; Lingoes, 1968; and Tversky & Zivian, 1966.) This model is an analog of two-way analysis of variance.

POLYNOMIAL CONJOINT MEASUREMENT. A subset of the models proposed by Tversky (1967) may be generated from our general model by defining the submodel

$$h_1'(h_2') = [h_2']^b \quad \text{and} \quad h_2'(x_{i.}, x_{j.}) = \sum_{a=1}^{r} (x_{ia} + x_{ja})^c$$

where b and c are integer constants. In this case, Equation (11) becomes

$$d_{ij} = \left[\sum_{a=1}^{r} (x_{ia} + x_{ja})^c \right]^b \tag{15}$$

The submodel represented by Equation (15) is actually a class of sub-models, with different submodels generated by different sets of assumptions concerning the constants r, b, and c. A few examples follow.

If we assume that $r = 1$, $b = 1$, and $c = 2$, then we see that

$$d_{ij} = x_{i1}^2 + 2x_{i1}x_{j1} + x_{j1}^2$$

which is simply a quadratic function of two variables. If we assumed that $r = 1$, $b = 1$, and $c = 3$, then we would obtain a formula for a cubic function of two variables. It should be clear that by the correct selection of the parameters b and c we can determine the degree of the polynomial under consideration, and that by changing the value of r we can modify the number of variables in the equation. Note that not all combinations of values for r, b, and c are sensible.

NONMETRIC FACTOR ANALYSIS. Several nonmetric analogs of factor analysis have been proposed (Lingoes & Guttman, 1967; Shepard, 1962). One possible analog, differing from earlier ones, will be presented here. It is specifically an analog of the Tucker and Messick points-of-view model (1963) as discussed by Cliff (1968) and Young and Pennell (1967). If one defines the submodel as

$$h_1'(h_2') = h_2' \quad \text{and} \quad h_2'(x_{i.}, x_{j.}) = \sum_{a=1}^{r} (x_{ia}x_{ja})$$

then Eq. (11) becomes

$$d_{ij} = \sum_{a=1}^{r} (x_{ia}x_{ja})$$

or, in matrix terms, $D = X_1X_2'$. This corresponds to the Tucker and Messick model which involves the matrix equation (using our symbols) $D = X_1\Gamma X_2'$, where Γ is a diagonal matrix of weights.

SUBJECTIVE EXPECTED UTILITY. According to the subjective expected-utility model (Savage, 1954), when a subject chooses between two gambles he makes his choice by maximizing the subjective expected utility of the choices. The subjective expected utility of a gamble is equal to the sum, over the various choice objects, of the product of the utility of an outcome and its subjective probability of occurrence.

For this submodel one defines

$$h_1'(h_2') = h_2' \quad \text{and} \quad h_2'(x_{i.}, x_{j.}) = \sum_{a=1}^{r} (x_{ia}x_{ja})$$

where there are r outcomes for each gamble, and where the $x_{i.}$ represent the utilities and the $x_{j.}$ the subjective probabilities. It should be obvious that the nonmetric analog of the factor analysis model and the subjective expected utility model are formally identical.

BRADLEY–TERRY–LUCE CHOICE MODEL. This model (Luce, 1959) specifies the relation of choice probabilities to the scale values of the objects when two choice objects are presented. The model states that

$$p(c, d) = \frac{v(c)}{v(c) + v(d)}$$

where $v(c)$ represents the scale values. The ordinal version of this model can be written

$$p(c, d) < p(e, f) \Leftrightarrow v(c) - v(d) < v(e) - v(f)$$

In the terminology used here, if we assume

$$h_1'(h_2') = h_2' \quad \text{and} \quad h_2'(x_{i.}, x_{j.}) = x_{i1} - x_{j1}$$

then

$$d_{ij} = x_{i1} - x_{j1}$$

where d_{ij} takes on the role of the choice probability between objects i and j, and x_{i1} and x_{j1} are the scale values of those objects. It should be noticed that this is equivalent to a one-dimensional Minkowski metric.

Specific Definitions

On the basis of notions fundamental to nonmetric multidimensional scaling, a model has been developed which indicates a method for constructing algorithms for polynomial conjoint analysis. It has been shown that this model includes, as special submodels, several of the common forms of nonmetric scaling, many of the forms of polynomial conjoint analysis, and several popular choice models. It should be obvious that, with the proper specification of the functional relationships indicated by Equations (10) or (11), a great range of polynomial conjoint models is possible.

Perhaps one of the major advantages of the model presented here is that it provides a means for minimizing the complex functions represented by Equations (10)–(13). The iterative minimization algorithms used in nonmetric scaling may be applicable to this new model. As has been pointed out by Guttman (1968) and Kruskal (1964a, b), algorithm construction consists of two major aspects. The first aspect is definitional, and the second is operational. The definitional aspect involves specifying the exact goal of the algorithm. The operational aspect involves specifying the programing methods and techniques involved in achieving the goal of the algorithm. In the previous sections of this paper we have dealt with only the initial phase of the definitional aspect of algorithm construction, since only the general goals of a set of possible algorithms have been presented. The next few sections of the paper will precisely define the goal of one specific algorithm by presenting a definition of goodness of fit of the model to the data, a derivation of the generalized partial derivatives of the goodness-of-fit index, a definition of the specific combination rules to be covered in the algorithm presented here, and a derivation of the partial derivatives specific to these combination rules.

Goodness of Fit

As was stated earlier, the general goal of the model just presented is to enable one to construct computer programs for computing the best possible solution to Equations (10)–(13). The notion of the best possible solution is represented by the relation between matrices $\tilde{D}$ and D. If, in fact, these two matrices are identical, then this is the best possible solution. Such perfect solutions will not always be possible. In fact, generally, only approximate solutions will be obtained. In such cases it is necessary to introduce some definition of the relative goodness of fit of a solution.

Since it has already been stated that the relation between D and $\tilde{D}$ is a least-squares relation, we use as an indicator of goodness of fit the definition

$$L^* = \sum_{i,j} (d_{ij} - \tilde{d}_{ij})^2$$

where the summation is over i and j as defined either in Equation (10) or (11), whichever applies. When the disparities involved in this formula are computed as suggested by Kruskal, it has been shown (Kruskal, 1965; Roskam, 1969) that

$$\sum_{i,j} d_{ij}\hat{d}_{ij} = \sum_{i,j} \hat{d}^2_{ij} \tag{16}$$

The proof of this relation can be seen by noting that

$$\sum_{i,j} d_{ij}\hat{d}_{ij} = \sum_{i,j} \left[(d_{ij} - \hat{d}_{ij}) + \hat{d}_{ij}\right]\hat{d}_{ij}$$

$$= \sum_{i,j} \left[d_{ij} - \hat{d}_{ij}\right]\hat{d}_{ij} + \sum_{i,j} \hat{d}^2_{ij}$$

and noting that the left-hand summation equals zero. This relationship permits us to rewrite the least-squares formula in an equivalent form:

$$L^* = \sum_{i,j} d^2_{ij} - \sum_{i,j} \hat{d}^2_{ij} \tag{17}$$

indicating that the sum of squared differences is equal to the difference of the sums of squares. It is interesting to note that the cross products of the distances and disparities do not enter into the computation of L^*.

While the definition of L^* represents the notion of a least-squares fit, it is obviously not scale independent. That is, if the scale of the distances or disparities were changed, the value of L^* would change. This is not a desirable feature. Therefore, L^* should be normalized somehow so as to make it independent of the scales involved. Several alternative normalization procedures have been proposed. Kruskal (1964a) proposed that the sum of squared distances be used as the normalization constant, producing this definition of the stress of the solution

$$S^2 = \frac{\sum_{i,j}(d_{ij} - \hat{d}_{ij})^2}{\sum_{i,j} d^2_{ij}} \tag{18}$$

This definition of stress normalizes L^* so that it is independent of the scale of the distances, but apparently not of the disparities. It can be shown that this deficiency is apparent only. Utilizing the relation noted in Equations (16) and (17) it is possible to rewrite Kruskal's stress as

$$S^2 = 1 - \frac{\sum_{i,j} \hat{d}^2_{ij}}{\sum_{i,j} d^2_{ij}} \tag{19}$$

Note that the disparity term (i.e., the term giving the differences between the original and the fitted distances) no longer explicitly appears in this equivalent version. This shows that the stress function is not affected by a change in unit of measurement of the disparities that is induced by a change in unit of measurement of the distances.

Notice from Equation (18) that $S \geq 0$, implying that

$$\sum_{i,j} d_{ij}^2 \geq \sum_{i,j} \hat{d}_{ij}^2$$

This relationship can be best understood when one realizes that the disparities consist of a series of values which are the means of their corresponding subscripted distances. It is well known that the sum of squared values is greater than summing the squared mean the same number of times.

An alternative normalization term is the sum of squared disparities, giving

$$U^2 = \frac{\sum_{i,j} (d_{ij} - \hat{d}_{ij})^2}{\sum_{i,j} \hat{d}_{ij}^2} \tag{20}$$

While it would appear at first glance that Equation (20) is only invariant over ratio-scale changes in the disparities, it can be shown from Equations (16) and (17) that

$$U^2 = \frac{\sum_{i,j} d_{ij}^2}{\sum_{i,j} \hat{d}_{ij}^2} - 1 \tag{21}$$

and that U, as S, is invariant over ratio-scale changes in both the disparities and distances.

A somewhat different way of looking at this same aspect of these two goodness-of-fit functions is to note that combining Equations (19) and (21) gives us the relationship between S and U as

$$S^2 = U^2/(1 + U^2) \tag{22}$$

or

$$U^2 = S^2/(1 - S^2) \tag{23}$$

From these equations it can be seen that if one of the functions is invariant over ratio-scale changes in the distances, then the other must be, and that the same can be said for the disparities. Because of the monotonic relationship between S and U, minimizing one is equivalent to minimizing the other. From this standpoint, then, it is not possible to choose between the two functions.

An alternative method for defining stress has been suggested by Kruskal (1965). He observed that certain kinds of degenerate solutions can be avoided if the sum of squared distances is replaced with the variance of the distances. Accordingly, he proposed that the stress of the solution should be redefined as

$$S_2{}^2 = \frac{\sum_{i,j} (d_{ij} - \bar{d}_{ij})^2}{\sum_{i,j} (d_{ij} - d)^2} \tag{24}$$

where the unsubscripted d indicates the mean of the distances. Comparing this definition of stress, referred to by Kruskal as stress formula two, with his stress formula one [Formula (18) above] indicated by the symbol S_1, we note that

$$S_1{}^2 = S_2{}^2 \left[1 - \frac{\sum_{i,j} d^2}{\sum_{i,j} d_{ij}^2} \right] \tag{25}$$

and that, except for solutions where all the distances are equal or zero (such solutions are degenerate), the value of stress formula two is larger than stress formula one. Such a relation between the two formulas has been previously noted on the basis of observations by both Kruskal and Carroll (1969) and Green and Rao (1969).

It would, of course, be possible to modify the definition of U in the same manner, giving what will be referred to here as L, the least-squares criterion, defined as

$$L^2 = \frac{\sum_{i,j} (d_{ij} - \bar{d}_{ij})^2}{\sum_{i,j} (\bar{d}_{ij} - \bar{d})^2} \tag{26}$$

where the unsubscripted $\bar{d}$ indicates the mean of the disparities. Comparing this with the definition of U [Formula (20)] we note that

$$U^2 = L^2 \left[1 - \frac{\sum_{i,j} \bar{d}^2}{\sum_{i,j} \bar{d}_{ij}^2} \right] \tag{27}$$

and that as with the two definitions of stress, the least-squares criterion L will be larger than U, except when all the disparities are equal or zero. Again this condition occurs only when the solution is degenerate.

Comparing the two formulas for stress and the formulas for U and the least-squares criterion, we note that all of them are equal to zero when the sum of squared distances and the sum of squared disparities are equal. This communality follows, of course, from the fact that the numerators of all the formulas are equivalent to Equation (17). We note, however, that the value of stress formula two can be reduced by increasing the variance of the distances, and that the value of the least-squares criterion can be reduced by increasing the variance of the disparities. This additional consideration in the latter two formulas underlies Kruskal's observation that the use of the variance term in stress formula two avoids certain kinds of degeneracies (Kruskal & Carroll, 1969). Kruskal's arguments also apply to using the variance of the disparities in the formula for L, since for the degeneracies considered by Kruskal the entire set of distances is equal to the entire set of disparities. Since the kinds of degeneracies being considered are particularly prevalent in the rectangular version of the polynomial conjoint measurement model, it is especially important to use the variance term as the normalization constant.

It is not clear whether the variance of the distances or the variance of the disparities is preferable as the normalization term. It has been shown by Roskam (1968), however, that the partial derivatives of the disparities vanish when the Kruskal monotonicity principle is used. For this reason, the least-squares criterion L was selected for the developments presented in the rest of this paper.

At this point a brief review is in order. Equations (10)–(13) represent the general polynomial measurement model. These equations can be viewed as a monotonic regression problem where it is desired to obtain a matrix of coefficients X such that some polynomial function of them (the matrix D) is a least-squares estimate of a monotonic transformation (the matrix $\tilde{D}$) of the data matrix S. Equation (26) represents the least-squares notion: We desire to regress the matrix D (and therefore also X) on the matrix $\tilde{D}$ (and therefore also S) in such a way as to minimize Equation (26). In order to do this we need to know three things: (a) the specific method for computing the matrix $\tilde{D}$; (b) the partial derivatives of the function L with respect to D; and (c) the partial derivatives of D relative to X (and, therefore, the polynomial relating D and X). Each of these three will be developed in succeeding sections.

Monotonic Transformation

The method for computing the matrix $\tilde{D}$, the monotonic transformation of the data matrix S, is identical to one of the methods for solving the same problem in nonmetric multidimensional scaling. Although there are several different programs for performing nonmetric multidimensional scaling, only three unique approaches to computing the transformation have been used. These are Kruskal's (1964a) monotonicity principle, Guttman's (1968) "rank-image" principle, and Shepard's (1962) original monotonicity principle (which could be termed an anti-rank-image principle). The approaches of Kruskal and Guttman have been thoroughly compared by Guttman (1968) and Roskam (1969), and it is sufficient for the purposes of the current paper to indicate that although the Guttman method usually provides one with a more "well-behaved" transformation (especially when there is a large number of ties in the data), the Kruskal method always provides the transformation minimizing goodness-of-fit functions like Equation (26). For this reason, and for reasons to become apparent in succeeding sections of this paper, the Kruskal method will be used here.

GENERAL PARTIAL DERIVATIVES

In this section the partial derivatives of L with respect to one of the coordinates, say x_{je}, will be obtained, without specifying the functional relationship between d_{ij} and x_{je}. Since no specific combination rule is involved in these partials, they are referred to as the general partial derivatives. Although it is necessary to know the specific form of the combination rule before it is possible to state the partial derivatives completely, the general partials are obtained in order to emphasize the subordinate role played by the combination rule.

Let us first define

$$A = \sum_{i,l} (d_{il} - \tilde{d}_{il})^2 \tag{28}$$

and

$$B = \sum_{i,l} (\tilde{d}_{il} - \tilde{d})^2 \tag{29}$$

giving us the definition of L as being

$$L = (A/B)^{1/2} \tag{30}$$

We see that the partial derivatives of L with respect to x_{je} can be expressed as

$$\frac{\partial L}{\partial x_{je}} = \frac{1}{2}\left(\frac{L}{A}\frac{\partial A}{\partial x_{je}} - \frac{L}{B}\frac{\partial B}{\partial x_{je}}\right) \tag{31}$$

where the derivatives of A are

$$\frac{\partial A}{\partial x_{je}} = 2\sum_{i,l}\left[(d_{il} - \tilde{d}_{il})\left(\frac{\partial d_{il}}{\partial x_{je}} - \frac{\partial \tilde{d}_{ie}}{\partial x_{je}}\right)\right] \tag{32}$$

and of B are

$$\frac{\partial B}{\partial x_{je}} = 2\sum_{i,l}\left[(\tilde{d}_{il} - \tilde{d})\frac{\partial \tilde{d}_{il}}{\partial x_{je}}\right] \tag{33}$$

We should now turn our attention to the partials of the disparities $\tilde{d}_{ij}$. It has been shown by Kruskal (1965) and Roskam (1969) that, when the disparities are computed by Kruskal's principle, the sum of the products of the residuals with the partials of the disparities vanishes. This does not apply to Guttman's rank-image principle. This is one reason, then, that the Kruskal method for computing the disparities is used. The formula for the partials of L with respect to x_{je}, when using the Kruskal monotonicity principle, is

$$\partial L/\partial x_{je} = (L/A) \sum_{i,l} [(d_{il} - \hat{d}_{il}) \, \partial d_{il}/\partial x_{je}] \tag{34}$$

It has been shown by Young and Appelbaum (1968) that Equation (34) can be rewritten equivalently as

$$\partial L/\partial x_{je} = (L/A) \sum_{i}^{p} [(d_{ij} - \hat{d}_{ij}) \, \partial d_{ij}/\partial x_{ie}] \tag{35}$$

Notice that Equation (35) is the partial derivative of the loss function L with respect to one of the coordinates x_{je}. Notice also that in its present form the derivatives cannot be computed because we do not yet know the function relating d_{ij} and x_{ie}.

So far the developments of the paper are necessary but not sufficient to obtain a solution to Equations (10)–(13). They are not sufficient because we do not yet know the combination rule relating the matrices D and X. If we did know such a rule, and if we did know the partial derivatives of D relative to X, we could write a computer program to solve the monotone regression problem represented by Equations (10)–(13).

Another way of viewing the developments to this point is to state that the definitional process is sufficiently complete to indicate the operations needed to write an "open ended" computer program; i.e., an algorithm which is complete except for a subroutine to compute the matrix D, and a subroutine to compute the partial derivatives of D. An open-ended program such as this would significantly reduce the programming effort on the part of the person performing the analysis. The program would already contain the necessary input and output facilities, and would already contain the methods for computing the monotonic transformation and obtaining the best solution.

While it would be possible, at this point, to proceed directly to a discussion of the operational aspects of such an open-ended program, it is felt that it is useful to state several combination rules which cover a wide range of possible applications of the polynomial conjoint model. Once these rules are stated, and once the partial derivatives of the rules are obtained, it will be possible to state the operations necessary for writing a computer program to solve the polynomial analysis model for a wide range of combination rules without any programming effort on the part of the user. Such a program can have in addition, of course, an open-ended feature, thereby providing a very flexible analytic tool to the researcher investigating measurement models other than those covered by the combination rules to be discussed.

In the next section six such rules will be proposed. It is felt that they cover a fairly wide range of useful and interesting polynomial conjoint models. Other definitions, of course, could have been proposed in addition to these. Roskam (1968), for example, has stated (in a different context) a set of combination rules, some of which are covered by the following developments.

COMBINATION RULES

Several examples of specific submodels of the general polynomial analysis model were presented in a previous section of this paper. These submodels represented specific definitions of the combination rule represented by Equations (10) and (11). It should be noted that these submodels involved defining

$$h_1(h_2) = (h_2)^b \quad \text{and} \quad h_2(x_{i.}, x_{j.}) = \sum_{a=1}^{r} h_3(x_{ia}, x_{ja})^c$$

giving a definition of the distance, or combination, rule as

$$d_{ij} = \left[\sum_{a=1}^{r} h_3(x_{ia}, x_{ja})^c \right]^b \tag{36}$$

where the function h_3 is a real single-valued function to be defined below. Six different definitions of h_3 will be given. These six definitions are used to define the additive, difference, and multiplicative combination rules, and the absolute value of these three rules. These six combination rules cover the entire set of specific submodels discussed previously as well as many additional submodels. The additive combination rule involves defining

$$h_3(x_{ia}, x_{ja}) = x_{ia} + x_{ja} \tag{37}$$

The difference combination rule involves defining

$$h_3(x_{ia}, x_{ja}) = x_{ia} - x_{ja} \tag{38}$$

The multiplicative combination rule involves defining

$$h_3(x_{ia}, x_{ja}) = x_{ia}x_{ja} \tag{39}$$

The absolute value versions of each of the three combination rules involves equations similar to (37)–(39). Specifically, the absolute additive combination rule involves defining

$$h_3(x_{ia}, x_{ja}) = |\, x_{ia} + x_{ja}\,| \tag{40}$$

The absolute difference combination rule involves defining

$$h_3(x_{ia}, x_{ja}) = |\, x_{ia} - x_{ja}\,| \tag{41}$$

The absolute multiplicative combination rule involves defining

$$h_3(x_{ia}, x_{ja}) = |\, x_{ia}x_{ja}\,| \tag{42}$$

Substituting Equation (37) into (36) gives the complete definition of the *additive combination rule*

$$d_{ij} = \left[\sum_{a=1}^{r} (x_{ia} + x_{ja})^c \right]^b \tag{43}$$

Substituting Equation (38) into (36) gives the complete definition of the *difference combination rule*

$$d_{ij} = \left[\sum_{a=1}^{r} (x_{ia} - x_{ja})^c \right]^b \tag{44}$$

Substituting Equation (39) into (36) gives the complete definition of the *multiplicative combination rule*

$$d_{ij} = \left[\sum_{a=1}^{r} (x_{ia}x_{ja})^c \right]^b \tag{45}$$

Substituting Equation (40) into (36) gives the complete definition of the *absolute additive combination rule*

$$d_{ij} = \left[\sum_{a=1}^{r} |\, x_{ia} + x_{ja}\,|^c \right]^b \tag{46}$$

Substituting Equation (41) into (36) gives the complete definition of the *absolute difference combination rule*

$$d_{ij} = \left[\sum_{a=1}^{r} |\, x_{ia} - x_{ja}\,|^c \right]^b \tag{47}$$

Substituting Equation (42) into (36) gives the complete definition of the *absolute multiplicative combination rule*

$$d_{ij} = \left[\sum_{a=1}^{r} \mid x_{ia} x_{ja} \mid^{c} \right]^{b} \tag{48}$$

It should now be noted that all the combination rules belong to the class of additive difference models (Beals, Krantz, & Tversky, 1968), and as such when $r \geq 3$ and when some special conditions hold, the dimensions are all measured on interval scales. Furthermore, if $c \geq 1$ and $b = 1/c$, then all the dimensions are measured on the same interval scale.

Specific Derivatives

Now that the various combination rules have been completely stated it is possible to derive the partial derivatives of L with respect to x_{je}. This will be done by first deriving the derivatives of the distances with respect to x_{ie}, and then substituting the derivatives into Equation (35).

In order to obtain the derivatives of the distances it is convenient to define

$$u_{ija} = h_3(x_{ia}, x_{ja})$$

We can then rewrite Equation (36) as

$$d_{ij} = \left(\sum_{a=1}^{r} u_{ija}^{c} \right)^{b} \tag{49}$$

whose derivatives are

$$\partial d_{ij}/\partial x_{ie} = b \left(\sum_{a=1}^{r} u_{ija}^{c} \right)^{b-1} \partial u_{ije}^{c}/\partial x_{ie} \tag{50}$$

Which, noting the relationship between d_{ij} and u_{ija}, can be written as

$$\partial d_{ij}/\partial x_{ie} = (b/d_{ij}^{(1-b)/b})(\partial u_{ije}^{c}/\partial x_{ie}) \tag{51}$$

For the additive and difference combination rules

$$\partial u_{ije}^{c}/\partial x_{ie} = c(x_{ie} + wx_{je})^{c-1} \tag{52}$$

(where $w = +1$ for the additive rule and $w = -1$ for the difference rule). For the multiplicative combination rule

$$\partial u_{ije}^{c}/\partial x_{ie} = cx_{ie}^{c-1}x_{je}^{c} \tag{53}$$

For the absolute additive and absolute difference combination rules

$$\partial u_{ije}^{c}/\partial x_{ie} = c \mid x_{ie} + wx_{je} \mid^{c-1} \operatorname{signum}(x_{ie} + wx_{je}) \tag{54}$$

and for the absolute multiplicative rule

$$\partial u^c_{ije}/\partial x_{ie} = c \mid x_{ie} \mid^{c-1} \mid x_{je} \mid^c \text{signum}(x_{ie}) \tag{55}$$

Substituting Equation 51 into Equation 35 we obtain

$$\frac{\partial L}{\partial x_{je}} = \frac{Lb}{A} \sum_{i=1}^{p} \left[\left(\frac{d_{ij} - \tilde{d}_{ij}}{d_{ij}^{(1-b)/b}} \right) \frac{\partial u^c_{ije}}{\partial x_{ie}} \right] \tag{56}$$

We should pause to note that Equation (56) shows the partial derivatives of L with respect to x_{je} when the combination rule is defined by Equation (36).

The final step in obtaining the complete partial derivatives is, for the additive and difference models, to substitute Equation (52) into (56) giving

$$\frac{\partial L}{\partial x_{je}} = \frac{Lbc}{A} \sum_{i=1}^{p} \left[\left(\frac{d_{ij} - \tilde{d}_{ij}}{d_{ij}^{(1-b)/b}} \right) (x_{ie} + wx_{je})^{c-1} \right] \tag{57}$$

For the multiplicative model, we substitute Equation (53) into (56) obtaining

$$\frac{\partial L}{\partial x_{je}} = \frac{Lbc}{A} \sum_{i=1}^{p} \left[\left(\frac{d_{ij} - \tilde{d}_{ij}}{d_{ij}^{(1-b)/b}} \right) x_{ie}^{c-1} x_{je}^c \right] \tag{58}$$

For the absolute additive and absolute difference models we substitute Equation (54) into (56) giving

$$\frac{\partial L}{\partial x_{je}} = \frac{Lbc}{A} \sum_{i=1}^{p} \left[\left(\frac{d_{ij} - \tilde{d}_{ij}}{d_{ij}^{(1-b)/b}} \right) \mid x_{ie} + wx_{je} \mid^{c-1} \text{signum}(x_{ie} + wx_{je}) \right] \tag{59}$$

For the absolute multiplicative model we substitute Equation (55) into (56) giving

$$\frac{\partial L}{\partial x_{je}} = \frac{Lbc}{A} \sum_{i=1}^{p} \left[\left(\frac{d_{ij} - \tilde{d}_{ij}}{d_{ij}^{(1-b)/b}} \right) \mid x_{ie} \mid^{c-1} \mid x_{je} \mid^c \text{signum}(x_{ie}) \right] \tag{60}$$

All the definitions necessary to write computer programs to perform a variety of polynomial conjoint analyses of similarities data have now been presented. By the proper selection of one of the various combination rules any of the specific submodels discussed earlier can be applied to a set of similarities data. If one desires to apply a model which does not correspond with any of the combination rules presented here, then he must do two things. First, he must write his complete combination rule in a form analogous to Equations (43)–(48). Finally, he must obtain an equation for the complete partial derivatives of L with respect to the configuration [as in Equations (57)–(60)]. This last step is done by deriving the partial derivatives of the combination rule with respect to the configuration [Equations (52)–(55)] and substituting them into Equation (56).

Operational Aspects

On the basis of notions fundamental to nonmetric multidimensional scaling a model has been developed which indicates the definitional and operational steps necessary for constructing algorithms for polynomial conjoint analysis.

In the previous sections of this paper the general and specific definitions necessary for such algorithms have been presented. With these definitions it is, at least, theoretically possible to solve Equations (10)–(13), by obtaining a minimum value for L in Equation (26). The partial derivatives represented by Equations (35) and (56)–(60) are necessary to obtain a solution.

In the remaining sections of this paper the operations corresponding to the definitions will be presented. These operations will indicate the methods for writing a computer program for polynomial conjoint analysis. Several authors (Guttman, 1968; Kruskal, 1964; Lingoes, 1966; Roskam, 1968) have indicated that there are three main computational problems which are encountered when writing a program to perform nonmetric analyses: the initial configuration, the monotonic transformation, and the minimization procedure. Each of these problems will be taken up in turn.

INITIAL CONFIGURATION

The most important operational characteristic of the procedure to be proposed here is that an iterative algorithm is used to minimize the least-squares function L. All existing methods for nonmetric analysis are iterative. As with all such algorithms there is no guarantee that the best solution will be obtained, although the method proposed here does guarantee exact convergence. Not all existing methods converge exactly on the (local) minimum, although most converge arbitrarily close to it. One of the best ways to increase the probability that the algorithm converges on the overall global minimum and not a local minimum is to provide the algorithm with a starting place (an initial configuration) which is near to the overall minimum. Although there is no way to prove that a particular method for computing the initial configuration will guarantee convergence on the global minimum, a general approach to computing an intuitively pleasing initial configuration will be discussed.

The method for computing the initial configuration proposed here is an iterative method based on the similarities. Other methods have been proposed, some of which are not related to the similarities (Kruskal, 1964b), others of which are based on the similarities (Guttman, 1968). The former methods have been called arbitrary, and the latter nonarbitrary. Of the nonarbitrary methods only the method of Young and Torgerson (1967) uses an iterative procedure. The procedure to be described here is essentially equivalent to the Young–Torgerson method.

One iteration in preparing the initial configuration involves five separate steps. The first step is to reduce the matrix of disparities $\tilde{D}$ to the matrix of coordinates X by a metric analog of the particular polynomial conjoint combination rule being used. Notice that the combination rule is usually applied to the matrix X of coordinates to obtain the matrix D of distances. Thus to obtain the coordinates, we apply the inverse of the combination rule to the disparities. Such an inverse of the combination rule may not exist (or may be too difficult to derive) for all rules, but a function which is approximately the inverse of the combination rule often suffices to prepare the initial configuration.

Once the matrix of coordinates has been obtained from the disparities, the second step of the procedure is simply to apply the combination rule to the coordinates, obtaining the matrix of distances D. Then the third step of the initial configuration iteration is performed: The monotonic transformation of the matrix D is derived which best fits the matrix of similarities S. This is a new estimate of the matrix $\tilde{D}$, which after normalization (the fourth step) serves as the basis for computing the least-squares index L (the fifth step). The value of L is compared with the value of L on the previous iteration, and if it decreased more than some finite amount the next iteration commences. Otherwise, (or if a maximum number of iterations has been exceeded) the process is terminated, and the matrix X is taken as the initial configuration for the nonmetric algorithm to follow. Note that the entire process is started directly from the similarities; i.e., on the very first iteration the first step involves reducing the matrix S of similarities to the coordinates X by applying the inverse combination rule. This is the only way in which the first iteration differs from the rest.

This procedure for deriving the initial configuration is called a quasi-non-metric procedure since it involves metric computations in the first step and nonmetric computations in the third step. Although the metric computations are originally performed on the similarities, this is only done in order to derive the initial configuration. Once the initial configuration has been derived, the procedure is fully nonmetric. Because of the metric use of the similarities it is possible that different solutions may be obtained for different ordinal transformations of the similarities. This local minimum problem is comparable to the well-known one that different solutions may be obtained from different initial configurations. Considerable experience with quasi-non-metric initial configurations suggests that in the vast majority of cases various monotonic transformations of the similarities data do not affect the form of the derived configuration. In fact, some Monte Carlo results of Green and Rao (1968) suggest that the derived configuration is less affected by monotonic transformations of the similarities when quasi-non-metric initial configurations are used than when arbitrary initial configurations are used. More research on this topic is needed, however.

At first glance it might appear that the iterative procedure is a stationary process since one applies an inverse function to the disparities and then eventually recomputes the disparities by applying the function itself. However, the process is not stationary for two reasons: (a) The inverse polynomial function produces a matrix of coordinates such that when the polynomial function is applied to these coordinates the disparities are only approximately reproduced. (This approximate reproduction results from the fact that the number of dimensions or variables in the coordinate matrix is smaller than the number of points.) (b) A monotonic transformation is applied to the distances to derive the disparities which serve as the basis for the next iteration. If a linear transformation were applied in place of the monotonic transformation the process would become stationary on the second iteration. In fact, the monotonic transformation does stabilize rapidly, and the process does converge very rapidly. Experience indicates that approximately five iterations are needed to converge on the initial configuration.

At this point the quasi-non-metric procedure is not well defined because the inverse functions have not been stated. The next part of this paper will develop the approximate inverse functions to be used in preparing the initial configuration for the additive, absolute difference and multiplicative combination rules.

ADDITIVE COMBINATION RULE. It is easy to see that the additive combination rule [Equation (43)] can be rewritten (using the disparities) as

$$\hat{d}_{ij}^{1/b} = \sum_{a=1}^{r} (x_{ia} + x_{ja})^{c} \tag{61}$$

and that the first step in computing the inverse of the additive combination rule is to obtain the bth root of the disparities. This leaves us with the problem of obtaining components which, when added together, approximately reproduce the matrix of disparities. A simple approximation for the initial coordinate of point i on dimension one is:

$$x_{i1} = \frac{1}{2(p-1)} \sum_{k=1}^{p} \tilde{d}_{ik}^{1/b} \quad \text{for} \quad k \neq i \tag{62}$$

If we assume that $c = 1$, then when such coordinates are added together a distance matrix is produced such that the residual differences between the distances and disparities sum to zero. A distance d_{ij} is defined as

$$d_{ij} = \frac{1}{2(p-1)} \sum_{k=1,k\neq i}^{p} \tilde{d}_{ik}^{1/b} + \frac{1}{2(p-1)} \sum_{l=1,l\neq j}^{p} \tilde{d}_{lj}^{1/b} \tag{63}$$

and the sum of the residuals, where a residual is defined as

$$r_{ij} = \tilde{d}_{ij} - d_{ij} \tag{64}$$

is

$$\sum_{i=1}^{p} \sum_{j=1,j\neq 1}^{p} r_{ij} = \sum_{i=1}^{p} \sum_{j=1,j\neq 1}^{p} \tilde{d}_{ij}^{1/b} - \frac{1}{2(p-1)} \sum_{i=1}^{p} \sum_{j=1,j\neq i}^{p} \sum_{k=1,k\neq i}^{p} \tilde{d}_{ik}^{1/b}$$

$$- \frac{1}{2(p-1)} \sum_{j=1}^{p} \sum_{i=1,i\neq j}^{p} \sum_{l=1,l\neq j}^{p} \tilde{d}_{lj}^{1/b} \tag{65}$$

$$= \sum_{i=1}^{p} \sum_{j=1,j\neq i}^{p} \tilde{d}_{ij}^{1/b} - \frac{p-1}{2(p-1)} \sum_{i=1}^{p} \sum_{k=1,k\neq i}^{p} \tilde{d}_{ik}^{1/b} - \frac{p-1}{2(p-1)} \sum_{j=1}^{p} \sum_{l=1,l\neq j}^{p} \tilde{d}_{lj}^{1/b} \tag{66}$$

and, since the double summations are all over the same elements regardless of the specific subscript, this sum is zero:

$$\sum_{i=1}^{p} \sum_{j=1,j\neq i}^{p} r_{ij} = \sum_{i=1}^{p} \sum_{j=1,j\neq i}^{p} \tilde{d}_{ij}^{1/b} - \sum_{i=1}^{p} \sum_{j=1,j\neq i}^{p} \tilde{d}_{ij}^{1/b} \tag{67}$$

If the model has more than one dimension, we can use the residuals to estimate the additional scale values just as we used the disparities to estimate the first dimension:

$$x_{i2} = \frac{1}{2(p-1)} \sum_{k=1}^{p} r_{ik} \quad \text{for} \quad k \neq i \tag{68}$$

for the second dimension and, after obtaining the new residuals by removing the additive effects due to the second dimension, for the third, etc., dimensions. These equations are appropriate for symmetric matrices, and if we substitute either p_1 (the number of rows in the rectangular matrix) or p_2 (number of columns) for p in Equations (62) and (68), they are appropriate for rectangular matrices. Since the diagonal submatrices of the supermatrix are zero, the residuals continue to sum to zero.

When this process has been performed for all r dimensions we have obtained a configuration X such that when the additive combination rule is applied to it we obtain the distances D which approximate the disparities D' in such a way that the residuals sum to zero.

ABSOLUTE DIFFERENCE COMBINATION RULE. One special case of the absolute difference combination rule Equation (41) is the well-known Euclidean metric. For this metric, the method for deriving the coordinates from a set of distances is well known (Torgerson, 1958, p. 254). This method has served as the basis for the quasi-nonmetric initial configuration procedure used by the Young–Torgerson programs. For a complete explanation of this procedure see Young (1968b). Extensive Monte Carlo experimentation indicates that this one inverse combination rule serves well for a wide range of difference combination rules. One slight modification is to raise the matrix of disparities to the $(2/b)$th power, thereby producing

$$\hat{d}_{ij}^{2/b} = \left[\sum_{a=1}^{r} | x_{ia} - x_{ja} |^c \right]^2 \qquad (69)$$

as the set of quantities to be analyzed by the Torgerson metric procedure. This modification transforms the disparities into quantities more related to Euclidean distances.

MULTIPLICATIVE COMBINATION RULE. A special case of the general multiplicative combination rule presented in Equation (39) corresponds to the standard factor-analysis problem. For this metric, the method for deriving the coordinates from the matrix of cross products D is well known. Again the same kind of modification is used to produce a set of quantities more appropriately analyzed by a factor-analytic method. This modification produces

$$\hat{d}_{ij}^{1/b} = \sum_{a=1}^{r} (x_{ia}x_{ja})^c \qquad (70)$$

as the quantities to be analyzed. For the preparation of the initial configuration, the value of c is assumed to be unity.

MONOTONIC TRANSFORMATION

The Kruskal monotonicity principle (1964a) is performed here by an algorithm computationally distinct from the Kruskal algorithm. This algorithm, based on the work of Torgerson and Meuser (1962), is simpler and more easily understood than the Kruskal algorithm, and it can be shown that it derives exactly the same monotonic transformation as that obtained by Kruskal's method. The algorithm proceeds by computing a trial value for a given disparity, checking to see if the trial value is monotonic with the similarities, adjusting it until all disparities under consideration are monotonic with the similarities, and then bringing in the next trial value for the next disparity.

To be more specific, it must be assumed that the similarities have been ordered according to magnitude. In the following discussion "first disparity" and "first distance" refer to the disparity and distance which correspond with the largest similarity. The algorithm works on computing the first disparity and then the second, and so on.

In the initial trial, the first disparity takes on the value of the first distance, while the second disparity takes on the value of the second distance. The values of the first and second disparities are then compared. If the first one is smaller than or equal to the second one, then the program goes on to compute the third disparity. If, on the other hand, the first is larger than the second, then each of the first two disparities is replaced by the arithmetic mean of both. These two now constitute a block of two equal disparities and the program goes on to compute the third disparity. It is possible that the algorithm will return to recompute new values for the first two disparities.

The third disparity, taking on the value of the third distance, is compared with the second disparity (or with the block of two disparities). If the order is correct, then the program goes on to the fourth disparity; if, however, the order is incorrect, then a new arithmetic mean is calculated, involving the third and second disparities (or the block of two disparities). The corresponding disparities are replaced with their mean.

Let us assume that the first two disparities were in the wrong order and have been replaced with their mean. Let us also assume that the third disparity is larger than the second and that the program is now about to compute the fourth disparity. The fourth disparity is initially set equal to the fourth distance and is compared with the third. If the order is correct, then the program goes on to the fifth; if not, the third and fourth disparities are replaced with their mean creating a new block of two equal disparities. Note that this block might be smaller than the first block, so the two blocks must be compared. If the second block is in fact smaller than the first, then a new block is formed by obtaining the overall mean of both blocks.

The general procedure, then, is to compare the current block of disparities with the previous one (where a block of disparities may only contain one entry); if it is larger, go on to the next disparity, but if it is smaller, then combine the two blocks into one by replacing each entry in each block with the mean of both blocks. This mean is actually a weighted mean, with weight being directly proportional to the number of entries in each block.

This procedure computes exactly the same transformation as that proposed by Kruskal (1964a). The approach differs in that the current block of disparities is never directly compared with the next largest block. In Kruskal's terms, the algorithm directly determines whether the current block is "down-satisfied." At the conclusion of the procedure all blocks will be "up-satisfied."

The actual algorithm is modified in the following manner in order to cope with tied similarities. If a tie exists in the similarities, the corresponding distances are replaced with their own mean. This modification corresponds to the "secondary" approach suggested by Kruskal. The primary approach may be opted for by the user if he so desires. This approach involves ordering the distances corresponding to the tied similarities into the best order. For reasons noted by Kruskal and Carroll (1969), it is not recommended that the primary approach be used with rectangular models.

Minimization Procedure

In this section the method for obtaining the smallest value of L [Equation (26)] will be discussed. Several alternative methods are available for minimizing functions when the partial derivatives of the function are known. Nonmetric analysis programs have generally used the method of steepest descents, or equivalent methods. This iterative method, also known as the method of gradients, involves computing on each iteration the partial derivatives (the gradient) of the function in order to determine the new coordinate values and the new value of the function. This process is repeated until the value of the function reaches the minimum. Note that each iteration utilizes a different configuration as the basis for computing the gradient. The value of the gradient, then, changes from iteration to iteration, although the expression for computing the gradient remains unchanged.

The gradient method suffers from one well-known problem. As the function approaches its minimum value the efficiency of the method drops off, with the convergence on the actual minimum value being very slow. For our particular problem this becomes very important if, in fact, the initial configuration does enable us to start relatively close to the minimum of the function. An alternative method (Davidon, 1968; Fletcher & Powell, 1963) is available, however, which does not suffer from this problem. It is known as the revised gradient method or the variance method. This method utilizes information that is acquired during the iterative process to (essentially) revise the expression for computing the gradient on each iteration. The information acquired during the iterative process is actually an estimate of the inverse of the matrix of second-order partial derivatives of L. Davidon refers to this matrix as the variance matrix. The revised gradient method is equivalent not only to modifying (on each iteration) the configuration which enters into computing the gradient, but also to modifying the actual expression by which the gradient is computed.

The revised gradient method is superior to the gradient method in several respects. Perhaps most importantly, the revised gradient method converges much more rapidly when the minimum value of the function is being approached. In fact, it has been shown by Fletcher and Powell that for quadratic (regions of) functions their method converges within pr iterations. In addition the revised gradient method provides (a) an estimate, on each iteration, of the minimum value of L; (b) an estimate, on each iteration, of the improvement in the value of L which is still possible; and (c) the variance–covariance matrix of the derived configuration. In order to provide us with these advantages, the procedure uses more space in the computer's memory, and requires more time for computations. Studies comparing the variance method with the gradient method indicate that in general the variance method is superior. In particular, it appears that if the major portion of the computation is involved in computing the gradient rather than the variance matrix, then the revised gradient method is superior. This is the case with the function being minimized here, as the computation of the partials is relatively more complex than updating the variance matrix.

Explanation of the algorithm is simplified somewhat if we rewrite the configuration X as a column vector with pr elements. We denote the configuration on iteration i as X^i, its gradient (partials) as the column vector G^i, and the approximation to the variance matrix as the symmetric matrix V^i (with pr rows and columns). Prior to the first iteration we set V^1 equal to the identity matrix. We then compute the quantities

$$S^i = V^i G^i \tag{71}$$

and

$$T^i = \alpha^i S^i \tag{72}$$

where α^i is the step size. Computation of the step size will be explained below. Next we compute the new configuration

$$X^{i+1} = X^i - T^i \tag{73}$$

From X^{i+1} we compute the distances and disparities, and then the value of L^{i+1}. Notice that for V^i equal to the identity matrix (as it is on the first iteration) Equations (71)–(73) define the ordinary gradient method. We could at this point simply iterate on these equations until the minimum value of L is obtained, without ever obtaining estimates of V^i. In some cases this might be advisable, and it appears reasonable to make this feature an option of the program, i.e., to provide the user with the option of using a simple gradient method or a revised gradient method.[1]

If the user desires to use the revised gradient method, a new estimate of the variance matrix V^{i+1} must be computed. We do this by computing G^{i+1}, the gradient of Equation (73), then finding the difference between the two gradients

$$U^i = G^{i+1} - G^i \tag{74}$$

and computing

$$Y^i = T^i T^{i\prime}/T^{i\prime} U^i \tag{75}$$

and

$$Z^i = -V^i U^i U^{i\prime} V^i / U^{i\prime} V^i U^i \tag{76}$$

The new estimate of the variance matrix

$$V^{i+1} = V^i + Y^i + Z^i \tag{77}$$

then may be computed. We can now return to Equation (71) and start a new iteration, noting that the configuration and its gradient have already been computed [Equation (73)].

The gradient revision part of this algorithm [Equations (74)–(77)] only involves one set of time consuming computations, obtaining the gradient matrix G^{i+1}. This matrix, of course, would have had to be computed on the next iteration in the simple gradient method. The remaining computations, Equations (75)–(77), while complex in appearance are actually computationally simple. Equation (75) simply involves multiplying one vector times its transpose, then dividing by a scalar. Equation (76) is somewhat more complex, although again, the denominator is simply a scalar. Perhaps the greatest disadvantage of this method is the size of the variance matrix V, which is a *pr* by *pr* symmetric matrix. For a program to perform analyses for up to 60 points in nine dimensions, as most do, a total of 146,070 locations must be reserved just for the variance matrix. While large, such a matrix is not prohibitive on third generation machines.

Any of several criteria can be used to terminate the iterative process. With the simple gradient process, the standard criteria of the absolute size of the function L and the rate of decrease of L can be used, as can the total number of iterations. With the revised gradient method two additional criteria are available. One of these is the distance between the current value and the predicted minimum value of L which can be computed as

$$\beta^i = (T^{i\prime} T^i)^{1/2} \tag{78}$$

and when it is sufficiently small the iterative process can be terminated. A second criterion for termination provided by the revised gradient method is the maximum entry in the vector represented by Equation (72), the vector by which the configuration is adjusted. When the largest absolute adjustment made to the configuration is small, then the iterative process should be stopped.

Fletcher and Powell (1963) have suggested that the efficiency of the method can be increased by using some approximation to the variance of the coordinates as the value of V^1 in place of the identity matrix. Davidon (1968) has suggested that an initial approximation to the variance matrix should involve a generous overestimate of the variance: i.e., V^1 should be a diagonal matrix whose elements are large compared to the variance of the coordinates. The problem of the initial variance matrix is, in essence, an additional "initial configuration" problem. It appears useful to be able to obtain some analytic expression of the variance of the coordinates, no matter how approximate the expression might be.

We now turn to α^i, the step size in Equation (72). Fletcher and Powell (1963) suggest using the method of cubic interpolation, based on a method by Davidon (1959). This procedure is rather time consuming, involving a relatively large number of computations, but experience has shown that it provides a very good estimate of the step size. The relative efficiency of Fletcher and Powell's (1963) algorithm to compute step size as compared with Kruskal's (1964a) less-involved algorithm is not known, though some preliminary information suggests that the comparison is favorable.

In outline form the step size method suggested by Fletcher and Powell involves computing a new configuration X^* according to the formula

$$X^* = X^i + \eta S^i \tag{79}$$

where η is defined as

$$\eta = \min[1, -2L/G^{i\prime}S^i] \tag{80}$$

We must then compute the value of L and the gradient of this new configuration. Denoting these as L^* and G^*, we can then compute the step size as

$$\frac{\alpha^i}{\eta} = 1 - \frac{G^{*\prime}S^i + w - z}{G^{*\prime}S^i - G^{i\prime}S^i + 2w} \tag{81}$$

where

$$w = (z - G^{i\prime}S^iG^{*\prime}S^i)^{1/2} \tag{82}$$

and

$$z = \frac{3(L^i - L^*)}{\eta} + G^{i\prime}S^i + G^{*\prime}S^i \tag{83}$$

It happens occasionally that the step size yields a value of L^{i+1} which is not less than L^i and L^* in which case a smaller value of η in Equation (80) must be used. This value can be reduced by arbitrarily dividing by some number such as 2. Empirically when the value $L^{i+1} > L^i$ and L^* occurs, it is on the first iteration (especially if the initial configuration is poorly determined), but seldom on other iterations (unless, of course, the minimum has been found).

Conclusions

On the basis of notions fundamental to nonmetric multidimensional scaling, a model has been developed for constructing algorithms for polynomial conjoint analysis. Several examples of specific cases of this model were presented, including nonmetric multidimensional scaling, nonmetric analysis of variance, nonmetric factor analysis, the subjective expected utility model, and the Bradley–Terry–Luce choice model. In addition to the characteristics of the general model, the definitions and operations necessary to write computer programs for a wide range of specific cases of the model were presented.

The polynomial conjoint analysis method provides a way of nonmetrically fitting a very wide range of descriptive models to a collection of data. Perhaps more importantly, a large number of different models in diverse areas of the behavioral sciences already conform to the notions of polynomial conjoint measurement. Savage's expected-utility model in economics (Savage, 1954), the Hullian and Spencian performance models in psychology (Hilgard, 1956), and the scaling models in psychometrics (Torgerson, 1958; Coombs, 1964) are but a few examples. All these models can be applied to data with the analytic method discussed here. When one of these models does not fit under the specific combination rules discussed here, the open-ended feature of the method can be used. Of equal importance is the fact that polynomial conjoint analysis may assist in providing answers to controversies concerning which model is best suited to a particular kind of data. In the area of generalization in learning, for example, at least three different models have been proposed to account for multidimensional generalization (Cross, 1965). These models correspond to the city-block, Euclidean, and dominance examples of the Minkowski metric. The analytic method proposed here provides a unified method for attempting to settle controversies such as these.

Polynomial conjoint measurement, and the associated analytic method proposed here, may also serve as a new means for evolving models of data. Generally, a model is stated a priori and then various attempts are made to fit it to the data. By using the polynomial conjoint approach, however, it may be possible to search through a large number of different models to evolve empirically an appropriate model. Of course, this is not radically different from current modeling practice, since most often a model which is proposed a priori is based in some manner on some previous set of data. The main difference is that, with the assistance of a powerful analytic tool, the empirical evolution of a model is made more efficient.

Finally, the overall structure of polynomial conjoint measurement theory provides us with what may be a very useful way of relating models in very diverse areas of behavioral science. If in fact the analytic method proposed here is as useful as it appears to be, and if specific polynomial conjoint models are found to describe data from many areas of the research in the behavioral sciences, then the structure of polynomial conjoint measurement theory becomes more than simply a theory of measurement. It becomes a general unifying theory of behavior.

Acknowledgments

This paper was supported in part by a PHS research grant No. MH-10006 from the National Institute of Mental Health, Public Health Service, and in part by a Science Development grant No. GU-2059 from the National Science Foundation. The author wishes to express his appreciation for the benefit he received from discussions with J. Douglas Carroll, Joseph Kruskal, Lincoln Moses, Roger Pennell, Amnon Rapoport, and Norman Cliff. POLYCON, a program based on the concepts presented in this paper, can be obtained by writing to the author at the Psychometric Laboratory, University of North Carolina, Chapel Hill, North Carolina 27514.

References

Attneave, F. Dimensions of similarity. *American Journal of Psychology*, 1950, **63**, 516–556.
Beals, R., Krantz, D. H., & Tversky, A. Foundations of multidimensional scaling. *Psychological Review*, 1968, **75**, 127–142.
Cliff, N. The "idealized individual" interpretation of individual differences in multidimensional scaling. *Psychometrika*, 1968, **33**, 225–232.
Coombs, C. H. *A theory of data*. New York: Wiley, 1964.
Cross, D. V. Metric properties of multidimensional stimulus generalization. In I. Mostofsky (Ed.), *Stimulus generalization*. Stanford, California: Stanford University Press, 1965. Pp. 72–93.
Davidon, W. C. Variance algorithm for minimization. *The Computer Journal*, 1968, **11**, 408–410.

Fletcher, R., & Powell, M. J. A rapidly convergent descent method for minimization. *The Computer Journal*, 1963, **6**, 163–168.

Green, P. E., & Rao, V. R. A note on the sensitivity of multidimensional scaling solutions to departures from monotonicity. Pittsburgh, Pennsylvania: Mimeographed working paper from Wharton School of Finance, 1968.

Guttman, L. A general nonmetric technique for finding the smallest coordinate space for a configuration of points. *Psychometrika*, 1968, **33**, 469–506.

Hilgard, E. R. *Theories of learning.* New York: Appleton–Century–Croft, 1956.

Kruskal, J. B. Multidimensional scaling by optimizing goodness-of-fit to a nonmetric hypothesis. *Psychometrika*, 1964, **29**, 1–27. (a)

Kruskal, J. B. Nonmetric multidimensional scaling: A numerical method. *Psychometrika*, 1964, **29**, 115–129. (b)

Kruskal, J. B. Analysis of factorial experiments by estimating monotone transformations of the data. *The Journal of the Royal Statistical Society*, 1965 (Series B, methodological), **27**, 251–263.

Kruskal, J. B., & Carmone, F. J. MONANOVA: A FORTRAN—IV program for monotone analysis of variance. *Behavioral Science*, 1969, **14**, 165–166.

Kruskal, J. B., & Carroll, J. D. Geometrical models and badness-of-fit functions. In P. R. Krishnaiah (Ed.), *International multivariate analysis, Dayton, Ohio*, 1968. New York: Academic Press, 1969. Pp. 639–670.

Lingoes, J. C. An IBM–7090 program for Guttman–Lingoes smallest space analysis—I. *Behavioral Science*, 1965, **10**, 183–184.

Lingoes, J. C. An IBM–7090 program for Guttman–Lingoes smallest space analysis—RI. *Behavioral Science*, 1966, **11**, 332.

Lingoes, J. C. An IBM 360/67 program for Guttman–Lingoes conjoint measurement— III. *Behavioral Science*, 1968, **13**, 421–422.

Lingoes, J. C., & Guttman, L. Nonmetric factor analysis: A rank reducing alternative to linear factor analysis. *Multivariate Behavioral Research*, 1967, **2**, 485–505.

Luce, R. D. *Individual choice behavior.* New York: Wiley, 1959.

Luce, R. D., & Tukey, J. W. Simultaneous conjoint measurement. *Journal of Mathematical Psychology*, 1964, **1**, 1–27.

McGee, V. E. The multidimensional analysis of 'elastic' distances. *The British Journal of Mathematical and Statistical Psychology*, 1966, **19**, 181–196.

McGee, V. E. Multidimensional scaling of N sets of similarity measures: A nonmetric individual differences approach. *Multivariate Behavioral Research*, 1968, **3**, 233–248.

Roskam, E. E. *Metric analysis of ordinal data. Psychology.* Voorschoten, Holland: VAM Press, 1968.

Roskam, E. E. A comparison of principles for algorithm construction in nonmetric scaling. Ann Arbor, Michigan: Michigan Mathematical Psychology Program Technical Report MMPP 69–2, 1969.

Savage, L. J. *The foundation of statistics.* New York: Wiley, 1954.

Shepard, R. N. The analysis of proximities: Multidimensional scaling with an unknown distance function. II. *Psychometrika*, 1962, **27**, 219–246.

Torgerson, W. S. *Theory and methods of scaling.* New York: Wiley, 1958.

Torgerson, W. S., & Meuser, G. Informal notes on Torgerson and Meuser's IBM 7090 program for multidimensional scaling. Department of Psychology, Johns Hopkins University, Mimeographed Report, 1962.

Tucker, L. R., & Messick, S. An individual differences model for multidimensional scaling. *Psychometrika*, 1963, **28**, 333–367.

Tversky, A. A general theory of polynomial conjoint measurement. *Journal of Mathematical Psychology*, 1967, **4**, 1–20.

Tversky, A., & Zivian, A. An IBM 7090 program for additivity analysis. *Behavioral Science*, 1966, **11**, 78–79.

Young, F. W. TORSCA–9: A FORTRAN IV program for nonmetric multidimensional scaling. *Behavioral Science*, 1968, **13**, 343–344. (a)

Young, F. W. A FORTRAN IV program for nonmetric multidimensional scaling. Chapel Hill, North Carolina: L. L. Thurstone Psychometric Laboratory Report No. 56, 1968. (b)

Young, F. W., & Appelbaum, M. I. Nonmetric multidimensional scaling: The relationship of several methods. Chapel Hill, North Carolina: L. L. Thurstone Psychometric Laboratory Report No. 71, 1968.

Young, F. W., & Pennell, R. An IBM system/360 program for points of view analysis. *Behavioral Science*, 1967, **12**, 166.

Young, F. W., & Torgerson, W. S. TORSCA, A FORTRAN IV program for Shepard–Kruskal multidimensional scaling analysis. *Behavioral Science*, 1967, **12**, 498.

Note

[1] Since the initial writing of this paper I have found that in practice the revised gradient procedure does not live up to its promise. I recommend instead using a conjugate gradients or simple gradients procedure using the cubic interpolation for step size. An IBM scientific subroutines conjugate gradients routine, called FMCG, is available.

INDIVIDUAL DIFFERENCES
AND MULTIDIMENSIONAL SCALING

J. Douglas Carroll

BELL TELEPHONE LABORATORIES, INC.
MURRAY HILL, NEW JERSEY

This paper will discuss individual differences in judgments of similarity, which presumably reflect differing "perceptual structures," and in judgments of preference (or other "dominance" judgments) which reflect different ways of using those perceptual structures (whether they themselves are the same or different).

Individual Differences in Perception

While we have always known that there were color-blind and non-color-blind people, people who have general or specific hearing loss, and the like, it is only recently that psychologists have recognized the possibility of individual differences in perception as a general and pervasive phenomenon not necessarily resulting from some physiological defect in one of the sense modalities. The first attempt to incorporate notions of individual differences into multidimensional scaling procedures was that of Tucker and Messick

(1963), who introduced what they called "points of view" analysis. This procedure amounts essentially to a factor analysis of the subjects by pairs-of-stimuli matrix of similarity (or dissimilarity) judgments, followed by an attempt to rotate the resulting structure to find clusters of subjects corresponding to different "points of view." Ross (1966) has criticized this procedure on the grounds of lack of mathematical justification for the factor analysis of subjects based on interpoint distances, while Cliff (1968) has answered this criticism by arguing, essentially, that the factor analysis should be regarded as only a vehicle for clustering subjects and finding "ideal" subjects. The present author would argue that, if this is the object of the analysis, a clustering rather than factor analysis of the subjects should be the first step of the analysis.

Kruskal (1968) and McGee (1968) have recently incorporated different ways of dealing with individual differences into their procedures. Kruskal has two approaches. The first assumes each subject to have a different monotone function (relating distances to similarity or dissimilarity judgments) but constrains them to have *identically* the same configuration (no degrees of freedom for weighting of dimensions or the like are allowed). The second assumes all subject to have the same monotone function, but allows each his own idiosyncratic configuration. These two represent two extremes of a continuum (or, perhaps, of two continua) of which there are, of course, many intermediate points. McGee's approach covers at least some of these intermediate points. McGee allows for either the case in which each subject has his own monotone function, or all are constrained to have the same. He then introduces a parameter that monitors the degree to which the configurations for different subjects are constrained to be similar. At one extreme, these configurations must be identical, at the other there is no constraint at all on how similar they must be. At intermediate values of this parameter, the configurations must be "intermediately" similar. McGee's approach, however, says nothing explicitly about how these configurations may depart from identity (the criterion of departure is simply a "sum of squared coordinate differences" criterion, which monitors degree, but not direction of departure from identity). The Tucker–Messick procedure also makes no explicit assumption about communality of dimensions among subjects.

The model to be discussed now (Carroll & Chang, 1970) does make a very explicit assumption about communality among dimensions. This model has been independently proposed by Horan (1969) and by Bloxom (1968). S. C. Johnson (personal communication) has also proposed a similar model for subjective clustering. It assumes that different individuals perceive the stimuli in terms of a common set of dimensions, but that these dimensions are differentially important or salient in the perception of different individuals. (Of course, the "importance" can be zero, in which case the corresponding dimension does not affect the subject's perception, or his perceptual judgments, at all.) One important point about this model is that it makes a difference *which* set of dimensions are differentially weighted by subjects (i.e., rotations are not permissible, even though the metric in each subject's perceptual space is assumed to be Euclidean). Thus the solution obtained is unique up to permutation of coordinate axes. We have found in quite a number of cases that these uniquely oriented axes are directly interpretable (without rotation) and that, when an a priori set of physical or other dimensions are known, they usually correspond in a one-to-one fashion to these a priori dimensions (see, e.g., the analysis reported in Carroll and Chang, 1970 of the data of Bricker and Pruzansky, 1969). Such correspondence would seem to be strong evidence in favor of such a model.

The Model

We assume a set of r dimensions or "factors" underlying the n stimuli. These are assumed to be common to all individuals. We shall use x_{jt} to represent the value of the jth stimulus on the tth dimension (so j ranges from 1 to n and t from 1 to r). Similarity judgments for each subject are assumed to be related in a simple way to a kind of modified Euclidean distance in this space. In particular, it is assumed that

$$s_{jk}^{(i)} = L(d_{jk}^{(i)}) \tag{1}$$

where $s_{jk}^{(i)}$ is the similarity of the jth and kth stimuli for the ith individual, and L is a linear function (with negative slope). The "modified" Euclidean distance for the ith subject is given by

$$d_{jk}^{(i)} = \left[\sum_{t=1}^{r} w_{it}(x_{jt} - x_{kt})^2 \right]^{1/2} \tag{2}$$

This formula differs from the usual Euclidean distance formula only in the presence of the weights w_{it}, which represent the saliences or importances mentioned above. Another way of looking at this formula is to say that the $d_{jk}^{(i)}$'s are ordinary Euclidean distances computed in a space whose coordinates are

$$y_{jt}^{(i)} = w_{it}^{1/2} x_{jt} \tag{3}$$

that is, in a space that is like the x space except that the configuration has been expanded or contracted (differentially) in directions corresponding

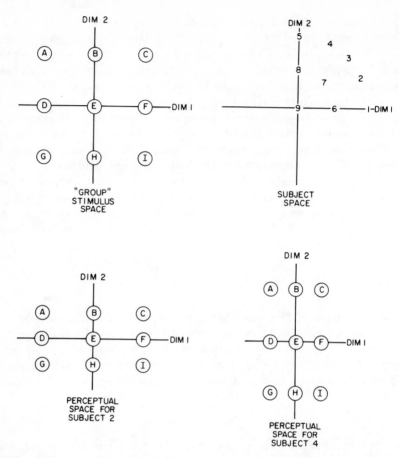

FIG. 1. Illustration of Carroll–Chang model for individual differences in multi-dimensional scaling. Weights (plotted in subject space) are applied to "group" stimulus space to produce individual perceptual spaces for Subjects 2 and 4, shown in bottom of figure. (For purposes of illustration the dimensions are multiplied by the weights themselves, rather than by their square roots as is more technically correct).

to the coordinate axes. This is the kind of transformation that would, for example, convert circles into ellipses with major and minor axes parallel to the coordinate axes, or spheres into (parallel) ellipsoids in three dimensions. The model is illustrated in Figure 1. There are two spaces in this model, a common or "group" stimulus space and a subject space, in which the weights for subjects are plotted as points. By applying Equation (3) we can get a separate space for each subject. Two of these are illustrated in the figure.

This model is sufficiently general to include a number of different models as special cases. Two completely different spaces could be accommodated, for example, by assuming a "common" space combining all the dimensions of the two separate spaces (the direct sum, in technical terms). The dimensionality of this "superspace" would be the sum of the two dimensionalities. Then, by assuming that one group of subjects attaches zero weights or saliences to the dimensions of the first space, while a second group attaches zero weights to those of the second, this model becomes equivalent to a model assuming two separate, disjoint, spaces for the two groups of subjects. Of course, the more interesting and exciting case is that in which some, but not complete, communality exists.

A limitation of this model, and of the method of analysis based on it, is embodied in the first assumption, which implies that this is a "metric" rather than a "nonmetric" procedure (i.e., it requires distances measured on at least an interval scale rather than on a merely ordinal scale). However, the method can be made at least "quasi-nonmetric" by procedures essentially the same as those used earlier by Torgerson (see, e.g., Young & Torgerson, 1967). We have found in a great many situations that this strong metric assumption does not seem to do a great deal of damage to the solutions obtained, so long as the "correct" dimensionality is used. The added redundancy afforded by having many different subjects evidently helps in this case.

The method we use to analyze data in terms of this model entails use of a procedure called "canonical decomposition of N-way tables." In the present case, we start with a three-way table of distances (derived from similarities or dissimilarities, à la Torgerson, 1958) between stimuli for individuals. This table, or rectangular solid, of data, will be $m \times n \times n$, for m individuals and n stimuli. By using procedures described by Torgerson (1958) we convert this cube of distances data to a cube of scalar products data (each subject's distances are independently transformed to scalar products by the Torgerson equations). It is this three-way table of scalar products between stimuli by subjects that is subjected to canonical decomposition analysis.

If we let $b_{jk}^{(i)}$ stand for the scalar product between the vectors (issuing from a common origin at the centroid of all the stimuli) for the jth and kth stimuli, then it is easy to show that

$$b_{jk}^{(i)} = \sum_{t}^{r} w_{it} x_{jt} x_{kt} \tag{4}$$

Canonical decomposition of three-way tables is a method that takes data in a three-way table whose general entry is z_{ijk} and analyzes it in terms of a model of the form

$$z_{ijk} = \sum_{t=1}^{r} a_{it} b_{jt} c_{kt} \qquad (5)$$

That is, given the z's and a specified value of r, the canonical decomposition finds the a's, b's, and c's yielding a best fit (in a least-squares sense) to the z's. It does this by a general numerical method called NILES (for nonlinear iterative least squares) due to the Swedish statistician Wold (1966). Roughly speaking, we note that if we hold the b's and c's constant, we can derive, by standard analytical methods, an exact least-squares solution for the a's. We can do the same for the b's, holding the a's and c's fixed, and similarly for the c's. By proceeding, iteratively, to improve our estimate of one set of parameters holding the other sets fixed, we will (hopefully) converge to the simultaneous least-squares solution for all the parameters. There is no proof that this process will converge, nor that, if it does, it will converge to the global (rather than a merely local) optimum solution. Nonetheless, it seems, empirically, to work extremely well, and to be almost wholly free of "local minima" and similar problems. This procedure can be regarded as a special kind of three-mode factor analysis (see Tucker, 1964, 1966) in which what Tucker calls the "core matrix" is eliminated, (or, equivalently, is constrained to be diagonal with ones on the diagonal) and can be extended in a straightforward way to N-way tables (Chang has currently programmed it for N as large as 7). The details can be found in Carroll and Chang (1970).

We use canonical decomposition of three-way tables to analyze data in terms of the model stated in Equations (1)–(3) by noting that Equation (4) is a special case of Equation (5). In this special case $z_{ijk} = b_{jk}^{(i)}$, $a_{it} = w_{it}$, and $b_{jt} = c_{jt} = x_{jt}$. If we define the z's in the way indicated above, and apply canonical decomposition the resulting B and C matrices will (after appropriate normalization) be, in fact, the same. No special constraint must be imposed to guarantee this; it will be assured by the basic symmetry of the (scalar products) data for each subject.

There are some other normalization conventions that should be mentioned. The first is a normalization of the data. Ordinarily, though not invariably, we normalize the *scalar products* for each subject to have unit sum of squares. This equalizes the total variance "to be accounted for" for each subject (as well as giving each subject equal weight in the analysis) and also leads to certain interpretive niceties. The second involves normalization of the *solution*. The stimulus dimensions are normalized so that the origin is at the centroid and the sum of squares of projections for each dimension is unity. This means that "variance accounted for" is reflected in the subject space. It also means that the distance from the origin in the subject space can be fairly directly interpreted in terms of variance accounted for or, better, as communality of that subject with the other subjects in the analysis. The origin in the subject space is not arbitrary, but has a very strong meaning. A subject precisely at the origin (such as subject 9 in Figure 1) is not accounted for at all in this analysis; he has nothing at all in common with the other subjects, or, perhaps, he is simply responding randomly. Also, since all the weights should be positive, the points in the subject space should all be in the positive orthant of that space. While there is no specific constraint to make this so, it almost always is the case when data are analyzed in this way. For some examples, see Wish, Deutsch, & Biener (this book, Volume II).

SOME "TEA-TASTING" DATA

Before going further with this description of algorithms and methodology, let us pause for a tea break. In this case, unfortunately, we will be only discussing an experiment on judgments of similarity and preference of various cups (or glasses) of tea, and these are only hypothetical cups at that! The subjects for this study were students from Columbia University.[1]

Twenty-five hypothetical cups of tea were described in terms of pairs of description words or phrases. The first set of descriptions referred to the temperature of the cup of tea. Five temperature related words or phrases—ice cold, cold, lukewarm, hot, steaming hot—were used. The second set of descriptions specified the amount of sugar: no sugar, $\frac{1}{2}$ teaspoon, 1 teaspoon, 2 teaspoons, 4 teaspoons. Subjects were shown a standard size styrofoam cup, in which they were to imagine tea of "moderate strength" with no cream or lemon. All 25 possible combinations of the two sets of descriptions were used to define the basic (verbally described) stimuli. The 300 possible pairs of stimuli were generated in a random order to form the basic questionnaire. There were a total of 12 subjects, divided randomly into two sets of subjects which responded to the items in opposite orders. Each of the 12 subjects was asked to give two kinds of judgments for each pair of stimuli. The first was a rating of dissimilarity (called "degree of difference") of the pair on a scale from 0 (for an indistinguishable pair) to 9 (for an extremely

[1] We thank Myron Wish for his advice on design of the study, as well as for great aid in collecting the data from students in his measurement class at Columbia, at no mean risk to his own life and limb. It was only the generally recognized docility of Columbia students (together with a solemn promise to talk about the data and data analysis in class later) that prevented a mutiny.

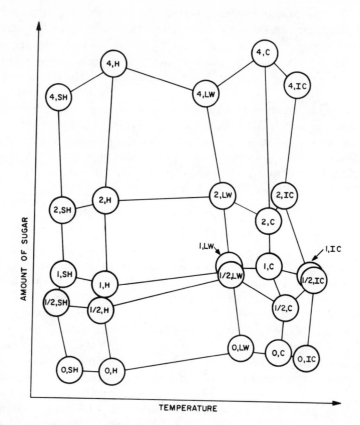

Fig. 2a. Unrotated two-dimensional solution from Carroll–Chang individual differences analysis of dissimilarities data on hypothetical cups of tea. In this and all figures involving these data the following coding is used: 0, ½, 1, 2, 4 refer to number of teaspoons of sugar; for temperature, IC ≡ ice cold, C ≡ cold, LW ≡ lukewarm, H ≡ hot, SH ≡ steaming hot. Thus, for example, "½, LW" means "a lukewarm cup of tea with ½ teaspoon of sugar."

dissimilar pair). The second was a paired comparisons preference judgment, which entailed circling either the letter *A* which appeared before one of the two stimuli or the letter *B* which appeared before the other. Subjects were asked to make the dissimilarity judgment before the preference judgment, and were carefully instructed so as to minimize the degree of confounding of the two judgments. Though one can justifiably criticize this procedure on the basis of the possibility of confounding of the two judgments, there is no evidence in the present case that such confounding ever occurred. One might suppose, for example, that subjects would have tended to judge dissimilarity with respect to preference (i.e., strength of the preference for the preferred stimulus) rather than general perceptual dissimilarity. It is abundantly clear, however, that this did *not* happen.

ANALYSIS OF DISSIMILARITIES BY INDSCAL

INDSCAL (individual differences scaling) was applied to the dissimilarities, producing the group stimulus space shown in Figure 2a, and the subject space (for 12 subjects) shown in Figure 2b. Note that the basic lattice structure embodied in the factorial design used to generate the stimuli is quite clearly in evidence (though a bit distorted) in the stimulus space, and, furthermore, that the "sides" of the lattice are very nicely parallel to the two coordinate axes. These axes are exactly as they came out of the analysis; no rotation whatsoever has been done. This preservation of structure tends to bolster the earlier assertions about uniqueness of axes

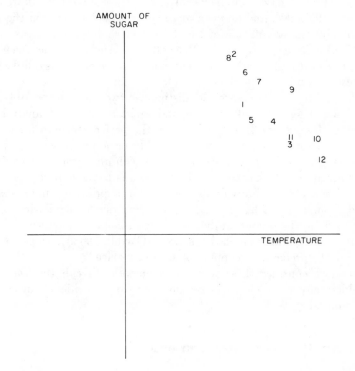

FIG. 2b. Subject space from individual differences analysis of dissimilarities data on hypothetical cups of tea.

as determined in the INDSCAL analysis. In the case of the "tea-tasting" data the axes correspond to a very high degree to the "natural" coordinate system, even though the amount of individual differences, as exhibited in the subject space, is relatively slight.

Individual Differences in Preference

A number of different models have been proposed to account for individual differences in preference. Foremost among these are the *vector* model, first proposed by Tucker (1960), and the *unfolding* model, proposed in the unidimensional form by Coombs (1950) and generalized to the multidimensional case by Bennett and Hays (1960). We shall presently consider a hierarchy of models, beginning with these two, going on to a further generalization of the unfolding model in which differential weights or saliences (which may even be negative) are assumed (or allowed) for different individuals, and an even more general model in which the possibility of differential rotation of the system of coordinate axes as well as differential weighting is allowed. We shall then briefly consider even more general models (and, in fact, show that none of these models is quite general enough to account for the data on preference for tea).

In the case of all these *models* we distinguish two different possible kinds of *analyses*. These we call *internal* and *external* modes of analysis. An *internal* analysis is one based entirely on the preference data for a set of individuals without reference to an outside or a priori set of stimulus dimensions. An *external* analysis is one in which an a priori set of dimensions is given and the purpose of the analysis is to *relate* preference judgments of the various individuals. When this a priori stimulus space is derived from a multidimensional scaling analysis of similarity or dissimilarity data, the present author has called this kind of external analysis "preference mapping of similarity space" (Carroll, 1968b). In general, we might call it "preference mapping of stimulus space."

Let us now consider these models, which we shall call the *linear–quadratic* hierarchy of models (for reasons soon to be evident), in order of their complexity.

THE LINEAR–QUADRATIC HIERARCHY OF MODELS

VECTOR MODEL. The vector model, illustrated in Figure 3, assumes (in common with all the models to be discussed here) a set of stimulus points

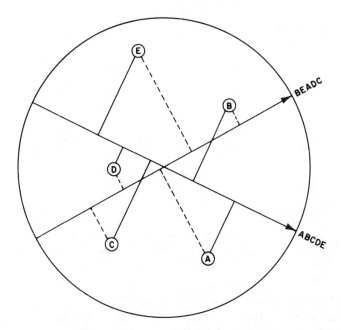

FIG. 3. Vector model for preference illustrated. Projections of stimulus points onto a subject's vector are assumed to define preference scale for that subject.

(such as A–E, in the figure) embedded in a multidimensional space. In this model, different subjects are represented by distinct *vectors*, or directed line segments. Two of these vectors are shown in Figure 3. The preference order for a given subject is assumed to be given by the projection of stimuli onto the vector representing that subject. As can be seen in the figure, quite different preference orders can be accommodated in such a model.

One way of interpreting vectors in this vector model is in terms of the relative *importance* of the dimensions to the preference judgment. The cosines of the angles the vector forms with the coordinate axes directly measure these relative importances. In the case of the vector model these *importances* act like coefficients in a linear combination of dimensions, as will be seen more directly and algebraically later.

An intuitively unattractive property of this vector model is that it assumes preference to change monotonically with all dimensions. That is to say, it assumes that if a certain amount of a given thing is good, even more must be even better (*ad infinitum*). We know that for most, if not all, quantities or attributes in the real world this is not true. (Money may be an exception, but even that is not obviously true; happiness or pleasure

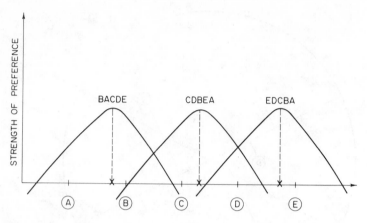

FIG. 4. Unidimensional unfolding model illustrated. Distance of stimulus from subject's "ideal point" (his optimal value on the unidimensional scale) is assumed to define (inversely) the preference scale for that subject.

are exceptions if one subscribes to a hedonistic theory of human motivation, but there is something vaguely circular about that conclusion.) Rather, for most dimensions there is an optimal value, and too much can be as bad as too little (or vice versa), as is implied in the cliché "too much of a good thing." This notion is directly contained in the "unfolding" model of Coombs (1950) and generalizations of this model to follow.

(SIMPLE) UNFOLDING MODEL. Coombs (1950) first introduced the uni-dimensional unfolding model, which is illustrated in Figure 4. Here the stimuli can be described in one dimension, as represented by their positions along the abscissa in the figure. Different subjects correspond to different "ideal points" which represent their respective optimal values on that stimulus continuum. In the unidimensional unfolding model, the farther a stimulus is from a subject's ideal point, the less the subject will like that stimulus. In Figure 4 three hypothetical subjects are represented by ideal points, and the preference order generated by these different ideal points is indicated. It is clear that, even in one dimension, quite different orders can be generated by this model. Coombs called this the "unfolding" model because the preference order for a given individual can be generated by *folding* the stimulus scale at that individual's ideal point. To recover the stimulus scale from the preference data, then, it is necessary simultaneously to *unfold* all these preference scales for individuals (what Coombs calls the I scales) to find the common, or joint, stimulus scale (the J scale). The three curves drawn above the abscissa in Figure 4 show hypothetical *preference functions* that go with the three individuals represented here. The important thing about them is that they are, to use Coombs' term, single peaked (have a single maximum, which occurs of course at the ideal point) and symmetric. The particular shape is not important, so long as these two conditions are met, nor do they all have to have the same shape.

Bennett and Hays (1960) generalized this model to the multidimensional case. The two-dimensional case of this "multidimensional unfolding" model is illustrated in Figure 5. Here the stimuli and subjects are both represented as points in the same multidimensional space. The points for individuals represent ideal stimuli, or optimal sets of stimulus values, for those individuals. In the Bennett and Hays model, the farther a given stimulus point is from an individual's ideal point the less the individual likes that stimulus. This notion of relative distance implies a metric on the space. Bennett and Hays assumed this to be Euclidean, an assumption we shall share. The assumption of the Euclidean metric means that the "iso-preference contours" (or loci of equal preference) are, in two dimensions, a family of concentric circles centered at the individual's ideal point. In three dimensions they are concentric spheres, and hyperspheres in higher dimensions.

While the unfolding model and the vector model seem, superficially, to be quite different, it is in fact the case that the vector model is a *special*

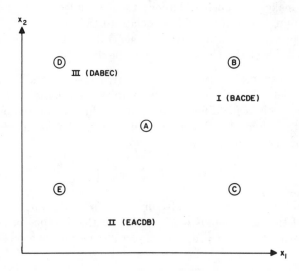

FIG. 5. Multidimensional unfolding model illustrated. Distance from subject's "ideal point" (inversely) defines his preference scale. Isopreference contours are concentric circles centered at "ideal points." They would be spheres or hyperspheres in higher dimensions.

case of the unfolding model. One can see this by conceptually moving the ideal point for an individual farther and farther out along a fixed line from the origin, while holding the stimuli constant. As one does this the rank order of distances from the ideal will approach (and will asymptotically be identical to) that of *projections* of stimuli onto a vector whose direction is the same as that of the line along which the ideal point is moved. This will be shown mathematically at a later point. One can see it geometrically by noting that, as the ideal point is moved farther and farther out, the family of circular isopreference contours looks (in the region occupied by the stimuli) more and more like a family of parallel straight lines perpendicular to the line joining the centroid to the ideal point, and asymptotically would be precisely such a family of straight lines. But the isopreference contours for the vector model comprise a family of parallel straight lines perpendicular to the vector.

If these geometric arguments have not yet convinced the reader, it may be instructive to construct a hypothetical scatter plot of stimuli in two dimensions, place an ideal point at a large distance from the stimuli, and compare distances from this ideal with projections on a vector in the direction of the ideal (from, say, the centroid, or center of mass, of the stimuli).

This *simple* unfolding model assumes that a given difference (on a dimension) makes as much difference to one subject as to another, as well as assuming that all individuals relate to the *same* set of dimensions within the space. We now consider two generalizations of this model that allow one or both of these assumptions to be dropped.

THE WEIGHTED UNFOLDING MODEL. In this first generalization of the unfolding model we continue, as in the simple unfolding model, to assume different ideal points for different individuals, but we also allow distinct individuals to weight the dimensions differently. That is, in place of the usual Euclidean distance formula of the form

$$d_{ij} = \left[\sum_{t=1}^{r} (y_{it} - x_{jt})^2 \right]^{1/2} \tag{6}$$

(where y_{it} is the tth coordinate of individual i's ideal point, x_{jt} is the tth coordinate of the jth stimulus point, and d_{ij} is the distance between ideal point i and stimulus point j in a space of r dimensions) we substitute the formula

$$d_{ij} = \left[\sum_{t=1}^{r} w_{it}(y_{it} - x_{jt})^2 \right]^{1/2} \tag{7}$$

where the weighting factor w_{it} can be thought of as the "salience" or "importance" of the tth dimension for subject i. For the moment we will assume the w_{ti}'s are all positive or zero, but we will later consider the case where they may be negative. The generalized version of the unfolding model following from Formula (2) assumes that one man's meat may be another man's irrelevancy; a dimension that is very important to one individual may be of no significance (at least for the judgment at hand) to another. It should be stressed that we need *not* assume these weights to reflect any differential *perceptual* discrimination of the dimensions. While a man may perceive perfectly well the difference between blondes and red-heads, this dimension may be irrelevant to his choice of dating (or mating) partners. To another, of no greater perceptual acumen, this dimension may make all the difference in the world. Of course, the weighted distance formula of Equation (2) does not and cannot distinguish between differential weights due to differences in perception, and those due to different "saliences" for preference of equally well discriminated dimensions.

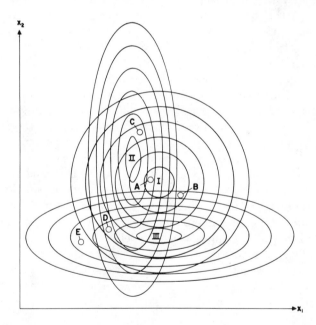

FIG. 6. Illustration of multidimensional unfolding model with differential weights. Subject I weights x_1 and x_2 equally, II weights x_1 more than x_2, while III weights x_2 more than x_1. Isopreference contours are ellipses with axes parallel to coordinate axes, and lengths of axes proportional to reciprocal of square root of weights. In higher dimensions these would be ellipsoids or hyperellipsoids. Generalized Euclidean distance from "ideal point" defines preference. Order implied for the three hypothetical subjects is I: ABCDE; II: CADBE; III: DEBAC.

This weighted unfolding model is illustrated in Figure 6. The only difference is that now the isopreference contours are ellipses, ellipsoids, or hyperellipsoids instead of circles, spheres, or hyperspheres. The larger the weight, the *smaller* the corresponding axis of the isopreference ellipse or ellipsoid, reflecting the fact that it takes a smaller change to make the same amount of difference [to be precise the ratios of the axes of the ellipses are reciprocally related to the square roots of the ratios of the weights that appear in Equation (7)]. In Figure 6, Subject I weights the two dimensions equally, subject II weights x_1 more than x_2 while III weights x_2 more than x_1. The preference orders for the three hypothetical subjects are also shown. These are generated by applying the generalized Euclidean distance defined in Equation (7), which can be characterized roughly as the number of rings of concentric ellipsoids out from the center (or ideal point).

THE GENERAL UNFOLDING MODEL (DIFFERENTIAL ROTATIONS AND WEIGHTS). In this first generalization we have assumed that, while individuals may differ both in ideal point and weighting of dimensions, the same basic set of dimensions are involved in the judgments of all individuals. The second generalization allows us to relax this assumption. While we shall assume all individuals to share in common a single perceptual space, we allow distinct individuals additional freedom in choosing a set of "reference axes" within that space. Thus each individual is allowed to rotate the reference frame of the perceptual space, and then to weight differentially the dimensions defined by this rotated reference frame (in addition to being permitted an idiosyncratic ideal point).

One point that should be made with respect to this model is that the rotation alone does not make the model different from the simple unfolding model (since orthogonal rotations leave Euclidean distances unchanged). It is only the rotation in combination with differential weighting of dimensions that makes this a genuinely new model.

Figure 7 illustrates isopreference contours that could arise from this most general unfolding model. For simplicity, only a single ideal point is shown, and all isopreference ellipses have the same eccentricities, but neither of these conditions would necessarily hold in general.

THE HIERARCHICAL STRUCTURE OF PREFERENCE MODELS. It has already been argued that the vector model is a special case of the simple unfolding model. It is clear that this simple unfolding model in turn is a special case of the weighted unfolding model (since the weights can, as a special case, be all equal to one), while the weighted model is a special case of the general unfolding model (since the rotation may be an identity). By transitivity

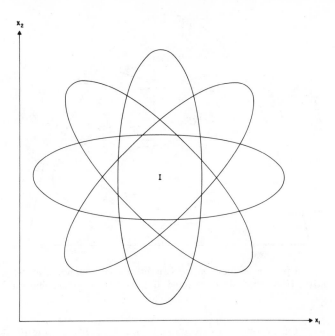

FIG. 7. Illustration of generalized unfolding model, in which differential rotations and differential patterns of weights are allowed. Shape of sample isopreference contours indicated, all (arbitrarily) about same "ideal point" and with same pattern of weights. Unlike previous model, isopreference ellipses need not be parallel to coordinate axes.

each simpler model is a special case of all the more general ones—hence the hierarchy of models alluded to earlier. The hierarchical relationship of these models will be seen more algebraically at a later point.

THE POSSIBILITY OF NEGATIVE WEIGHTS. While the weights (w's) have heretofore been spoken of as though they were assumed to be positive, in the preference domain it is possible to argue that we may sometimes want to allow negative weights. A negative weight, in this context, means that there is a *minimally* (rather than maximally) preferred value for that dimension, as is certainly true for some dimensions. We shall argue later that such a minimally preferred value characterizes many subjects in the case of the temperature dimension for tea (i.e., many subjects like hot and cold but not lukewarm tea). In the unidimensional case a negative weight simply means that the preference functions are inverted, or that the folding of the J scale produces the *negative* of the I scale. In the multidimensional case, however, negative weights may lead to more interesting

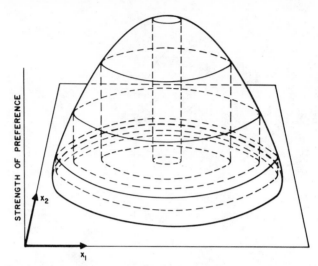

FIG. 8. Typical preference function for two-dimensional unfolding model with both weights positive. Horizontal slices projected into x_1-x_2 plane define elliptical isopreference contours.

consequences. Of course, if *all* dimensions have negative weights it is just as though the preference scales were inverted in direction (so that the "ideal point" is transformed into an "anti-ideal"). If, however, some dimensions have positive and others have negative weights, the situation is more complex. Instead of either an "ideal point" or an "anti-ideal point" we now have a saddle point, that is a point that is optimal with respect to some dimensions and "pessimal" with respect to others.

This is shown more graphically in Figures 8, 9, and 10. Figure 8 shows a

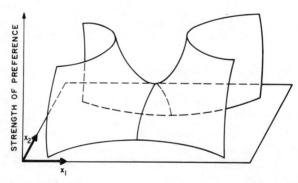

FIG. 9. Saddle-shaped preference function when one dimension (x_1) has negative and other (x_2) has positive weight.

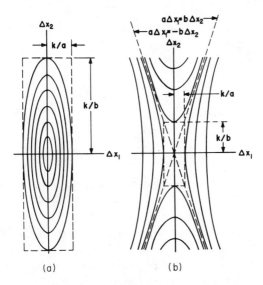

FIG. 10. Isopreference contours contrasted for positive–positive versus positive–negative situation. In latter case isopreference contours become a family of hyperbolas, while "ideal point" is replaced by saddle point at intersection of two asymptotes. Isopreference contours for: (a) $d^2 = \pm[a^2(\Delta x_1)^2 + b^2(\Delta x_2)^2]$ and (b) $d^2 = \pm[a^2(\Delta x_1)^2 - b^2(\Delta x_2)^2]$.

prototypical preference function for the usual case of both weights positive in the two-dimensional case. (Horizontal slices are taken through this response surface, and the intersections projected down onto the x_1, x_2-plane to generate the elliptical isopreference contours). Figure 9 shows a section of a typical saddle-shaped preference function for the case in which one dimension (x_1) is negatively weighted while the other (x_2) has a positive weight. Figure 10 contrasts the isopreference contours appropriate for the two cases. In the case of the positive–negative pattern of weights the isopreference contours comprise a family of hyperbolas, as shown. The two straight lines which are asymptotes of the hyperbolas define the locus of points equal in preference to the saddle point, which is the point at which the two lines intersect.

INTERNAL ANALYSIS OF PREFERENCE DATA

METHODS BASED ON THE VECTOR MODEL. The kind of data we are assuming at the moment are data from paired comparisons preference experiments. Thus we may assume a set of paired comparisons matrices, one for each subject. These matrices can be considered to be of the form

$$P_i \equiv \| p_{i,jk} \|, \qquad i = 1, 2, \ldots, m \quad j, k = 1, 2, \ldots, n \qquad (8)$$

where

$$p_{i,jk} = \begin{cases} +1 & \text{if individual } i \text{ judges } j > k \\ -1 & \text{if individual } i \text{ judges } j < k \\ 0 & \text{if no response or indifference} \end{cases}$$

In many cases P_i will be perfectly skew symmetric (i.e., $p_{i,jk} = -p_{i,kj}$) but we do not assume it necessarily to be so. This covers the case in which stimuli may be presented in both orders.

Our model assumes stimulus points are projected onto individual vectors. The projection of a point onto a unit-length vector is given by the scalar product of the vector from the origin to the point with the unit-length vector. Thus, letting X_j represent the vector issuing from the origin (or any fixed point) to the jth stimulus point, and Y_i represent the *unit-length* vector for subject i, then $\hat{s}_{ij}$, the estimated preference scale value (or "subjective utility") of stimulus j for subject i is defined as

$$\hat{s}_{ij} = Y_i \cdot X_j \qquad (9)$$

where the dot implies the scalar product, or inner product, operation. If $X \equiv \| x_{jt} \|$ is the $n \times r$ matrix of stimulus coordinate values, and $Y \equiv \| y_{it} \|$ is the $m \times r$ matrix of coordinates of the termini of subject vectors, then $\hat{S} \equiv \| \hat{s}_{ij} \|$, the $m \times n$ matrix of preference scale values is defined by

$$\hat{S} = YX' \qquad (10)$$

Given any such matrix $\hat{S}$ of scale values we may define the *preference differentials*

$$\delta_{i,jk} \equiv \hat{s}_{ij} - \hat{s}_{ik} \qquad (11)$$

If the matrix of scale values agreed perfectly with the original paired comparisons data $\delta_{i,jk}$ would have exactly the same sign as $p_{i,jk}$ for all i, j, and k, (unless, of course $p_{i,jk} = 0$). Thus, if there were perfect agreement, the product $p_{i,jk}\delta_{i,jk}$ would always be positive or zero. This fact suggests the following two *criteria of agreement* between the data and the given configuration:

$$C_1 = \sum_i w_i \left[\frac{(\sum \sum_{j \neq k} p_{i,jk}\delta_{i,jk})^2}{\sum \sum_{j \neq k} \delta_{i,jk}^2} \right] \qquad (12)$$

and

$$C_2 = \sum_i w_i \left[\frac{\sum \sum_{j \neq k} (p_{i,jk}\delta_{i,jk})_+{}^2}{\sum \sum_{j \neq k} \delta_{i,jk}^2} \right] \tag{13}$$

where $(x)_+$ means *the positive part* of x; i.e., $(x)_+$ equals the maximum of x and zero. The w_i's are introduced in case it is desired to weight subjects differently in the analysis, and are not critical to the development (they should not be confused with the w_{it}'s that appear elsewhere).

Since the p's are defined to be ± 1 or 0, it is clear that for each subject the first criterion simply adds up the δ's agreeing with his data, subtracts the sum of the δ's disagreeing, squares the resulting number and normalizes by dividing by the sum of squares of the δ's to get a measure of agreement for that subject. These individual agreement indices are then weighted (if desired) and this weighted sum forms the overall measure of agreement C_1 [Equation (12)].

C_2 [Equation (13)] is similar except that the numerator adds up the *squares* of the δ's agreeing with the subject's (paired comparisons) data, and simply ignores those δ's that disagree. The individual measure of agreement used in C_2 (the term in brackets) can be interpreted directly as the proportion of the total variance of the preference scale for subject i that "agrees with" the data.

On many grounds C_2 would seem to be a better measure of agreement than C_1. In particular, if a solution with a perfect fit to the paired-comparisons data is possible, maximizing C_2 should find it, whereas this cannot be proved to be true for C_1. However, some Monte Carlo experiments Chang and the author did a few years ago showed that, in practice, the procedure based on criterion C_1 gives better fits to the "true" solution in essentially all cases except those involving perfect (i.e., error free) data. Since the real world very seldom provides perfect data, the solution based on C_1 is recommended. Apart from this empirical superiority, the solution based on C_1 exhibits a numerical superiority, since it can be found by "analytical" procedures, while the one based on C_2 requires an iterative numerical algorithm which may not always converge to the global maximum.

The procedure for maximizing C_1 can be described as follows. First, define $S \equiv \| s_{ij} \|$ by

$$s_{ij} = (w_i)^{1/2} \sum_{k \neq j} (p_{i,jk} - p_{i,kj}) \tag{14}$$

Factor S into a product of the form

$$S = U\beta V' \tag{15}$$

and set

$$Y = U_r \beta_r \tag{16}$$

and

$$X = V_r \tag{17}$$

where U_r and V_r represent the matrices made up of the first r columns of U and V, respectively, and β_r is the diagonal matrix containing the first r rows and columns of β. If desired, the rows of Y can be normalized to unit length, to make them correspond to unit vectors. The factoring referred to is done by the procedure outlined by Eckart and Young (1936). The Eckart–Young procedure produces matrices X and Y such that the matrix $\hat{S} = YX'$ is the rank r matrix yielding the best least-squares approximation to S. Briefly, U is the matrix with characteristic vectors of SS' defining its columns, while the columns of V are characteristic vectors of $S'S$ (in both cases ordered according to size of the characteristic roots). β is the diagonal matrix of square roots of characteristic roots (which is the same for both of these matrices) again ordered in magnitude from greatest to smallest.

This method of analysis or similar methods have been discussed by Slater (1960) and, recently, by Bechtel (1969). This method, as well as the numerical solution based on C_2, have been called "nonparametric multi-dimensional analyses" of paired comparisons data (Carroll & Chang, 1964) because neither of them require explicit parametric assumptions (regarding distributions or the like) for justification. It can be argued that the procedure based on C_1 is "nonparametric" in this sense even though it leads to what looks very much like a "metric" analysis (i.e., a linear factor-analytic solution). A computer program has been written by Chang (see Chang & Carroll, 1968) for carrying out this analysis. This program, called MDPREF, will also accept directly judged preference scale values as input (these would define the matrix S directly, bypassing paired-comparisons matrices altogether).

Some data that very nicely illustrate the MDPREF procedure, and also show that it can be applied to any kind of *dominance* data (not necessarily preference data only) were collected by Roger Shepard and Maureen Sheenan some years ago. These data entailed paired-comparisons judgments by 50 subjects of *size* of 16 rectangles that varied (in a 4 × 4 factorial design) in height and in height-to-width ratio. MDPREF produced the solution shown in Figure 11 (only four subject vectors are shown, the distribution of the others being indicated by dots). Two things are clear. First, the dimensions (known a priori) underlying these stimuli have pretty well been reconstructed in the stimulus configuration (derived from the preference data *alone*). Approximately a 45° rotation of the coordinate system

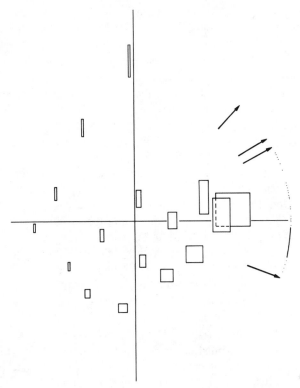

FIG. 11. Configuration derived from internal vector model analysis of data from Shepard and Sheenan study (unpublished) of individual differences in judged size of rectangles. Only four subject vectors are shown, the distribution of the rest being indicated by black dots.

would reproduce pretty well the lattice structure by which the stimuli were generated (although a couple of the rectangles appear slightly out of place). The first dimension, which can be roughly called the "consensus" dimension (it would correspond very closely to the preference order for an "average" individual) corresponds pretty closely to area. The second thing that is clear, however, is that subjects vary greatly in what they mean by "size" (or what they assume the experimenter to mean). Some equate "size" to height, some to area, some to width, and some to height-to-width ratio. (This variation is not too surprising, since subjects were deliberately left uninstructed as to what "size" meant, and many tried unsuccessfully to persuade the experimenter to define the term more fully). Recently Ross and DiLollo (1968) have proposed a "vector model for psychophysics" in which such essentially semantic transformations (sometimes operating, perhaps, at an "unconscious" level) may account for many so-called "adaptation level" effects.

That it is possible to discover the perceptual dimensions underlying preference or other dominance judgments via this kind of internal analysis of the preference data has also been demonstrated by McDermott (1969). McDermott used MDPREF to analyze a set of paired-comparisons preference data on a set of stimuli comprising simulated telephone circuits perturbed by various linear and nonlinear distortions. She also collected similarity data from an independent sample of subjects on the same set of stimuli, which were scaled by a nonmetric scaling procedure. Three interpretable dimensions were found in both analyses. Canonical correlation analysis showed that these dimensions matched very well. Even more striking is the fact that when a second kind of dominance data of a much more limited nature (i.e., on loudness) were analyzed in this way, *two* dimensions were found that matched very closely two of the dimensions from the separate analyses of the preference and similarity data. This correspondence of dimensions from the three solutions was shown by application of a generalized canonical correlation analysis for three (or more) sets of data (Carroll, 1968a), as well as by ordinary two-way canonical correlation of all pairs of the three solutions.

It would be overoptimistic, however, to suppose that this "vector model" analysis can always unearth the underlying perceptual dimensions. On the one hand, it may be the case that *no* purely internal analysis of preference data can find all the relevant perceptual variables, simply because some of these variables may not contribute to individual differences in preference judgments. It is only insofar as such dimensions are used differently by different subjects that an internal analysis can reveal these dimensions. On the other hand, even though all the dimensions do contribute to individual differences, the vector model (which is basically a linear model) may be too simple. If the "true" model is at least as complicated as one of the unfolding models discussed above, this analysis may fail completely to uncover the appropriate structure.

Such failure seems clearly to occur in the case of the "tea-tasting" preference data, indicating the need for a more complicated model. When these data were analyzed by MDPREF the structure shown in Figure 12 emerged in the first two dimensions. These two dimensions seem to distinguish the "steaming hots" from everything else, and also exhibit a direction (about a 45° rotation of the *y*-axis) yielding a moderate correlation with sweetness but hardly provide a satisfactory recovery of total structure. The reason is that a model even more complicated than any of

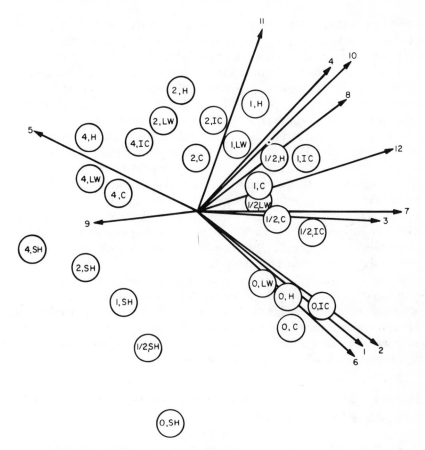

Fig. 12. Configuration obtained from internal vector model analysis of preference data from tea-tasting experiment. Coding of stimuli is same as in Figure 2a. Numbering of subjects is same as in Figure 2b.

those considered thus far (entailing, in some cases, bimodal or doubly peaked preference functions) seems to be required for these data. To account for these data at all well in terms of the vector model requires about six dimensions, rather than the two perceptual dimensions known a priori and recovered quite adequately by the individual differences scaling of dissimilarities. The lesson to be learned is that one should proceed with caution when using this or any other internal analysis of preference data.

METHODS BASED ON THE UNFOLDING MODEL. A number of investigators have recently proposed methods for the simple (unweighted) case of the unfolding model. (See, e.g., Kruskal & Carroll, 1969; Lingoes, 1966; Roskam, 1968; Young and Torgerson, 1967.) These procedures all start with preference scale values (the s's) rather than with raw paired-comparisons data. Most of them are nonmetric in the sense of assuming the data scale values to measure preference only ordinally. Many of these have theoretical problems due to the "badness-of-fit" measure being optimized that can lead to theoretical degeneracies that yield a nominally perfect "badness-of-fit" value but convey no information. This is discussed by Kruskal and Carroll (1969) who propose a way out of this problem, yielding a method that works very nicely with artificial data but has so far performed less than fully satisfactorily with real data (this may be due to the particular "badness-of-fit" measure being used, but may also be due to problems in the iterative numerical algorithm). To summarize the situation vis à vis internal analyses via the simple unfolding model: The problem is theoretically tractable, but there are difficulties with development of practical algorithms for data analysis.

If this is the situation with respect to simple unfolding, it would seem impetuously optimistic to hope for any kind of favorable prognosis for the weighted or generalized unfolding models or for more general models. However, a new procedure called polynomial factor analysis (Carroll, 1969) may well provide a vehicle for such more general analyses. This procedure will be discussed in detail in a later section.

EXTERNAL ANALYSIS OF PREFERENCE DATA VIA THE
LINEAR–QUADRATIC HIERARCHY OF MODELS

We now turn to a consideration of methods for external analysis, i.e., for relating preference data to a given stimulus space, in terms of a hierarchy of models ranging, in order of increasing complexity, from the vector model to the generalized unfolding model. It will be convenient, however, to consider the most complex and general model first. We shall simply refer to these as models I through IV (I being the generalized unfolding model and IV the vector model). A unified algebraic treatment of these models and a unified method of analysis is possible, as will be seen.

We shall first consider *metric* analyses, but then show that these can be made nonmetric in a straightforward manner. Briefly, all of these models imply certain linear or quadratic regression equations, as will be shown. It turns out to be possible to solve these regression equations by standard procedures, and then, by further analysis of the regression coefficients, to determine parameters of the models. The metric or nonmetric character of the analysis depends on whether the regressions are done metrically or nonmetrically. There is also the possibility of communication between certain levels of the model hierarchy in this analysis, in the form, for example, of the "rotation to canonical reference frame" that will be described below.

MODEL I: THE GENERAL MODEL. It is assumed that we are given a matrix

$$X \equiv \| x_{jt} \|, \qquad j = 1, 2, \ldots, n, \quad t = 1, 2, \ldots, r \qquad (18)$$

representing the coordinates of n stimuli in r dimensions (as determined, for example, by a multidimensional scaling solution). We will also use $X_j \equiv (x_{j1}, x_{j2}, \ldots, x_{jr})$ to represent the jth point.

In addition, we are given a data matrix

$$S \equiv \| s_{ij} \|, \qquad i = 1, 2, \ldots, m, \quad j = 1, 2, \ldots, n \qquad (19)$$

where s_{ij} represents the preference scale value of the jth stimulus for the ith individual. We assume for now that preference is measured in such a way that the *smaller* the scale value the more highly preferred is the stimulus (although this assumption is not critical since the preference scale can easily be reversed in direction by, say, multiplying all values by minus one).

The unfolding model assumes the preference scale value to be monotonically related to distance between X_j and the "ideal point" Y_i in psychological space. We shall, for present purposes, make the stronger assumption that the scale value is *linearly* related to the *square* of the (Euclidean) distance, i.e.,

$$s_{ij} = a_i d_{ij}^2 + b_i + e_{ij} \qquad (20)$$

where a_i and b_i are arbitrary constants (except that $a_i \geq 0$) and e_{ij} is an error term. This same basic assumption holds in models I, II, and III; these models differ only in the way in which d_{ij}^2 is defined.

In model I we assume that both X_j and Y_i are operated on by an orthogonal transformation matrix T_i, and then squared distances are computed from the transformed values. Thus, we define

$$X_j^* = X_j T_i \qquad (21)$$

$$Y_i^* = Y_i T_i \qquad (22)$$

and then, in keeping with Equation (7), we compute the squared (weighted) distances

$$d_{ij}^2 = \sum_{t=1}^{r} w_{it}(x_{jt}^* - y_{it}^*)^2 \qquad (23)$$

Equation (23) can be written in matrix form as

$$d_{ij}^2 = (X_j^* - Y_i^*)W_i(X_j^* - Y_i^*)'$$
$$= X_j^*W_i(X_j^*)' - 2Y_i^*W_i(X_j^*)' + Y_i^*W_i(Y_i^*)' \qquad (24)$$

where W_i is a diagonal matrix whose diagonals are the weights w_{it}. Substituting Equations (21) and (22) in Equation (24), we get

$$d_{ij}^2 = X_jT_iW_iT_i'X_j' - 2Y_iT_iW_iT_i'X_j' + Y_iT_iW_iT_i'Y_i' \qquad (25)$$

Defining

$$R^* \equiv T_iW_iT_i' \qquad (26)$$

and letting c_i^* represent the last term in Equation (25) (since that term is a constant with respect to X_j), we have

$$d_{ij}^2 = X_jR_i^*X_j' - 2Y_iR_i^*X_j' + c_i^* \qquad (27)$$

Substituting Equation (27) in Equation (20) we have

$$s_{ij} \approx a_i[X_jR_i^*X_j' - 2Y_iR_i^*X_j' + c_i^*] + b_i$$
$$= a_iX_jR_i^*X_j' - 2a_iY_iR_i^*X_j' + c_i \qquad (28)$$

or, if we define

$$R_i = a_iR_i^* \qquad (29)$$

and

$$B_i = -2Y_iR_i \qquad (30)$$

we have

$$s_{ij} \approx X_jR_iX_j' + B_iX_j' + c_i \qquad (31)$$

which is the equation of a general quadratic function of X. In summational notation, Equation (31) can be written as

$$s_{ij} \approx \sum_t \sum_{t'} r_{tt'}^i (x_{jt}x_{jt'}) + \sum_t b_{it}x_{jt} + c_i \qquad (32)$$

which makes explicit the nature of the quadratic regression assumed between s_{ij} and x_{jt}. We can solve for estimates of the components $r_{tt'}^i$ of R_i and for the components b_{it} of B_i by solving for the coefficients of this quadratic regression. These coefficients can be solved for most simply by treating the problem as a multiple linear regression problem in which, in addition to the independent variables $x_1, x_2, \ldots, x_r$ we include the *dummy* independent variables $x_t \cdot x_{t'}$ ($t \leq t'$). Then the regression coefficient for the variable x_t will be an estimate of b_{it}, the regression coefficient for the dummy variable x_t^2 will be an estimate of $r_{tt'}^i$, and *one-half* the regression coefficient for $x_t \cdot x_{t'}$ $(t < t')$ will be an estimate of $r^i_{tt'}$ (and also, by symmetry of R_i, of $r^i_{t't}$). Having estimated R_i and B_i in this way, we can solve for an estimate of Y_i with the equation

$$Y_i = -\tfrac{1}{2} B_i R_i^{-1} \qquad (33)$$

which is derived from Equation (30).

We may, furthermore, solve for T_i and W_i by solving for characteristic roots and vectors of R_i; T_i will be the transpose of the matrix of characteristic vectors (i.e., *columns* of T_i are characteristic vectors of R_i) while W_i is the diagonal matrix of characteristic roots (thus, w_{it} is just the tth characteristic root of R_i).

NEGATIVITY OF THE w'S. In the above equation we tacitly assumed the weights w_{it} to be positive (or zero), but there is nothing in the solution for model I or II that constrains them to be nonnegative. In the case of model I, they will be so if and only if the matrix R_i is positive definite or semi-definite, which it may not be in practice. This possibility of negative weights might be a serious problem, except that a reasonable interpretation attaches to negative w's, as discussed above. This interpretation is simply that if w_{it} is negative, then, with respect to dimension t, the ideal point for individual i indicates the *least preferred*, rather than the most preferred value, and the farther a stimulus is *along that dimension* from the ideal point, the more highly preferred is the stimulus. It certainly seems reasonable that there are dimensions that operate in this manner, at least for some individuals. To a person who likes both iced tea and hot tea, for example, the dimension of temperature (of tea) might be such a case; there is, we might suppose, a midway point ("tepid tea") which is least preferred, and the farther the temperature moves from that point toward the two extremes, the more preferred is the potion. Of course, we would assume in such a case that the preference curve would begin descending fairly precipitously as temperature becomes so extreme in either direction as to approach the pain threshold, but this "negative" unfolding model may still describe such a situation quite accurately within a wide range of stimulus variation. It thus seems reasonable not to restrict the w's to nonnegativity, but, rather to let them fall as the data dictate. It will be seen later how this works out with real data on tea preferences.

MODEL II. Model II differs from model I in that it does not assume a different orthogonal transformation for each individual, although it does assume differential weighting of dimensions (but the *same* dimensions for all individuals). In effect, model II is the special case of model I in which T_i is restricted to be the identity transformation for all individuals. This means, as can be seen from Equations (26) and (29), that R_i is just of the form $a_i W_i$; i.e., a diagonal matrix whose diagonal elements are proportional to the weights w_{it}. Then the analog of Equation (31) for model II is (absorbing the constant a_i into the w's)

$$s_{ij} \approx X_j W_i X_j' + B_i X_j' + c_i \tag{34}$$

while, corresponding to Equation (30) is

$$B_i = -2Y_i W_i \tag{35}$$

so that we may solve for Y_i by the equation

$$Y_i = -\tfrac{1}{2} B_i W_i^{-1} \tag{36}$$

which has a particularly simple form, since the inverse of the diagonal matrix W_i is just the diagonal matrix which has diagonal elements that are the reciprocals of the w_{it}'s.

Equation (34) in summation notation can be written as

$$s_{ij} \approx \sum_{t=1}^{r} w_{it} x_{jt}^2 + \sum_{t=1}^{r} b_{it} x_{jt} + c_i \tag{37}$$

Comparing Equation (37) with Equation (32), we see that model II implies a similar quadratic regression, but with the important difference that the quadratic equation has no cross-product terms; it involves only linear terms and squares. Thus, while model I allows $[r(r-1)/2] + 1$ free parameters for each subject, model II allows only $2r + 1$. Furthermore, it is clear that model I is more general in the sense that model II is a special case of it.

We may estimate the quantities w_{it} and b_{it} of Equation (37) in much the same manner as we estimated the comparable quantities for model I. In the case of model II, however, we need include only linear and squared terms; i.e., $x_1, x_2, \ldots, x_r$ and $x_1^2, x_2^2, \ldots, x_r^2$. No cross-product terms are required. Then the regression coefficient for x_t estimates b_{it}, while that for x_t^2 estimates w_{it} (note that it is *not* necessary to find characteristic roots and vectors of any matrix). Given estimates of b_{it} and w_{it}, we may estimate y_{it}, the tth coordinate of Y_i with the equation

$$y_{it} = -\tfrac{1}{2} b_{it}/w_{it} \tag{38}$$

which is equivalent to the matrix Equation (36), because of the diagonality of W_i.

INITIAL ROTATION TO A CANONICAL REFERENCE FRAME. Because model II does not allow for any rotation of the given reference frame, it seems appropriate to begin the analysis with a choice of reference frame that is already optimal in some sense. The particular set of reference axes in terms of which the initial description of the perceptual space is given may be wholly arbitrary, or suited to some purpose other than this analysis. We therefore begin this second analysis with a frame chosen in the following manner: A set of scale values for an "average subject" are defined as the arithmetic mean of the scale values of all subjects included in the analysis, and the procedure prescribed for model I is applied to the data for this "average subject." The transformation of axes appropriate for the "average subject" is applied to the initial reference frame, and the new reference frame thus derived is used for the analysis based on model II. The justification for this is that, if the same orthogonal rotation (as given by a common matrix T) is appropriate for all subjects, that same rotation will be appropriate for the "average subject." This is true even if the weighting matrices (the W_i) are quite different, as can be seen by averaging Equation (31) over subjects and noting that each R_i is of the form TW_iT'. Presumably the transformation derived for this "average subject" will be a better estimate of the "true" matrix than that for any individual subject.

MODEL III. Model III is the "simple" unfolding model, but with one modification. This allows the possibility that some or all of the dimensions have negative weight, making model III equivalent to model II, with the weights, $w_{it} = \pm 1$. Since these are independent of i, we will call them u_t, where $u_t = \pm 1$. Letting U be the $r \times r$ diagonal matrix with diagonals u_t, the analog of Equations (31) or (34) becomes

$$s_{ij} \approx a_i X_j U X_j' + B_i X_j' + c_i \tag{39}$$

or, in summational form,

$$s_{ij} \approx a_i \left[\sum_{t=1}^{r} u_t x_{jt}^2 \right] + \sum_{t=1}^{r} b_{it} x_{jt} + c_i \tag{40}$$

Since the term in square brackets is independent of i, it may be simply entered as a *single* extra "pseudo-independent variable" in the regression equation (with s_i, the set of preference scale values for individual i, as the dependent variable). Solving this multiple regression equation in $r + 1$ independent variables gives us, immediately, a_i and the values b_{it}. We may then solve for the coordinates of the "ideal point" (or saddle point) using the equation

$$y_{it} = -\tfrac{1}{2}(b_{it}/a_i u_t) \tag{41}$$

If a_i should turn out to be negative for some individual, it means that the pattern of signs of the saliences is reversed for that individual.

CANONICAL REFERENCE FRAME AND WEIGHTS. As we defined a "canonical reference frame" for model II by applying the rotation appropriate to the "average subject" when analyzed in terms of model I, so we apply a set of "canonical weights" to the dimensions for the analysis in terms of model III. These canonical weights are the weights appropriate for the average subject as analyzed in terms of model II. In practice, the dimensions are multiplied by the square roots of the absolute values of the w_t's for the average subject. If, for any t, w_t is negative, u_t is defined to be -1; otherwise u_t is $+1$. This is only done, of course, if the model II analysis (in "phase II") precedes the model III analysis (in "phase III") which is not necessarily the case. It is possible to enter any one of these phases without first applying the previous phase(s). If phase II is entered, skipping phase I, no "canonical rotation" is applied. If phase III is entered immediately, no "canonical weights" are applied, and the u_t's are all $+1$.

MODEL IV. Model IV is the simple linear, or "vector" model. The analog of Equation (31), (34), or (39) is simply

$$s_{ij} \approx a_i Y_i X_j' + c_i \qquad (42)$$

where, for this model, Y_i is the row vector of coordinates of the unit vector onto which the stimulus points are projected. This equation is closely analogous to the earlier Equation (9), but matrix multiplication replaces the (equivalent) scalar product notation, and the constants a_i and c_i are introduced.

If we define $B_i \equiv a_i Y_i$, Equation (42) becomes

$$s_{ij} \approx B_i X_j' + c_i \qquad (43)$$

or, in summational notation,

$$s_{ij} \approx \sum_{t=1}^{r} b_{it} x_{jt} + c_i \qquad (44)$$

So that the regression equation for this situation contains only linear terms, the quadratic terms that appeared in the regression equations for the various unfolding models being, effectively, set to zero. Having estimated the b's by multiple regression methods we may, if desired, estimate the y's by simply normalizing the b's to unit length, i.e.,

$$y_{it} = b_{it} \Big/ \left(\sum_{t'=1}^{r} b_{it'}^2 \right)^{1/2} \qquad (45)$$

STATISTICAL TESTS OF SIGNIFICANCE. Because, under the linear assumptions we have made, the fitting of these various models is equivalent to solving certain linear or quadratic regression equations, we may use the standard test for significance of a multiple correlation coefficient to test significance of the fit of each model to the data. Furthermore, these models are embedded in a strict hierarchical structure based on the level of generality, as can be seen algebraically in the fact that each of Equations (31), (34), (39), and (42) is a special case of each of the equations preceding it (in the sense that a less general model can be obtained by assigning special values to certain of the parameters of a more general model). This hierarchy of generality can be expressed symbolically as $I > II > III > IV$, where $A > B$ means that B is a special case of A. Because of this hierarchical embeddedness of the models, it is possible to test statistically whether a more general model is accounting for significantly more variance than a less general model. Comparisons of this sort are possible between any two models in the hierarchy (although, of course, these will not be independent of one another). The situation is formally equivalent to testing whether the addition of new independent variables in a stepwise regression scheme accounts for a significant extra amount of variance.

NONMETRIC PREFERENCE MAPPING OF STIMULUS SPACE. So far our "preference mapping of stimulus space" has been done metrically, which is reflected most directly in the fact that linear relations are assumed in Equation (20), and in all the regression equations. Suppose we replace Equation (20) with

$$\check{s}_{ij} = d_{ij}^2 + e_{ij} \tag{46}$$

where

$$\check{s}_{ij} = M_i(s_{ij}) \tag{47}$$

with M_i an arbitrary (nondecreasing) monotone function, and furthermore interpret "$s_{ij} \approx$" to mean "$\check{s}_{ij} - e_{ij} =$" with $\check{s}_{ij}$ as defined above. If we could, then, solve for the various parameters of the implied regression equations, *and* for the monotone function M_i, yielding a best least-squares fit, our procedure would be fully *nonmetric*. A fairly simple (in principle) algorithm will do this. The first step is to solve for the parameters of the appropriate *linear* regression equation to predict the s_{ij}'s. One then applies the algorithm for least-squares monotone regression described by Kruskal (1964) to find a first estimate of the monotone function M_i. Call this function $M_i^{(1)}$. We then compute $\check{s}_{ij}^{(1)} = M_i^{(1)}(s_{ij})$, and replace s_{ij} with $\check{s}_{ij}^{(1)}$ to compute a new set of regression coefficients. Then a new monotone function $M_i^{(2)}$ is computed as before (going back, now, to the original s_{ij}'s) and $\check{s}_{ij}^{(2)} = M_i^{(2)}(s_{ij})$ now replace the s_{ij}'s for computation of still another set of regression coefficients. This iterative process continues until it converges (i.e., until no more change occurs in the monotone function or regression coefficients). When this occurs the resulting monotone function and regression coefficients provide the appropriate (least-squares) estimates. The regression coefficients can then be used to estimate the parameters of the corresponding model. Note that it is not necessary to estimate the ideal points, rotation matrices, weights, or other parameters at each iterative cycle, this can all be done strictly by manipulating parameters of the appropriate regression equation. Note, also, that the scheme described is quite general and could be applied to any multiple regression situation in which the predictor variables are measured on interval scales while the criterion variable is measured only on an ordinal scale, or is so treated. This general procedure might be called "nonmetric multiple regression."

If this nonmetric procedure is applied, of course, the F tests for significance of the various models or for comparison of different models are no longer valid, although they may still be useful as a general indication of goodness of fit (or improvement in fit).

Chang (Carroll & Chang, 1967) has programmed this procedure for external analysis of data in terms of the hierarchy of models. The current version of this program, as mentioned, can begin at any phase, and will then do the analyses for that model and all less general models. The program will do these analyses either metrically or nonmetrically.

APPLICATION TO THE "TEA-TASTING" DATA. External analysis in terms of the hierarchy of linear–quadratic models was applied to the preference data from the "tea-tasting" experiment. The stimulus space (defining the X matrix) was the one in Figure 2 derived by applying INDSCAL (individual differences scaling) analysis to the dissimilarities data. The analysis was applied to the full set of 25 stimuli, and also to the subset of 20 stimuli derived by omitting the "steaming hots." (The reason for this omission will be seen shortly.) Each of these analyses was done in two ways: (1) *metrically*, starting with phase I and (2) *nonmetrically*, starting with phase II. The first, metric, analysis was done primarily to allow use of the F tests of significance to determine which model was most appropriate to apply to these data. In both cases model II was clearly most appropriate; i.e., the difference between model II and models III and IV were significant statistically (especially so in the case of the smaller set of 20 stimuli) while there was no evidence of a statistical difference between models I and II. It should be recalled in this context that the INDSCAL analysis does *not* allow arbitrary rotations (and, in fact, that the reference axes determined by this analysis corresponded essentially perfectly to the a priori dimensions of temperature and sweetness). In this light it seems particularly appropriate and confirmatory of the validity of these models that our analysis of the preference data in effect rejected any rotation of this reference frame. In effect, the reference frame given by INDSCAL was the "right" one for all our subjects. This purely statistical result can be seen more directly by inspection of the orthogonal rotations determined for individual subjects in phase I. A measure of the degree to which this reference frame is used by an individual subject is provided by the cosine of the angle of rotation in the two-dimensional space (after a possible permutation to pair old and new axes optimally). When the full set of 25 stimuli are analyzed, the median cosine for the 12 subjects is .99923, while the smallest cosine for all the subjects is .92388. For the smaller set of 20 stimuli, these figures were .99591 and .95810, respectively. These results from the metric analyses provided the rationale for doing the nonmetric analyses beginning immediately with phase II (and, thus, model II).

The reason for doing two separate analyses, one with all 25 stimuli included and the second including only a subset (excluding the "steaming hots") is that, at least for some subjects, exactly the phenomenon alluded to earlier seems to have occurred. That is, "steaming hot" is too hot for some subjects (who are of the type who like hot and iced but not lukewarm tea). This means that while a "negative" unfolding model holds pretty well within the range from iced to hot, there is a precipitous drop in the preference function from "hot" to "steaming hot," so that, in fact, the preference function for these subjects is bimodal, or doubly peaked. The unfolding model, even when allowed the possibility of positive or negative weights, cannot possibly accommodate a preference function of this form. Concentrating for the moment on the situation with respect to temperature alone, a function at least as complex as a cubic seems to be required to fit all subjects adequately. Such a function will have, for at least some subjects, a minimum (say at "lukewarm") and a maximum (say at "hot"). If forced to fit data of this complexity with the quadratic function implicit in the weighted unfolding model, the method can, as it were, "choose" to fit the portion of the curve near the minimum, thus looking like a negative un-folding model with an "anti-ideal" for temperature near "lukewarm," or to fit the part near the maximum, thus looking like a positive unfolding model with an "ideal" near "hot" (or it could, conceivably, strike some compromise between these two). A quadratic, however, cannot possibly fully account for such a relation. By leaving out the "steaming hots" we are restricting ourselves to a set of stimuli for which this more restricted model should provide an adequate fit. We might expect it, then, to yield a better fit as well as providing more readily interpretable results. This is confirmed

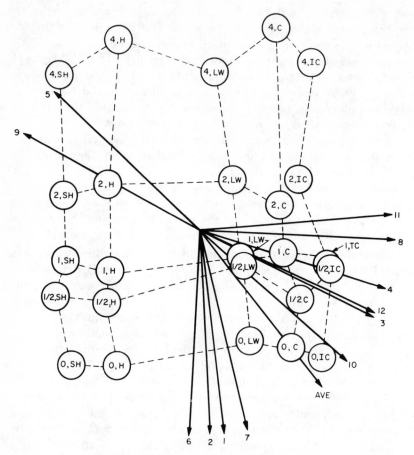

Fig. 13. External vector model analysis relating subjects' preference data to stimulus space from individual differences scaling of dissimilarities. Coding as in Figure 12.

in the fact that the root mean square of the correlations (between the predicted values from the fitted models and the monotone functions of the data) was higher for the restricted set than for the full set (.9761 versus .9435) for the model II nonmetric analysis. If these values are squared to convert them to a figure more nearly analogous to "variance accounted for," the resulting figures are .9528 and .8902, respectively. One might suspect that this increase is due only to the fact that fewer data points are involved in the analysis of the smaller set (leading to fewer "degrees of freedom" in the data). Actually, though, this loss of "degrees of freedom" is counteracted to a large extent by the marked *restriction of range* in the smaller set, which, by itself, would tend to lower the correlation. That these effects approximately balance each other is indicated by the fact that the analogous root mean-square correlations for the nonmetric *vector model* analysis are about equal (with the figure for the 20 stimuli actually being slightly *smaller* than the one for the 25 stimuli). The rms correlations in this case are, respectively, .8759, and .8626. This suggests that the greater root mean-square correlation for the 20 stimuli is indicative of a real improvement in fit of the model in that case. Other evidence (e.g., from plots of some individuals' preference data as a function of temperature alone, holding sweetness constant) supports this conclusion.

Figures 13 and 14 show the results of the application of the analysis in terms of the vector model. Note that the directions of many subjects' vectors change radically when the "steaming hots" are eliminated. Perhaps

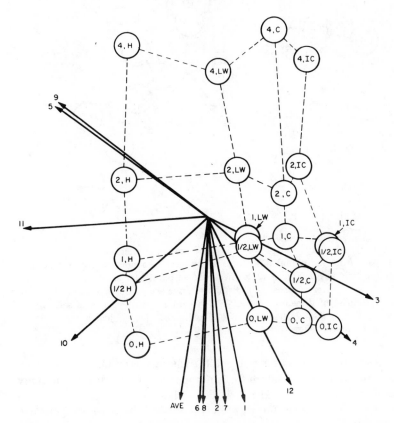

FIG. 14. Same as Figure 13, but five "steaming hot" stimuli were omitted.

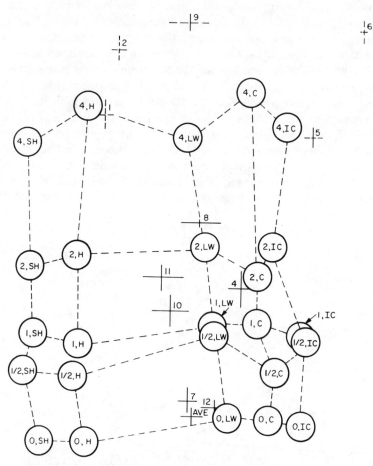

Fɪɢ. 15. External analysis of preference data in terms of weighted unfolding model. Stimulus space from individual differences analysis of dissimilarities data. Coding of stimuli and subjects as in Figure 12. Subjects "ideal point" (or saddle point, or "anti-ideal point") is at center of cross. Lengths of two arms are proportional to square roots of (absolute values) of dimension weights. If weight is positive, arm is solid line; if weight is negative, arm is dashed line. The "ideal point" for Subject 3 is not plotted, since it is too far out of range.

the most radical change is for Subject 11, whose vector undergoes a complete 180° rotation. The vectors for a number of other subjects (notably, Subjects 8, 10, and 12) undergo large, although not quite so radical, changes. Even the vector for the "average" subject has changed fairly markedly; enough so that the stimulus with the highest projection has changed from "no sugar, ice cold" to "no sugar, hot." These changes do not seem particularly surprising, however, when it is recognized that the vector model is simply not appropriate to these data (either for the full or restricted set of stimuli).

Figures 15 and 16 display the results of the nonmetric analysis in terms of model II, the weighted unfolding model (an analysis in terms of model III, the simple unfolding model, was done, but will not be reported, since this model was clearly inappropriate to these data). In both of these figures the ideal point (or saddle point, or anti-ideal) for a subject appears at the

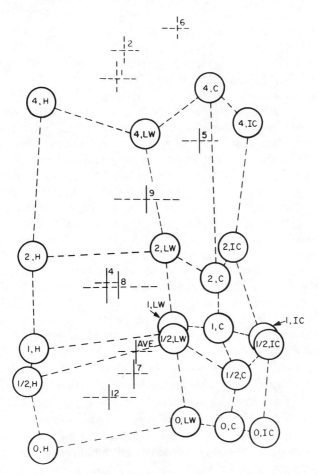

FIG. 16. Same as Figure 15, except that five "steaming hot" stimuli were omitted. "Ideal points" for Subjects 3, 10, and 11 are out of range, and so are not plotted.

intersection of the two arms of the cross appearing next to the number for that subject. The lengths of the two arms are proportional to the square roots of the (absolute values) of the weights for the two dimensions for that subject. (If both weights are positive, a circle in the original space would be transformed into an ellipse whose axes are proportional to these lengths, and distances between the "ideal point" and stimuli would then be computed in this transformed space. The isopreference contours, in the original, or "common" space, would be ellipses with precisely the *inverse* ratio of axes. In this two-dimensional case, the relative lengths of the axes of these isopreference ellipses or hyperbolas can be seen by rotating the cross 90°.)

As with the analysis in terms of the vector model, there seem to be fairly radical changes when the five "steaming hot" stimuli are omitted. Only Subjects 1 and 2 remain fairly stable between the two analyses, with Subjects 5 and 6 being moderately so (these latter two change somewhat in position, but keep the same sign pattern of weights). Subject 9 retains the same sign pattern of weights, but changes position from well outside the range of stimuli to a much more intermediate point (although, curiously, this change affects primarily the indicated optimum for sweetness, leaving the preference function with respect to temperature essentially unchanged). Two subjects, 10 and 11, move from the middle of the space with a positive–positive pattern of weights, to well outside the stimulus range (so much so that they are not plotted in Figure 16) with a positive–positive and negative–positive pattern of weights, respectively. They were both about in the middle of the range of stimuli with respect to dimension 2 (sweetness) but far out and *on opposite sides* with respect to dimension one (temperature). If one subject's point is on the extreme left of a dimension with a positive weight, his "preference function" is essentially equivalent to that for a second subject on the extreme right with a negative weight. ("Extreme" means here "beyond the range encompassed by the stimuli.") The first *likes* the left, the second *dislikes* the right; both are acting essentially like a subject whose "preference function," *with respect to that dimension,* is given by a vector model with the vector oriented to the left. In the present case Subject 10 is on the left of dimension one with a positive weight, while Subject 11 is on the right with a negative weight. They both, therefore, "act like" vector-model subjects with respect to dimension 1. These subjects probably cannot be regarded as "pure" vector model types. However, since the F tests referred to earlier indicate fairly highly significant differences between the vector model and weighted unfolding model for these subjects ($p < .001$ and $p < .05$, respectively). What may be needed to account for their data (in relation to the restricted set of 20 stimuli) is a kind of *mixed* vector and unfolding model—that is, a model that is linear (or vector-like) with respect to some dimensions, and quadratic (or "ideal-point-like") with respect to others. This kind of mixed model was first proposed to the author by Kruskal (personal communication) to accommodate just such bothersome cases as this. Unfortunately, we have not yet implemented a procedure that would allow for such mixed models, but this may be a useful direction in which to move in the future. In the present case, this mixed model would be interpreted, for Subjects 10 and 11, as follows: These subjects like *hot* tea, (the hotter the better), but prefer some intermediate, moderate, amount of sugar (around $\frac{1}{2}$ to 1 teaspoon, as it happens). Of course we know, from the result when the "steaming hots" are included, that it is not *really* true that they like their tea "the hotter the better." When we say that a vector model describes their preferences with respect to the temperature dimension, all we mean is that it describes their preferences for the range of stimuli at hand. If the preference function is monotonic for the range of stimuli presented, we probably cannot expect to distinguish between a vector and unfolding model for that dimension. Even if we could make this distinction, we cannot expect to estimate the location of the "ideal" or "anti-ideal" point reliably.

One other subject is missing on Figure 16, and is also not plotted on Figure 15. This is Subject 3, who has a positive–negative pattern of weights for both the full and restricted stimulus set. Subject 3 is (for both sets of data) well outside the range of stimuli on dimension 1, and just "on the edge," as it were, on dimension two (with an "anti-ideal" value just about in the middle of the "4 teaspoon" region). This subject is somewhat closer to a pure vector model, but there is still a significant improvement for the weighted unfolding model ($p < .05$).

The remaining subjects, 4, 7, 8, 12, and the "average" subject all stay pretty much in the midst of the stimuli relative to both dimensions, but change from a weight pattern of positive–positive to one of negative–positive. The change from positive to negative weight on the temperature dimension for these subjects is evidently due to the elimination of the "precipitous drop" referred to earlier, from "hot" to "steaming hot." The fact that the positions of these subjects do not change too much indicates that, when all 25 stimuli were included, some kind of a compromise was reached between an "anti-ideal" and "ideal" for temperature, which apparently did not provide a very good account of what was really going on (although on purely statistical grounds the fit may look fairly good).

It is of interest to note that, in the analysis involving the restricted stimulus set, every subject except Subjects 3 and 10 (two of the three who were vectorlike with respect to temperature) had a negative weight for the temperature dimension. Furthermore, all the subjects except 1, 2, 3, and 6 have positive weights for sweetness, with ideal values somewhere between 0 and 4 teaspoons. The four subjects with negative weights for sweetness are all at the edge of or outside the range of the stimuli on dimension two (and all on the same side, namely the "very sweet" side). These subjects are all acting very nearly vectorlike with respect to the sweetness dimension, and might just about as well be at the other end (the "no sugar" end) with a positive weight. (One might suppose they really have anti-ideals around 4 to 8 teaspoons of sugar, but this would imply that they like 16 teaspoons of sugar better than 8, an unlikely conclusion).

A very clear result, as can be seen in Figure 16, is that all six of the real subjects (4, 5, 7, 8, 9, and 12), plus the average subject, whose points lie within the range of the stimuli on *both* dimensions, have a negative–positive pattern of weights, indicating an anti-ideal for temperature somewhere around lukewarm, and an ideal for sweetness varying pretty much from 0 to 4 teaspoons. It would not be stretching the truth, then, to say that, for the analysis of the restricted set of 20 stimuli, all subjects are either of the "mixed-model" type, or exhibit this negative–positive pattern of weights.

This external analysis in terms of the linear–quadratic hierarchy of models seems, then, to provide a pretty good account of the restricted set of 20 stimuli. Suppose, however, that we had not known enough to eliminate certain of the stimuli. How would we have provided an adequate analysis in this case? In another direction, suppose we did not have dissimilarities data that could be scaled to provide an a priori stimulus space. Is there a way to uncover the stimulus space via a purely internal analysis of the preference data? We shall now discuss a couple of methods that show promise in these directions. The first, parametric mapping, may be very useful in providing a stimulus space to which external analysis of the kind we have described may be applied. The second, polynomial factor analysis, may be able to provide the stimulus space and *at the same time* a parameterization of the subjects (though not necessarily the most interpretable one for many purposes). As such, polynomial factor analysis holds promise as a very general method of multidimensional unfolding.

PARAMETRIC MAPPING AND THE STIMULUS SPACE

We have already seen from the application of MDPREF to the "tea-tasting" preference data that a multivariate technique closely related to linear factor analysis cannot adequately recover the perceptual structure of these stimuli. Is it possible that a nonlinear procedure can do this? After all, no matter how complex the individual preference functions are, they

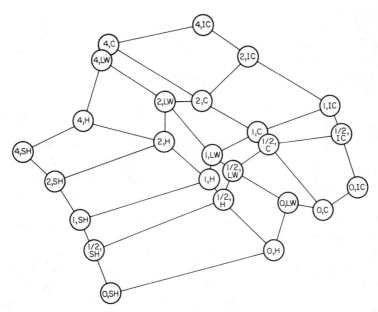

Fig. 17. Parametric mapping solution derived from tea-tasting preference data. Configuration from individual differences scaling of dissimilarities (INDSCAL configuration) provided starting values.

presumably *are* (possibly different and possibly nonlinear) functions of the underlying "perceptual space." Parametric mapping (Shepard & Carroll, 1966) is such a procedure, which requires only the very general assumption that the preference functions are relatively "smooth" or "continuous" (the quotes indicate a sense of these words not corresponding directly to their precise mathematical definitions). Parametric mapping was applied to these data, and the best solution obtained is shown in Figure 17. While it took some "finagling" to get this solution (for some reason there seemed to be a local minimum that corresponded very closely to the MDPREF solution) it did yield the best value of κ (the "departure from continuity" criterion being optimized in parametric mapping) of any solution we obtained. The main "finagling" that occurred involved using the INDSCAL solution as starting configuration and experimenting with different initial values of the parameter e (actually, we used a new version of the program that allows a different value of e for each stimulus point, but that is "another story" that will not be told here). It can be stated with relative confidence that, *in principle*, this is *the* parametric mapping solution, even if, in fact, it may be a little hard to find it. The main problem with this procedure as with a number of the new computer-implemented methods of analysis, seems to lie more in numerical analysis than in psychology or statistics. Probably, the best general solution to this problem lies in improved methods of generating starting configurations. This is particularly difficult for parametric mapping, because of its own great generality of assumptions, but we are working on it (some suggestions Shepard has made for building up a structure one point at a time may provide at least a partial solution).

One thing we may note about this parametric mapping solution is that it seems to have somewhat changed the configuration given by the INDSCAL solution, but has retained the lattice structure implicit in the stimuli (while rotating the lattice to an arbitrary orientation). The changes (e.g., an increase in the distance between the "hots" and the "steaming hots") evidently have the effect of making the structure more consistent with the preference data. Maintenance of the lattice structure, however, confirms that parametric mapping is *in principle* able to uncover at least the topological properties of the perceptual structure about as well as a scaling of dissimilarities data. We may take this as a kind of "existence proof" confirming the existence of this perceptual information in the preference data and the potential of very generally based nonlinear procedures for recovering this information.

POLYNOMIAL FACTOR ANALYSIS AS A VERY GENERAL UNFOLDING TECHNIQUE

Polynomial factor analysis (Carroll, 1969) is a nonlinear factor analytic procedure less general than parametric mapping but much more specific in its assumptions about the relation between the underlying, or "latent," factors, and the observable, or "manifest," variables comprising the data. Polynomial factor analysis is based on the principle of explicitly minimizing a least-squares criterion of fit of the model to data.

In the present case, the data consist of the preference scale values s_{ij}. In this context, the polynomial factor analysis (PFA) model can be stated, in general terms as

$$s_{ij} \approx \sum_{l=1}^{M} b_{il} z_{lj} \tag{48}$$

where the z_{lj}'s comprise a set of evaluated elementary polynomial functions in a set of r underlying or "latent" variables (or factors) x_{jt}. That is,

$$z_{lj} = f_l(x_{j1}, x_{j2}, \ldots, x_{jr}) \tag{49}$$

where the M functions f_l $(l = 1, 2, \ldots, M)$ are elementary polynomial functions, which are, at present, restricted to be products of integral powers of $x_1, x_2, \ldots, x_r$. (It is very easy to generalize this to allow the z's to be any polynomial functions, or, indeed, any differentiable functions of the x's). For example, if we wanted a model that assumed s_i to be a general quadratic function of two "latent variables," the z's would be defined as

$$z_{1j} = x_{j1}^0 x_{j2}^0 = 1, \qquad z_{4j} = x_{j1}^2 x_{j2}^0 = x_{j1}^2$$

$$z_{2j} = x_{j1}^1 x_{j2}^0 = x_{j1}, \qquad z_{5j} = x_{j1}^0 x_{j2}^2 = x_{j2}^2 \qquad (50)$$

$$z_{3j} = x_{j1}^0 x_{j2}^1 = x_{j2}, \qquad z_{6j} = x_{j1}^1 x_{j2}^1 = x_{j1}x_{j2}$$

Note that the set of exponents of the x's serve to specify the model completely. The PFA program, as currently written, takes a matrix E of exponents, as part of its input. For the model specified above, this would be a 6×2 matrix of the form

$$E \equiv \begin{bmatrix} 0 & 0 \\ 1 & 0 \\ 0 & 1 \\ 2 & 0 \\ 0 & 2 \\ 1 & 1 \end{bmatrix} \qquad (51)$$

By changing E we can very easily change the particular polynomial model assumed. Note that, generally, the constant term must be included unless it is specifically intended to exclude it. Note, too, that the exponents must be integers (which may, however, be negative, so long as zero values of x are avoided). Nonintegeral values would create problems of definition for negative x's (although, possibly, noninteger values could be allowed together with a positivity constraint on the x's). A final note is that 0^0 is defined to be 1.

The general quadratic model we have specified in Equations (50) and (51) is, as we have seen earlier, equivalent to the generalized unfolding model. Given such a model, specified by an appropriate E matrix, and a matrix of data (the S matrix, here) PFA proceeds, by a steepest descent numerical method, to find the X matrix providing the best least-squares fit to the data. The matrix B of regression coefficients can also be solved for if desired.

Thus, if S contains preference scale values, and PFA is applied with the model specified in Equations (50) and (51), the effect would be that of a kind of generalized "unfolding" of the preference data, in terms of the most general of the unfolding models in the linear–quadratic hierarchy of models discussed above. (If desired, the regression coefficients could be further analyzed as described earlier to provide estimates of the orthogonal rotations, "ideal points," and dimension weights for various subjects.) By dropping the last row of the E matrix, which specifies the interaction term, the analysis could be done in terms of model II in the hierarchy, the weighted unfolding model (and, again, ideal points and weights could be estimated, if desired, from the coefficients in the B matrix). Unfortunately, model III, the simple unfolding model, is not presently possible in PFA, since it would require a component of the form $\sum_t x_t^2$, which is not currently possible (but the possibility of such additive composites could easily be added). This is not too critical, however, since other procedures exist for simple unfolding, as discussed earlier (although the possibility of negative signs might be useful).

Of course, by eliminating all terms except the linear (i.e., all except the second and thirds rows of the E matrix) we could do the analysis in terms of the vector model. This would be equivalent, however, to a linear factor analysis (or Eckart–Young analysis), which could be done more efficiently by other, more standard procedures (such as are incorporated, e.g., in MDPREF).

PFA is currently a metric procedure, but could easily be made nonmetric by addition of an extra phase in the iterative procedure in which a monotonic regression (of the predicted values on the data) is performed with the monotone transformation of the data then replacing the data values to provide improved estimates of X and B. This should yield an exact nonmetric, rather than a quasi-nonmetric solution. As such, it would provide a nonlinear generalization of the Kruskal–Shepard method of nonmetric linear factor analysis (described in Shepard, 1966).

In applying PFA as an unfolding procedure to the "tea-tasting" data, it was decided first to analyze the data in terms of the weighted unfolding model, since our earlier external analysis had indicated this as the most appropriate of the linear–quadratic hierarchy of models. This means that the E matrix was like the one in Equation (51), but with the last row omitted. The configuration from the INDSCAL analysis was used as starting configuration.

The configuration shown in Figure 18 resulted. The proportion of variance accounted for by this solution was .8869. This compares to .7315 for the metric external analysis in terms of model II, when the INDSCAL solution provided the stimulus space. (It is appropriate to compare this figure with the comparable figure from the metric, rather than the nonmetric, external analysis, since PFA is currently a metric technique.)

The most striking change in the configuration of points shown in Figure

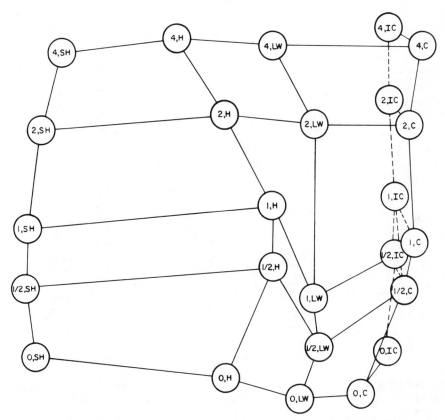

Fig. 18. Polynomial factor analysis (PØLYFAC) solution for tea-tasting preference data when only quadratic terms (with no interaction terms) were included. INDSCAL starting configuration was used.

18 is the "folding back" of the "ice colds" that is so clearly in evidence (as indicated, in part, by the dotted lines showing parts of the lattice structure that are, as it were, behind the rest). In addition to this the "steaming hots" have moved away from the "hots," much as in the parametric mapping solution. Evidently both of these changes improve the fit of the weighted unfolding model to the data. The change in the "ice colds" tends to bring them closer to the "hots," which are most likely to be at the peak of a positive–positive preference function fit for this model.

As suggested earlier, however, even this fairly general model apparently fails to provide an adequate fit to the present data. Something approaching a cubic seems to be required for the temperature dimension. For this

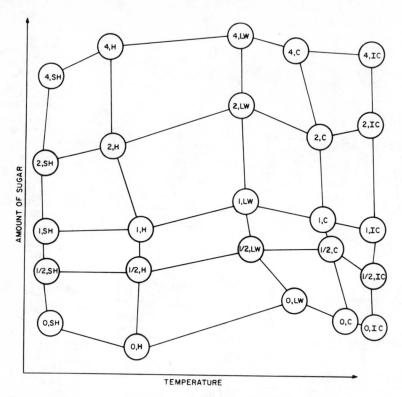

Fɪɢ. 19. Polynomial factor analysis solution when additional cubic term was allowed for Dimension 1. INDSCAL starting configuration used.

reason, an additional polynomial factor analysis solution was attempted, this one including a cubic term for Dimension 1. Thus the E matrix was like the one in Equation (52), except that the last row was replaced with the entry (3, 0). The configuration that resulted is shown in Figure 19 (again, the INDSCAL solution provided the starting configuration). The proportion of variance accounted for by this solution was .9454, bv far the best figure attained in any of the metric analyses. It might be noted, parenthetically, that the proportion of variance accounted for by the INDSCAL starting configuration was .8650 when this model was used (this is the figure for the zeroth iteration of the PFA run). Thus this mixed quadratic–cubic model does almost as well with the INDSCAL configuration as the doubly quadratic weighted unfolding model does after optimizing the configuration. Such a use of PFA for "zero iterations" provides a general way of doing *external* analyses in terms of more general regression equations such as the one used here. The parameterization provided by

PFA is perhaps not the best, however, since it provides only the regression coefficients, but does not parameterize subjects in terms of ideal points and the like.

The configuration obtained by using PFA with this mixed quadratic–cubic model appears to be the most "regular" one resulting from any of the analyses. It may be concluded from this that none of the models in the linear–quadratic hierarchy is sufficiently general to account for the preference data from the "tea-tasting" experiment. An additional conclusion is that polynomial factor analysis appears to be a very promising technique for analysis of complex preference data. It provides a very general mode of "unfolding" analysis that has potentially wide application for data, not only in the preference domain, but for multivariate data of many different kinds.

Acknowledgments

Many people were instrumental in the work reported here, and in the preparation of the paper. The author would like to single out for special acknowledgment: Myron Wish, whose advice and other help related to the "tea-tasting" experiment were invaluable; Roger Shepard and Maureen Sheenan, who generously allowed use of their data and data analysis on subjective judgments of size of rectangles; Carolyn Brown, who assisted in many phases of data analysis and preparation of figures for this paper; and, most particularly, Jih-Jie Chang, who wrote most of the computer programs used for the various data analyses reported here, and provided other essential help.

References

Bechtel, G. Individual differences in the linear multidimensional scaling of choice. Paper presented at meeting of the Psychometric Society, Princeton, New Jersey, April 1969.

Bennett, J. F., & Hays, W. L. Multidimensional unfolding: Determining the dimensionality of ranked preference data, *Psychometrika*, 1960, **25**, 27–43.

Bloxom, B. Individual differences in multidimensional scaling. Research Bulletin 68–45. Princeton, New Jersey: Educational Testing Service, 1968.

Bricker, P. D., & Pruzansky, S. Comparison of sorting and pairwise similarity judgment techniques for scaling auditory stimuli. Paper presented at 78th meeting of the Acoustical Society of America, San Diego, November 1969.

Carroll, J. D. A generalization of canonical correlation analysis to three or more sets of variables. *Proceedings of the 76th Annual Convention of the American Psychological Association*, 1968, **3**, 227–228. (a)

Carroll, J. D. A general method for preference mapping of perceptual space. *Bulletin of the Operations Research Society of America*, 1968, **16**, 282 (Abstract). (b)

Carroll, J. D. Polynomial factor analysis. *Proceedings of the 77th Annual Convention of the American Psychological Association*, 1969, **4**, 103–104.

Carroll, J. D., & Chang, J.-J. Non-parametric multidimensional analysis of paired-comparisons data. Paper presented at the joint meeting of the Psychometric and Psychonomic Societies, Niagara Falls, October 1964.

Carroll, J. D., & Chang, J.-J. Relating preference data to multidimensional scaling solutions via a generalization of Coombs' unfolding model. Paper presented at meeting of Psychometric Society, Madison, Wisconsin, April 1967.

Carroll, J. D., & Chang, J.-J. Analysis of individual differences in multidimensional scaling via an *N*-way generalization of "Eckart–Young" decomposition, *Psychometrika*, 1970, **35**, 283–319.

Chang, J.-J., & Carroll, J. D. How to use MDPREF, a computer program for multidimensional analysis of preference data. Unpublished report, Bell Telephone Laboratories, 1968.

Cliff, N. The "idealized individual" interpretation of individual differences in multidimensional scaling. *Psychometrika*, 1968, **33**, 225–232.

Coombs, C. H. Psychological scaling without a unit of measurement. *Psychological Review*, 1950, **57**, 148–158.

Eckart, C., & Young, G. The approximation of one matrix by another of lower rank. *Psychometrika*, 1936, **1**, 211–218.

Horan, C. B. Multidimensional scaling: Combining observations when individuals have different perceptual structures. *Psychometrika*, 1969, **34**, 139–165.

Kruskal, J. B. Nonmetric multidimensional scaling: A numerical method. *Psychometrika*, 1964, **29**, 115–129.

Kruskal, J. B. How to use MDSCAL, a program to do multidimensional scaling and multidimensional unfolding. Unpublished report, Bell Telephone Laboratories, 1968.

Kruskal, J. B., & Carroll, J. D. Geometric models and badness-of-fit functions. In P. R. Krishnaiah (Ed.), *International symposium of multivariate analysis, Dayton, Ohio, 1968*. New York: Academic Press, 1969. Pp. 639–670.

Lingoes, J. C. An IBM-7090 program for Guttman–Lingoes smallest space analysis—RI. *Behavioral Science*, 1966, **11**, 332.

McDermott, B. J. Multidimensional analyses of circuit quality judgments. *The Journal of the Acoustical Society of America*, 1969, **45**, 774–781.

McGee, V. E. Multidimensional scaling of *N* Sets of similarity measures: A nonmetric individual differences approach. *Multivariate Behavioral Research*, 1968, **3**, 233–248.

Roskam, E. I. *Metric analysis of ordinal data in psychology*. Voorschoten, Holland: VAM Press, 1968.

Ross, J. A remark on Tucker and Messick's "points of view" analysis. *Psychometrika*, 1966, **31**, 27–31.

Ross, J., & DiLollo, V. A vector model for psychophysical judgment. *Journal of Experimental Psychology (Monograph Supplement)*, 1968, **77** (3, Pt. 2).

Shepard, R. N. Metric structures in ordinal data. *Journal of Mathematical Psychology*, 1966, **3**, 287–315.

Shepard, R. N., & Carroll, J. D. Parametric representation of nonlinear data structures. In P. R. Krishnaiah (Ed.), *International symposium of multivariate analysis, Dayton, Ohio, 1965*. New York: Academic Press, 1966. Pp. 561–592.

Slater, P. The analysis of personal preferences. *British Journal of Statistical Psychology*, 1960, **13**, 119–135.

Torgerson, W. S. *Theory and methods of scaling.* New York: Wiley, 1958.

Tucker, L. R. Intra-individual and inter-individual multidimensionality. In H. Gulliksen and S. Messick (Eds.), *Psychological scaling: Theory and applications.* New York: Wiley, 1960. Pp. 155–167.

Tucker, L. R. The extension of factor analysis to three-dimensional matrices. In N. Frederiksen and H. Gulliksen (Eds.), *Contributions to mathematical psychology.* New York: Holt, Rinehart, and Winston, 1964. Pp. 109–127.

Tucker, L. R. Some mathematical notes on three-mode factor analysis. *Psychometrika,* 1966, **31,** 279–311.

Tucker, L. R., & Messick, S. An individual difference model for multidimensional scaling. *Psychometrika,* 1963, **28,** 333–367.

Wish, M., Deutsch, M., & Biener, L. Differences in perceived similarity of nations. This book, Volume II.

Wold, H. Estimation of principal components and related models by iterative least squares. In P. R. Krishnaiah (Ed.), *International symposium of multivariate analysis, Dayton, Ohio, 1965.* New York: Academic Press, 1966. Pp. 391–420.

Young, F. W., & Torgerson, W. S. TORSCA, A FORTRAN IV program for Shepard–Kruskal multidimensional scaling analysis. *Behavioral Science,* 1967, **12,** 498.

NONMETRIC MULTIDIMENSIONAL
TECHNIQUES FOR SUMMATED RATINGS

David Napior

UNIVERSITY OF CALIFORNIA
IRVINE, CALIFORNIA

In 1932, Likert introduced a measurement strategy called the "method of summated ratings." The method articulates a series of simple procedures for the collection and numerical representation of social data. Likert's strategy gained substantial currency in empirical social research due to the relative ease with which it could be administered to large numbers of subjects and the rapidity of its coding and scoring system. The trend toward larger sample sizes in social research has, if anything, amplified the virtues of the data collection phase of the method of summated ratings. Unfortunately, the computational algorithm recommended by Likert for item selection and derivation of scores for respondents requires investigators to make assumptions about the dimensional, distributional, and metric properties of their data that frequently cannot be supported; however, computational and computer developments have made possible the adoption of numerical procedures that permit more realistic assumptions about Likert-type data than is possible with the originally recommended scoring algorithm. Before turning to a discussion of these developments, let us briefly review the elements of Likert's measurement strategy.

157

Likert's Method of Summated Ratings

The data collection phase of the method of summated ratings begins with the solicitation of responses to a battery of multiple-choice items. For each item in the battery, the subjects are confronted with a dimension of appraisal and an *ordered* set of response alternatives, ranging, say, from -2 to $+2$ or strongly disagree to strongly agree. Respondents supposedly choose the alternative for each item that best describes their relation to the item in question. For example, Table 1 presents 16 items in the Likert format. The items describe potential activities and attitudes of members of the role network of elementary school teachers. The items were part of a larger battery administered to primary school teachers in Ciudad Guayana, Venezuela (Gross, McGinn, Napior, & Jewell, 1968). The teachers were requested to indicate on a one-to-four scale of response the extent to which they felt there was a need for change in the activity or attitude described in each item.

In general, Likert-type inventories consist of one set of items similar in format to those in Table 1 for each variable or dimension of interest to the investigator. The use of multiple items for each variable to be measured is recommended as a means of improving the reliability of the measurement process.

The standard quantitiative analysis of responses to Likert-type items approaches the measurement of each variable as a separate, independent process. For any given variable, the investigator specifies a priori those items which can be construed as multiple indicators of the phenomenon to be measured. Each subject is then scored on each item in the set. A respondent's score on a given item is equal to the scale value of the response alternative he selected.

Two alternative procedures are used in the assignment of scale values to response categories. The most frequently used approach is simply to assign sequential integers as scale weights to each of the response categories within a given item. Using this procedure, the response alternatives for each of the need-for-change items in Table 1 would have scale values of 1, 2, 3, and 4, corresponding, respectively, to "no need for change," "some need for change," "considerable need for change," and "great need for change." A second procedure for assignment of scale weights assumes that a continuous normal distribution underlies the observed distribution of choices of discrete response alternatives. If we let p_i represent the proportion of the sample of subjects who have chosen response category i for a particular item and let c_i represent the cumulative proportion choosing a category below category i plus one-half the proportion within category i (i.e.,

TABLE 1

LIKERT-TYPE ITEMS DEALING WITH TEACHERS' PERCEPTIONS OF NEED FOR CHANGE
IN THE BEHAVIOR OF MEMBERS OF THEIR ROLE NETWORK

Instructions

We are interested here in the views teachers have concerning the need for change in the behavior of people with whom they associate as a teacher. Please answer Question 1 by circling the ONE number which best represents your feeling for each of the following items.

Question 1

To what extent do you feel that there is a need for change in the following aspects of the behavior of the people with whom you associate as a teacher?

1 = no need for change
2 = some need for change
3 = considerable need for change
4 = great need for change

1. Your principal's attitude toward teachers. 1 2 3 4

2. Your principal's dedication to his work. 1 2 3 4

3. Your principal's comprehension of what goes on in classrooms. 1 2 3 4

4. Your principal's interest in new educational ideas. 1 2 3 4

5. Parents' attitudes toward teachers. 1 2 3 4

6. Parents' interest in the academic progress of their children. 1 2 3 4

7. Parents' knowledge of what goes on in schools. 1 2 3 4

8. Parents' willingness to cooperate with the schools. 1 2 3 4

9. Other teachers' knowledge of the subjects they teach. 1 2 3 4

10. Other teachers' interest in improving their skills as a teacher. 1 2 3 4

11. Other teachers' interest in new educational ideas. 1 2 3 4

12. Other teachers' willingness to devote time to the preparation of lessons. 1 2 3 4

13. Your students' attitude toward teachers. 1 2 3 4

14. Your students' interest in academic achievements. 1 2 3 4

15. Your students' moral standards. 1 2 3 4

16. Your students' willingness to do school work at home. 1 2 3 4

$c_i = \sum_{j=1}^{i-1} p_j + \frac{1}{2}p_i$), then we can equate the scale weights of the categories to the value of the normal deviates corresponding to each of the cumulative midpoints, the c_i. In the development of the method of summated ratings, Likert found that scores based upon the relatively simple assignment of sequential integers as weights tended to correlate almost perfectly with scores derived with the more complicated normal deviate system. He therefore recommended the use of the integer system in the majority of problems (Likert, 1938).

Once all respondents have been assigned a score for the variable under consideration, quantitative procedures are then applied to determine the degree of correlation between item scores and the summary score. Items which fail to correlate at an acceptable level with the summary score are eliminated from the measure and a new summary score is calculated for each respondent on the basis of his responses to the reduced set of component items. This procedure is generally repeated until all items in the measure display an adequate degree of covariation with the summary score; hence, indicating unidimensionality in the sense that the items display a moderate degree of internal homogeneity.

The numerical procedures of the method of summated ratings are subject to two important criticisms. First, the item analysis procedure is arbitrarily unidimensional when a multidimensional approach to the data would often prove to be more fruitful. Secondly, the scoring system requires a number of unnecessary assumptions about the distributional and metric properties of the data.

Multidimensional Item Analysis

The unidimensional approach to item analysis yields deceptive results in two ways. First, by forcing an early subjective decision about the particular variables or underlying continua that will be used to represent the larger body of data, it unnecessarily defers the beginning of the empirical aspect of the measurement process. The a priori segmentation of the data in terms of these variables and the disconnected treatment of responses within each segment is frequently a less-fruitful attack than one which takes the body of data as a whole and allows the underlying segmental structure to reveal itself. Secondly, the unidimensional approach to item analysis can deceive the investigator by persuading him to terminate the item analysis process too quickly. If an a priori set of component items consists of two or more relatively independent clusters of items contributing roughly equal portions to the total variance of the set, each item may still correlate adequately

TABLE 2

PRODUCT–MOMENT CORRELATION COEFFICIENTS BETWEEN SIXTEEN ITEMS DEALING
WITH TEACHERS' PERCEPTIONS OF NEED FOR CHANGE AND A SUMMARY SCORE
DERIVED FROM RESPONSES TO THE SAME SIXTEEN ITEMS

Item/number	r	Item/number	r
1	0.64	9	0.54
2	0.53	10	0.62
3	0.63	11	0.60
4	0.67	12	0.52
5	0.62	13	0.58
6	0.60	14	0.67
7	0.64	15	0.57
8	0.57	16	0.63

with a summary measure using all the items even though the items would exhibit a much higher degree of association with a summary score derived from the subset of items in their own clusters. In short, the variable by variable approach to item analysis will frequently begin empirical analysis too late and stop it just short of the discovery of interesting multidimensional subtleties.

As a working example of the potential flaws of unidimensional item analysis, let us examine the 16 questions dealing with teachers' perceptions of need for change (Table 1). Confronting these items on a face validity basis, we clearly could treat all 12 as indicators of the degree to which teachers desire changes in the behavior of members of their role network. Table 2 presents the product-moment correlation between each item and a summary score based on the mean of the responses to all 16 items using the integer system of weights. Although not overwhelmingly high, the magnitude of the coefficients is high enough to warrant inclusion of all the items in a single measure; nevertheless, an equally reasonable approach to this data might be to use subsets of the 16 items to obtain several independently derived summary scores. The most obvious such segmentation involves four subsets of four items each, treating teachers' perceived need for change in the behavior of principals, parents, other teachers and pupils as separate scaling problems. Another plausible consideration would be to distinguish between need for change in the behavior of colleagues (i.e., administrators and other teachers) and clients (i.e., parents and pupils). Finally, it is feasible that one might want to cut across role boundaries to build scales for perceived need for change in: (a) the interest of others in educational innovation (items 4 and 11); (b) the commitment of others to the educational enterprise (items 2, 5, 8, 10, 12, 14, and 16); (c) the attitudes of others toward teachers (items 1, 5, and 13); and (d) the knowledge of others about the academic process (items 3, 7, and 9). Given these divergent possibilities, it follows that an a priori segmentation may misrepresent the structure of the data. One way to avoid an a priori commitment or to support empirically such a commitment is through multidimensional analysis.

We should note at this point that, theoretically, it is not advisable to undertake the analysis of items and analysis of subjects as two distinct tasks, as we are apparently endorsing. Several multidimensional models have been implemented for scaling items and scoring respondents simultaneously (Coombs, 1964; Lingoes, 1966a, 1966b, 1967; Shepard & Kruskal, 1964; Young, 1968); however, at present the working versions of these techniques are impractical for sample sizes larger than 100. Since Likert-type inventories are commonly administered to much larger samples, we are constrained to undertake an alternative strategy. This strategy has two stages: (1) the segmentation of the set of items into unidimensional subsets through multidimensional analysis of the pairwise associations among items, and (2) application of Guttman's least-squares scaling procedure (Guttman, 1950) within each unidimensional subset to obtain, simultaneously, scale weights for response alternatives and scores for subjects on the dimension under consideration.

Our first task, then, is the establishment of appropriate techniques for multidimensional analysis of interrelations among *items*. We begin with the computation of estimates of the degree of pairwise association among all the items under consideration. The most frequently used measure of pairwise association has been Pearson's product-moment correlation coefficient. Attendant upon use of Pearson's r are two assumptions that Likert-type data often fail to meet: (a) the relationship between the pair of items being correlated should be linear; (b) the numerical representation of the responses to the items should have the properties of an interval scale (Carroll, 1961).

If the investigator feels that his data do not meet these assumptions and that the departure will seriously distort the accuracy of estimates of degree of association given by Pearson's r, rank-order correlation procedures are indicated. Although Spearman's ρ and Kendall's τ are probably the most familiar approaches to rank-order correlation, they both prove awkward in the handling of tied responses. Since ties are necessarily abundant in Likert-type data, we recommend the use of the Goodman–Kruskal gamma (Goodman & Kruskal, 1954). It requires only ordinal information from the responses, ranges between -1 and $+1$, similar to Pearson's r, Spearman's

TABLE 3

GOODMAN–KRUSKAL γ'S FOR SIXTEEN ITEMS DEALING WITH TEACHERS'
PERCEPTIONS OF NEED FOR CHANGE

Item 1	2	3	4	5	6	7	8	9	10	11	12	13	14	15
1			principals											
2 .67														
3 .69	.73													
4 .67	.67	.74		parents										
5 .40	.28	.24	.38											
6 .33	.21	.27	.27	.58										
7 .41	.16	.31	.38	.60	.63									
8 .26	.13	.20	.32	.62	.58	.75		other teachers						
9 .36	.32	.38	.41	.26	.28	.25	.21							
10 .36	.25	.38	.45	.29	.36	.34	.31	.62						
11 .34	.23	.35	.47	.27	.23	.32	.28	.60	.83					
12 .39	.38	.36	.34	.24	.29	.31	.23	.54	.47	.45		pupils		
13 .35	.32	.29	.31	.39	.36	.34	.31	.25	.31	.28	.39			
14 .34	.31	.33	.35	.43	.49	.48	.44	.28	.40	.37	.33	.63		
15 .29	.26	.25	.34	.42	.38	.45	.31	.22	.28	.28	.28	.46	.61	
16 .30	.25	.29	.36	.38	.46	.45	.41	.32	.43	.37	.28	.50	.70	.62

parents and pupils

ρ and Kendall's τ, and has a simple probabilistic interpretation as the probability of "like" order minus the probability of "unlike" order of responses to the items given two respondents drawn at random from the sample.

Table 3 presents the Goodman–Kruskal γ's for the 16 items dealing with teachers' perceptions of need for change in the behavior of members of their role network. The coefficients are all positive, ranging from a high of .83 to a low of .13. If one circles the coefficients in the top quartile (i.e., $\gamma \geq .45$), as we have done in Table 3, it can be seen that the items tend to form four mutually exclusive clusters corresponding to need for change in behavior of (a) principals (items 1–4); (b) parents (items 5–8); (c) other teachers (items 9–12); and (d) pupils (items 13–16). The exceptions to the rule occur mainly in γ's describing relationships between items pertaining to "parents" and "pupils." This finding is not surprising since parents and pupils are probably closely associated in the teachers' minds.

Although the superficial visual examination of the matrix of γ's has been revealing for the simple data we have used as an example, more complex multidimensional structure often requires more sophisticated analytical treatment. We find it convenient at this point to distinguish among two approaches to multidimensional item analysis: (1) clustering models and (2) geometric models.

Clustering Models

Clustering models attempt to place items in mutually exclusive groups in such a way as to best represent measures of similarity among them. Clustering techniques vary along three important dimensions: (1) metric versus ordinal assumptions about input; (2) score matrix versus association matrix as input; (3) hierarchical versus nonhierarchical solutions.

In order to give some idea of the information to be gained from clustering techniques, we have applied one of the many available procedures to the association matrix in Table 3. The program we have used is Johnson's diameter method (Johnson, 1967). This is a nonmetric technique which operates on the association matrix rather than the original score matrix in order to produce a hierarchical clustering of items. Figure 1 presents the solution. The item numbers are indicated across the top of the figure. The fifteen tiers of horizontal lines indicate the progress of the clustering procedure as it works from the "weak" clustering in which each item is a separate cluster (step 0) to the "strong" clustering in which all items are collapsed into a single cluster (step 15). Hierarchical solutions have the

Step number	Item number															
	1	2	3	4	9	10	11	12	6	5	7	8	13	15	14	16
0																
1							———									
2							———						———			
3			———				———						———			
4			———				———						———			———
5		———	———				———				———				———	
6		———					———				———				———	
7		———					———				———				———	
8		———				———					———				———	
9		———				———					———				———	
10		———				———				———				———		
11		———				———				———				———		
12	principals			teachers				parents			pupils					
13	principals			teachers				clients								
14	colleagues						clients									
15																

Fig. 1. Hierarchical clustering solution for sixteen items dealing with teachers' perceptions of need for change.

distinguishing characteristic that once two items appear together in the same cluster as one proceeds from the weak to the strong solution, they cannot appear in different clusters in subsequent steps.

Examination of the hierarchical solution in Figure 1 reveals that when only four clusters remain (step 12), items 1–4 (principals), items 5–8 (parents), items 9–12 (other teachers), and items 13–16 (pupils) comprise four separate groups. At step 13, we have parents and pupils collapsed into a single cluster, principals in another and other teachers in the third. At step 14, clients (i.e., parents and pupils) form one cluster while colleagues (i.e., principals and other teachers) form another.

The hierarchical solution in Figure 1 is clearly a refinement upon a simple visual scan for recognizable clusters in the association matrix; however, the utility of clustering techniques such as Johnson's diameter method is limited by the discrete nature of their solutions. Accurate reflection of complex or subtle structural relationships may not be possible with the discrete groupings of items produced by clustering approaches to multidimensional analysis. The geometric models to which we now turn have the advantage of offering users a somewhat more refined picture of the structure of their data.

GEOMETRIC MODELS

Multidimensional geometric models attempt to position items in a spatial configuration in such a way as to represent best, simultaneously, all pairwise relations among items. The basic assumption underpinning these models is the notion that an accurate correspondence can be established between structural aspects of the association matrix and certain geometric properties of the derived configuration, such as distances between points, angles between vectors, or projections of vectors upon vectors.

Conceptually, one of the simplest geometric models is the technique known as multidimensional scaling (Kruskal, 1964a, 1964b; McGee, 1966; Shepard, 1962a, 1962b; Torgerson, 1958) or smallest space analysis (Guttman, 1968; Lingoes, 1965). In Torgerson's original formulation, multidimensional scaling was designed specifically for the analysis of judgments of similarity among triads of stimuli under the assumption of normally distributed variations (Torgerson, 1958, Chapter 11). Later developments of so-called nonmetric multidimensional scaling extended the range of applications to include any data for which one could draw a broad analogy between various notions of social and psychological distance and the more familiar concept of spatial distance between physical objects. Semantic distance in psycholinguistics and social distance in sociometric

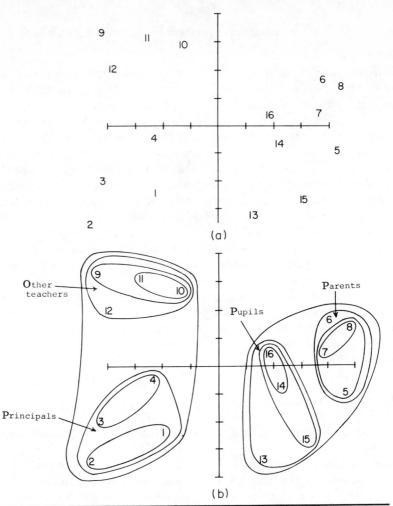

| | Dimension | | | Dimension | |
Item	1	2	Item	1	2
1	−.61	−.55	9	−1.02	.80
2	−1.12	−.90	10	−.33	.71
3	−1.03	−.45	11	−.59	.83
4	−.60	−.16	12	−.91	.51
5	1.03	−.21	13	.37	−.83
6	.95	.41	14	.52	−.22
7	.80	.13	15	.81	−.73
8	1.23	.47	16	.49	.19

stress = 0.14

Fig. 2. Nonmetric multidimensional scaling configuration for sixteen items dealing with teachers' perceptions of need for change. (a) two-dimensional configuration; (b) hierarchical clustering solution embedded in two-dimensional multidimensional scaling solution.

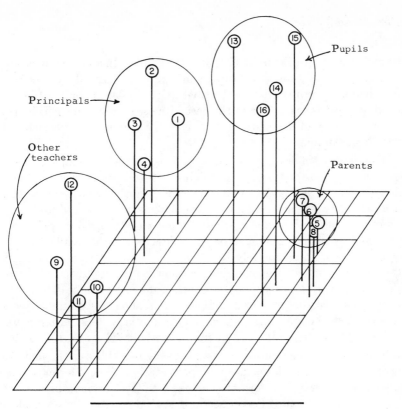

| | | Dimension | |
Item	1	2	3
1	−.62	.69	−.19
2	−.87	.83	.01
3	−.86	.60	−.15
4	−.69	.37	−.28
5	.72	.33	−.59
6	.92	−.05	−.38
7	.75	.12	−.38
8	.91	.00	−.66
9	−.71	−.85	−.12
10	−.37	−.82	−.21
11	−.54	−.81	−.41
12	−.71	−.72	.47
13	.23	.10	.99
14	.54	.07	.53
15	.68	.29	.76
16	.61	−.14	.57
	stress = .07		

Fig. 2c. Three-dimensional configuration.

167

research are two of the more prominent examples. In addition, measures of similarity, correlation, association, and agreement have all been converted into distances or dissimilarities by inverting each datum, or, if a theoretical maximum exists, as is true in the case of most correlation coefficients and other measures of association, by taking the complement of each datum and the maximum.

The goal of multidimensional scaling is to find a compact, accurate geometric representation of the original "distances" between items. The degree of accuracy is determined by the extent to which the Euclidean distances between the positions of pairs of items in the derived configuration reproduce either the *value* or the *rank order* of the original pairwise distances. The degree of compactness is a function of the number of dimensions required to adequately represent the data: The fewer dimensions, the more compact the solution. Nonmetric multidimensional scaling programs, in attempting to reproduce the rank order rather than the value of the input, require only ordinal information about the original distances; nevertheless, the solutions obtained have essentially the same scale properties as configurations obtained by metric methods (Shepard, 1962a, 1962b).

The utility of the multidimensional scaling model lies in the fact that it gives a compact multidimensional representation of the information in the association matrix in a format that has intuitive meaning because of its strong analogy to our ideas concerning spatial distance between physical objects. Of course, the more compact the derived configuration (i.e., the fewer the number of dimensions), the greater the potential for serious distortion of the data. The principle of parsimony advocates attaining the highest compression possible while retaining satisfactory fit.

Figure 2a presents a two-dimensional configuration derived from application of Kruskal's nonmetric multidimensional scaling program, M-D-SCAL, (Kruskal, 1964a, 1964b) to the association matrix in Table 3. Several strategies exist for the interpretation of spatial configurations. First, we can look for substantively meaningful clusters or "local structure" in the solution. Items that are relatively close to each other in the Euclidean sense are considered to be members of a common group or cluster. The problem here is to interpret the meaning of "close." One particularly useful tool for delimiting clusters in a spatial configuration is to embed the solution derived from a clustering analysis in the configuration space (Shepard, this book, Volume I). Figure 2b presents the two-dimensional solution in Figure 2a with the hierarchical clustering solution of Figure 1 embedded in it. The clusters defined in this way can readily be assigned substantively meaningful labels as we have shown earlier in our discussion of the hierarchical cluster solution and, in addition, we obtain a more complete picture of the relative positioning of the items than was possible using clustering analysis alone. For example, it is interesting to note that in the two-dimensional solution the distinction between the parents cluster (items 5–8) and the pupils cluster (items 13–16) is not very clear. If we attempt a three-dimensional representation of the same data (Figure 2c), the solution has much lower stress and also renders a somewhat sharper differentiation of the parents cluster from the pupils cluster.

Although search for clusters has been an effective interpretive strategy for the data in our example, other kinds of structural paradigms can be successfully captured in multidimensional scaling solutions (Degerman, this book, Volume I; Shepard, this book, Volume I). Included among these is what has been, in the past, the most common of all interpretive strategies: search for axes, directions, or dimensions in the solution that have a compelling substantive significance. It is important to remember when using this approach that the direction and origin of the orthogonal reference axes obtained by multidimensional scaling programs are arbitrary from a mathematical point of view and should be rotated and translated in order to find a substantively meaningful position in which to fix them. Furthermore, restraint should be exercised in attempting to interpret multidimensional scaling solutions in terms of axes or dimensions, since multidimensional scaling does not seek vector representation of the data. The occurrence of interpretable axes in multidimensional scaling configurations is a function of properties of the data more than it is a function of properties of the mathematical procedures employed. This is not true of all geometric models. The geometric model underlying factor analysis, for example, is designed to yield a solution interpretable in terms of axes or dimensions even at the expense of distorting nonlinear relationships that actually appear in the data matrix.

In factor analysis, unlike multidimensional scaling, the Euclidean distance between two points is not directly related to the values in the association matrix; instead, the values can be reproduced from cosines of angles between item vectors. More precisely, if we let p_i and p_j represent the length of vectors drawn from the origin to the positions of items i and j in the factor solution, and if we let θ_{ij} represent the angle inclination between these two vectors, then the goal of factor analysis is to position items in a space of a given dimensionality so that the value of the expression $p_i p_j \cos \theta_{ij}$ approximates as closely as possible the numerical value or rank order of the original measure of pairwise association between items i and j, for all possible pairs of i and j, simultaneously. In visual terms, this means that highly related items will have a relatively small angle of inclination between them (i.e., form a relatively straight line), while unrelated items

TABLE 4

Nonmetric Factor Analysis Configurations for the Sixteen Items Dealing
with Teachers' Perceptions of Need for Change

	(a) Four-dimensional solution—unrotated[a] Dimension					(b) Four-dimensional solution—orthogonal rotation[b] Dimension			
Item	1	2	3	4	Item	1	2	3	4
1	−.68	−.43	.27	−.05	1	−.22	−.78	−.18	.15
2	−.62	−.53	.28	.07	2	−.07	−.84	−.13	.18
3	−.70	−.45	.14	.01	3	−.13	−.80	−.21	.16
4	−.70	−.45	.14	−.04	4	−.18	−.76	−.30	.15
5	−.62	.27	.17	−.27	5	−.67	−.20	−.15	.22
6	−.62	.32	.12	−.19	6	−.63	−.14	−.17	.30
7	−.68	.38	.19	−.33	7	−.80	−.15	−.16	.25
8	−.61	.40	.16	−.37	8	−.79	−.09	−.15	.18
9	−.59	−.14	−.46	−.10	9	−.14	−.21	−.71	.14
10	−.65	−.08	−.55	−.09	10	−.17	−.15	−.81	.20
11	−.61	−.12	−.52	−.10	11	−.15	−.18	−.77	.16
12	−.55	−.08	−.23	−.03	12	−.17	−.24	−.48	.21
13	−.58	.15	.02	.30	13	−.19	−.20	−.18	.58
14	−.71	.34	.04	.45	14	−.27	−.14	−.17	.84
15	−.59	.22	.05	.32	15	−.23	−.17	−.15	.64
16	−.66	.28	−.02	.38	16	−.24	−.13	−.22	.74
root =	6.45	1.70	1.17	.93					

[a] Coefficient of alienation is .18; coefficient of deformation is .03.
[b] Kaiser (1958).

will tend to have vectors separated by a wide angle of inclination (i.e., lie at right angles to each other).

The vector representation attempted by factor analysis leads investigators to rely relatively heavily on various rotational schemes for interpretive purposes. Two fundamentally different rotation strategies exist: Procrustean (Hurley & Cattell, 1962) and simple structure (Kaiser, 1958). Procrustean rotations are appropriate in instances when the investigator has prior evidence leading him to believe that the factor solution should take a certain form. He then may choose to position the configuration axes so that the derived solution matches as closely as possible the hypothetical solution. "Simple structure" rotations proceed from the assumption that there are no conditions external to the factor analysis to guide the process. The basic principle behind rotation to simple structure is the notion that

TABLE 4 (continued)

(c) Four-dimensional solution—oblique rotation[c]
Dimension

Item	1	2	3	4	
1	−.10	−.85	.04	−.04	
2	.10	−.94	.09	.03	principals
3	.33	−.87	−.00	−.18	
4	−.03	−.79	−.12	−.04	
5	−.71	−.07	.02	.01	
6	−.65	.00	−.02	.12	parents
7	−.88	.01	.02	.00	
8	−.89	.07	−.01	−.07	
9	.15	−.03	−.78	−.04	
10	.00	.07	−.90	.01	other teachers
11	.02	.02	−.85	−.02	
12	−.04	−.11	−.56	.08	
13	.02	−.08	−.03	.63	
14	.01	.04	.04	.96	pupils
15	−.02	−.03	.02	.70	
16	.00	.05	−.05	.81	

Correlations among oblique factors

Factor	1	2	3	4
1	—			
2	.46	—		
3	.48	.54	—	
4	−.62	−.48	−.53	—

[c] Hendrickson & White (1964).

the most meaningful configuration is one which allows each factor to correlate highly with only a few variables. The reasoning here is that since we intend to classify the data in terms of the "underlying dimensions" corresponding to configuration axes, it follows that we should be more interested in factors that discriminate as sharply as possible between items than ones which correlate indiscriminately with a wide range of items.

Tables 4a, b, and c present the results of application of the Guttman–Lingoes nonmetric factor-analysis program (Lingoes & Guttman), to the association matrix in Table 3. Guttman–Lingoes nonmetric factor analysis is a recent reformulation of the factor problem with advantages over the traditional metric procedures. First, by seeking a solution capable of reproducing only the rank-order pattern of the data matrix, it is able to relax considerably assumptions concerning the scale properties of the association matrix that are required by traditional factor analysis. Secondly, solutions reflecting order relations can generally be more compact (i.e., have fewer dimensions) than solutions reflecting metric values. Thirdly, and perhaps most important, the nonmetric solution is designed to represent nonlinear relationships in the input without the attenuation and distortion inherent in the representations of traditional factor analysis. This means that nonmetric factor analysis can be used to reveal or to test hypotheses about nonlinear patterns such as circumplices or radices in the data, whereas a metric analysis would obscure such patterns. Finally, the quibbling over which of the various theorems on communalities to embrace for a correct factor solution can be avoided. Nonmetric factor analysis regards Thurstone's minimum-rank formulation of the factor problem as empirically impractical since it rarely affords adequate compression of the original matrix. Once it has been accepted that compression of the matrix to minimum rank is not practical as an empirical research strategy, the algebraic aspects of the traditional factor model become dysfunctional and the problem can be reformulated without reference to communalities (Lingoes & Guttman, 1967).

Examination of Tables 4a, b, and c reveals structure in the association matrix very similar to that revealed through hierarchical clustering and multidimensional scaling approaches, although the factor solution appears to require a greater dimensionality than the multidimensional scaling solution. If we circle all factor loadings greater than a 0.50 as has been done in Table 4c, four mutually exclusive sets of items can be readily identified. The four sets contain exactly the same items as the four clusters in the multidimensional scaling and hierarchical clustering representation of the data on teachers' perceptions of need for change (Figure 2b).

Before turning to a discussion of procedures for obtaining scale weights and scores for Likert-type inventories, let us briefly review the major differences in the two basic approaches to multidimensional item analysis. Clustering models solve for essentially discrete arrangements of items in groups that are representative of the observed relations in the data matrix. The derived solutions, however, tend to provide inadequate information about the more subtle and ambiguous patterns in the data. Geometric models offer a more refined representation of the data by locating the items in a metric space. Multidimensional scaling offers solutions that can achieve great compression of the data without severe distortion; furthermore, two- and three-dimensional configurations can be interpreted quite easily using physical models and intuitive visual processes. The vector representation of the data attempted by factor analysis generally requires a solution of greater dimensionality than a multidimensional scaling analysis of the same data; however, factor solutions of dimensionality greater than three can frequently be interpreted by examination of the numerical values of the factor loadings, a property not generally shared by multidimensional scaling solutions.

Scale Weights and Scores

Let us assume that the problem of multidimensionality in the item space has been satisfactorily handled in such a way as to reveal several mutually exclusive sets of items, each of which represents a unidimensional facet or variable. The problem now remains to assign scores to individuals that indicate their position on each variable. A directly related problem is the assignment of scale values or "weights" to the response categories of the items.

Although resulting in highly correlated scores of the same variable, Likert's "sigma" and "integer" scoring procedures described in the beginning of the paper rely on somewhat different formal models. In the integer procedure, it is assumed that a single scale of weights is appropriate for all items. This assumption implies that there is no scale of items, as such. For example, a "4" response to item 1 in Table 1 is assumed to have identical meaning or value as a "4" response to any of the other items to be used in the table. Since each item is equal in scale value and identical in response scale, a subject's score can be computed by taking the sum or mean of his item scores.

There are two serious criticisms of this approach. First, the appropriateness of a single scale of weights for all items is not safely taken for granted. This is especially true when the distribution of responses to items are skewed in different degrees. Items with a disproportionately high frequency of response in categories with high weight will then have a disproportionate influence on the summary score. Secondly, the use of integers as weights results in an overly discrete distribution of scores for the variable being measured. If these scores are to be used as criterion variables in future analyses, a more continuous metric would be desirable.

Likert's sigma scoring procedure is derived from a model in which it is possible for scale weights of the response categories to vary from item to item; however, the model also assumes that these differences are for the most part corrections for artifacts of the inventory. In theory, there is an identical normal distribution underlying the discrete responses to each item. Since all items have identical theoretical response distributions, empirical variation in the distribution of the discrete responses is artifactual and should be standardized away by assigning appropriate normal deviates as scale weights for response categories.

In situations where the investigator is reluctant to burden himself with the metric and distributional assumptions of either the integer or sigma scoring procedures, we recommend Guttman's long-ignored least-squares scaling model (Guttman, 1950; Torgerson, 1958). Guttman proceeded from the initial assumption that internal consistency should be the primary criterion of success in the derivation of both category weights and respondent scores. Saying nothing about weights, he postulated that the most internally consistent set of scores to assign people on the basis of their responses to the items are those that satisfy the following condition:

> All people who fall in one category of an item should have scores as similar as possible among themselves, and as different as possible from the scores of the people in other categories of the item; this should be true to the best possible extent for all people simultaneously [Guttman, 1950, p. 314].

Similarly, saying nothing about scores, he postulated that the most internally consistent values to assign the categories are those that satisfy the following condition:

> All categories characterizing one person should have numerical values as similar as possible among themselves, and as different as possible from the value of categories that do not characterize this person; this should be true to the best extent possible for all people simultaneously [Guttman, 1950, p. 314].

Although the derivation of scores and weights may be treated as separate projects, Guttman showed that the two solutions are equivalent in that a simple relationship exists between the optimum scores and the optimum weights: The most internally consistent score for an individual turns out to be proportional to the mean of the weights of the categories which he selected, and the most internally consistent weight of a category is proportional to the mean of the scores of the subjects who selected it.

Since the number of categories is generally smaller than the number of respondents, we chose to solve for category weights first and to use the derived weights to compute the subjects' scores. We begin by defining the pairwise incidence matrix, H, as follows: (1) Number the response categories from 1 to N, where N is the number of items times the number of response alternatives for each item; (2) let N_j be the number of subjects responding to category j; (3) let N_k be the number of subjects responding

TABLE 5

SCALE WEIGHTS FOR RESPONSE CATEGORIES OF SIXTEEN ITEMS DEALING WITH
TEACHERS' PERCEPTIONS OF NEED FOR CHANGE

Item	No need for change	Some need for change	Consider-able need for change	Great need for change
(a) Principals				
1	−2.38	1.17	2.45	3.97
2	−2.06	1.44	3.33	5.18
3	−2.46	.77	2.52	5.47
4	−2.60	.31	2.51	4.42
(b) Parents				
5	−4.34	−.96	1.57	3.14
6	−4.49	−2.41	.53	2.92
7	−5.00	−2.55	.67	2.80
8	−5.95	−2.32	.18	2.81
(c) Other teachers				
9	−2.32	−.59	2.78	6.84
10	−3.38	−.88	.95	5.73
11	−3.09	−1.15	.37	5.34
12	−1.71	−.52	2.56	5.10
(d) Pupils				
13	−2.98	−.09	2.71	3.67
14	−4.80	−1.53	1.20	3.70
15	−3.80	−.46	1.98	3.58
16	−4.68	−1.78	1.18	3.13

to category k; (4) let N_{jk} be the number of subjects responding to both categories j and k; (5) then the general element of the pairwise incidence matrix H is equal to $N_{jk}/(N_jN_k)^{1/2}$. The solution to the problem posed is the latent vector corresponding to the second largest latent root of the matrix H. This gives the weights which maximize the variance ratio of the variance between people to the total variance, the formal equivalent of Guttman's internal consistency criterion.

Table 5 presents the category weights for the 16 items dealing with teachers' perceptions of need for change in behavior of members of their role network. The 16 items were divided into four groups of four items each on the basis of our multidimensional analysis of their interrelations. Each cluster of four was then scaled separately using Guttman's least-squares scaling procedure. As might be expected, the rank order of the category weights within each item proceeds from lowest for the response, "no need for change," to highest for the response, "great need for change," with "some need for change" and "considerable need for change" falling second and third, respectively. It should be emphasized that this rank order of category weights is an empirical finding. Guttman's least-squares scaling model makes no assumptions about the rank order of categories. The order observed in the solution is a function of the data and not required, a priori, by the model. When the data are not unidimensional, or are plagued by other types of inconsistency, reversals in the expected rank order of categories within items will frequently occur.

The one a priori constraint that Guttman's least-squares scaling procedure does place on the solution is that the mean score for each item should be zero. This implies that from the point of view of the final solution, items as a whole are equal in scale value; but the scale value of particular response categories may vary from item to item in order to account for empirical, but theoretically artifactual, variation in item difficulty.

Summary

The ease and accuracy with which Likert inventories can be administered to large numbers of people have enabled the method of summated ratings to become a popular measurement strategy in survey research and other areas of the empirical social sciences. Unfortunately, the computational algorithm recommended by Likert for item selection and derivation of scores for respondents requires investigators to make assumptions about the dimensional, distributional, and metric properties of their data that frequently cannot be supported; however, computational and computer hardware advances have made it possible to avoid the burden of these assumptions. In place of Likert's item selection and scoring procedures, we recommend a two-stage analysis of the data. In the first stage, we apply multidimensional modes of analysis to the matrix of pairwise associations among items in order to reduce the number of a priori decisions involved in item selection. The multidimensional analysis is intended to result in the delineation of several unidimensional subsets of items. In the second stage, we apply Guttman's least-squares scaling procedure to the responses to the items in each of the unidimensional subsets. In many situations Guttman's least-squares scaling model should prove to be a significant improvement upon Likert's integer and sigma scoring procedures. Guttman's system makes far fewer assumptions than does Likert's about metric and distributional properties underlying responses to items and yields scale weights and scores equal in utility to those rendered by either of Likert's systems.

References

Carroll, J. B. The nature of the data, or how to choose a correlation coefficient. *Psychometrika*, 1961, **26**, 347–372.

Coombs, C. H. *A Theory of Data*. New York: Wiley, 1964.

Degerman, R. The geometric representation of some simple structures. This book, Volume I.

Goodman, L. A., & Kruskal, W. H. Measures of association for cross-classifications. *Journal of the American Statistical Association*, 1954, **49**, 732–764.

Gross, N., McGinn, N., Napior, D., & Jewell, W. Planning for Educational Change: An Application of Sociological and Psychological Perspectives. Unpublished monograph, 1968.

Guttman, L. The principal components of scale analysis. In S. A. Stouffer (Ed.), *Measurement and predication*. Chapter 6. Princeton, New Jersey: Princeton University Press, 1950.

Guttman, L. A general nonmetric technique for finding the smallest coordinate space for a configuration of points. *Psychometrika*, 1968, **33**, 469–506.

Hendrickson, A. E., & White, P. O. Promax: A quick method for rotation to oblique simple structure. *British Journal of Statistical Psychology*, 1964, **17**, 65–70.

Hurley, J. R., & Cattell, R. B. The Procrustes program: Producing direct rotation to test a hypothesized factor structure. *Behavioral Science*, 1962, **7**, 258–262.

Johnson, S. C. Hierarchical clustering schemes. *Psychometrika*, 1967, **32**, 241–254.

Kaiser, H. F. The varimax criterion for analystic rotation in factor analysis. *Psychometrika*, 1958, **23**, 187–200.

Kruskal, J. B. Multidimensional scaling by optimizing goodness of fit to a nonmetric hypothesis. *Psychometrika*, 1964, **29**, 1–27. (a)

Kruskal, J. B. Nonmetric multidimensional scaling: A numerical method. *Psychometrika*, 1964, **29**, 115–129. (b)

Likert, R. A technique for measurement of attitudes. *Archives of Psychology*, 1932, No. 140.

Likert, R. A technique for measurement of attitudes. In G. Murphy and R. Likert (Eds.), *Public Opinion and the Individual*. Chapter 2. New York: Harper, 1938.

Lingoes, J. C. An IBM 7090 program for Guttman–Lingoes smallest space analysis—I. *Behavioral Science*, 1965, **10**, 183–184.

Lingoes, J. C. An IBM 7090 program for Guttman–Lingoes multidimensional scalogram analysis—I. *Behavioral Science*, 1966, **11**, 76–68. (a)

Lingoes, J. C. An IBM 7090 program for Guttman–Lingoes smallest space analysis—RI. *Behavioral Science*, 1966, **11**, 332. (b)

Lingoes, J. C. An IBM 7090 program for Guttman–Lingoes multidimensional scalogram analysis—II. *Behavioral Science*, 1967, **12**, 268–270.

Lingoes, J. C., & Guttman, L. Nonmetric factor analysis: A rank reducing alternative to linear factor analysis. *Multivariate Behavioral Research*, 1967, **2**, 485–505.

McGee, V. E. The multidimensional analysis of "elastic" distances. *The British Journal of Mathematical and Statistical Psychology*, 1966, **19**, 181–196.

Shepard, R. N. The analysis of proximities: Multidimensional scaling with an unknown distance function—I. *Psychometrika*, 1962, **27**, 125–140. (a)

Shepard, R. N. The analysis of proximities: Multidimensional scaling with an unknown distance function.—II. *Psychometrika*, 1962, **27**, 219–245. (b)

Shepard, R. N. A taxonomy of some principal types of data and of multidimensional methods for their analysis. This book, Volume I.

Shepard, R. N., & Kruskal, J. B. Nonmetric methods for scaling and for factor analysis. *American Psychologist*, 1964, **19**, 557–558.

Torgerson, W. S. *Theory and methods of scaling.* New York: Wiley, 1958.

Young, F. W. Torsca-9: A Fortran IV program for nonmetric multidimensional scaling. Chapel Hill, North Carolina: Thurstone. Psychometric Laboratory Report, No. 56, 1968.

LINEAR TRANSFORMATION OF MULTIVARIATE DATA TO REVEAL CLUSTERING

Joseph B. Kruskal

BELL TELEPHONE LABORATORIES, INC.
MURRAY HILL, NEW JERSEY

A major problem in data analysis is how to find any structure in a set of multivariate observations. If each observation is represented as a point in multidimensional space, this means finding the structure of a configuration of points in high-dimensional space. To find linear relationships among the variables, linear regression, principal components, and factor analysis are often used. To find nonlinear relationships, polynomial and more general regression procedures are used, and other techniques such as the recently introduced method of nonlinear principal components (Gnanadesikan & Wilk, 1969).

One very simple and important kind of structure is clustering. Whenever the points cluster together, knowledge of this fact is almost sure to be useful to the man who is interested in the data. Though clustering is used here to include both the simple situation of points clustering around point centers, and the more general situation in which they cluster around lines,

179

curves, curved manifolds, and so on, the primary interest here is simple point clusters.

Some structure-seeking methods depend on the distances between the points. For example, many cluster-seeking techniques look for collections of points whose interpoint distances are small in some sense. Similarly, the method of parametric mapping (Shepard & Carroll, 1966) starts by calculating the matrix of interpoint distances of the original configuration, and subsequently works only with that.

Naturally such distance-using methods are very sensitive to linear transformations of the data, since such transformations can radically alter the interpoint distances. For example, suppose we collect information about people from one small neighborhood in a large city. It may well happen that by using only the variables "income" and "years of education" there is strong clustering, because the neighborhood contains apartment buildings differing considerably in character. However, suppose the data include information on height, weight, hair color, and age, and suppose we calculate interpoint distances based on all six variables. We will probably find no evidence of the clusters, because the variables which are irrelevant to the clustering dilute those which display it. Thus to find the clusters, it may be necessary to transform the multivariate observations by a matrix which gives weight zero to the irrelevant variables.

The problem we attack in this paper is how to find the linear transformation which will reveal a hidden cluster structure. Our general approach is to construct an "index of condensation" which depends on the collection of interpoint distances. This index is intended to indicate, for a given configuration of points, the extent to which these points are condensed around point centers or low-dimensional structures. This index does *not* depend on a tentative assignment of points to clusters and does *not* depend on any tentative description of the low-dimensional structures around which the condensation presumably occurs.

It is practical to optimize this index of condensation over the space of linear transformations (i.e., to find the linear transformation which makes the index as large as possible or as small as possible, whichever is appropriate). Since any linear transformation is described by a matrix, the index of condensation can be viewed as a function defined on matrices. By iterative numerical procedures, we can seek one (or several) matrices which optimize it. By this means we can use the index of condensation to pick out one or several linear transformations of the data for further analysis by some structure-seeking method (such as cluster analysis or parametric mapping).

In some cases, we might want to optimize the index over some limited set of linear transformations. For example, the permissible linear transformations might be limited to rescaling of the axes (i.e., transformations which correspond to diagonal matrices), so that the transformation does not introduce linear combinations of the original variables, but merely permits the units of measurement of each variable to be adjusted. Where the units of measurement are already felt to be appropriate, and the problem is merely seen as picking out the right subset of variables (in order to display structure), the linear transformations might be restricted to the perpendicular projections onto coordinate subspaces (i.e., transformations which correspond to diagonal matrices having 1's and 0's down the diagonal). Since this set of transformations is finite, the computational procedure used in this case might consist of no more than running systematically through all subsets of variables (or some given class of subsets) and calculating the index of condensation corresponding to each subset, as a way of picking out interesting subsets for further examination. Another interesting possibility is to optimize over the linear transformations which project the original set of points down to a spherical set of points in ν dimensions (where dimensionality is used in the conventional sense, and spherical is used in a sense described below). This procedure permits the data analyst to use his intuition as to how many dimensions are appropriate, and it does not compare configurations of different "shape" (which may be helpful if it turns out ultimately to be difficult properly to compensate for the effect of "shape"). In practice, the natural way to do this optimization would be first to use a single fixed transformation to make the data spherical in the full number of initial dimensions. Then the optimization would be restricted to all orthogonal projections onto ν dimensions. In matrix terms, this means all $n \times \nu$ suborthogonal matrices.

The Shape of a Set of Points

The notion of the "shape" of a set of points will be used frequently in what follows. This phrase is used here to refer to certain information contained in the sample covariance matrix of the points. (The common meaning of shape is, of course, much broader.) Since I conceive that shape does not change under rigid rotation, the usable information in the covariance matrix is entirely summarized by the eigenvalues of the covariance matrix (or their square roots). It is the sequence of eigenvalue square-roots itself, arranged in order of descending magnitude, which I consider as describing the shape.

A more modern way of describing the sequence of eigenvalue square-roots is based on the canonical form of a (real rectangular) matrix X under orthogonal equivalence (also called the singular value decomposition of X). A theorem (which dates back to the 1860s) states that there exist orthogonal matrices P and Q and a diagonal matrix M such that $X = PMQ$. Furthermore, we may require that the diagonal elements of M satisfy $m_{11} \geq m_{22} \geq \cdots \geq 0$; and if we do so, then M becomes unique. The diagonal values of M are called by various names, such as the singular values of X. Their squares equal the eigenvalues of X^TX and of XX^T, except that different numbers of zero values may be present. (See Forsythe & Moler, 1967, for a fine exposition of orthogonal equivalence and its applications in numerical analysis.)

Suppose each row of X gives one point in the set of points, and suppose that the centroid of the points is at the origin (i.e., the column sums of X are all zero). Then the shape of the set of points, as described above, consists precisely of the sequence of singular values of X.

To illustrate why the sequence of singular values is called the shape, we list some of the inferences which can be drawn from it. If just k of the singular values are nonzero, then the points lie in a k-dimensional flat subspace. If the nonzero values are all equal, then the points are often called spherical. If j values are much larger than the remaining nonzero values, then we may say that the points are approximately j dimensional. If the points are (exactly or approximately) three dimensional, and the first two eigenvalues are approximately equal and substantially larger than the third, the points are roughly lens shaped. If the points are three dimensional, and the second and third largest eigenvalues are approximately equal and substantially less than the first, the points are roughly cigar shaped.

Internal Dimensionality of a Set of Points

If a set of points is spread diffusely in several dimensions, then we consider that it has "internal dimension" (which is not necessarily an integer) to match its nominal dimension. However, if the points cluster tightly around a twisted curve, then we consider that the internal dimension of the set is close to 1; and if the points cluster tightly around a few point centers, we consider that its internal dimension is close to 0. As a first step in developing an index of condensation, we might like to devise a measure of internal dimensionality which formalizes this intuitive concept.

An interesting paper by Trunk (1968) proposes a definition of dimensionality which uses similar ideas, though it is quite elaborate. His interest is in estimating the dimension of the observations per se, and not in transforming the data.

The indices of condensation actually studied in this paper are not based directly on internal dimensionality. Nevertheless, similar concepts are involved, and the following discussion should help to clarify the concept of internal dimensionality.

We restrict our potential definition of internal dimensionality to concepts which depend only on the interpoint distances, considered as an unstructured set of values. If the points of a set cluster tightly around a twisted curve, what is there about the collection of interpoint distances which distinguishes such a configuration from a more diffuse set of points?

Consider the interpoint distances from a fixed point to other points (of the set) within a sphere of radius r around it. If the sphere is big enough to contain the entire thickness of the scatter around the curve, but small enough so that the curve does not bend very much within it, the number of points within the sphere is approximately proportional to r, just as it would be if the curve were straightened out into a straight line. The same reasoning applies with any point of the collection as the sphere center. Thus we see that the number of interpoint distances $\leq r$ is proportional to r, for values of r which are "small but not too small." By contrast, for a configuration of points spread diffusely in two- or three-dimensional space, the number of interpoint distances $\leq r$ is proportional to r^2 or r^3, again for "medium–small" values of r. For a configuration of points tightly clustered around point centers, the number of interpoint distances $\leq r$ is constant (i.e., proportional to $r^0 = 1$) if r exceeds the cluster diameters but is less than the intercluster distances.

From this discussion, we see that the behavior of sample cumulative distribution function (cdf) of the interpoint distances may offer information about the internal dimensionality of the collection of points. In particular, for points which cluster around a p-dimensional structure with p small, the cdf may behave like r^p for medium–small values of r.

Of course, there are many obstacles to using this information, among which is deciding how big "medium–small" is. We shall not discuss this particular approach further, but shall shift over to another approach, which also relies on the cdf of the interpoint distances.

Two Indices of Condensation

The first index of condensation which we have actually worked with so far is based on the coefficient of variation of the interpoint distances.

(Recall that the coefficient of variation C is the standard deviation divided by the mean.) To see why this basis makes some kind of sense, imagine several rather loosely grouped clusters, and then consider what happens as every point in each cluster moves toward the center of its own cluster. The within-cluster distances all get smaller. Some between-cluster distances get smaller and some larger, but they seem to share no systematic tendency. Hence the standard deviation gets larger and the mean gets smaller, both of which contribute to C getting larger. This leads to the notion that a large value of C tends to indicate condensation.

Furthermore, it has been generally known (and we shall develop this notion quantitatively in full detail) that for diffuse configurations in r dimensions, C decreases as r increases. (Indeed, Shepard (1962, pp. 131, 135) discusses this phenomenon and makes explicit use of it.) This also suggests that large C corresponds to more condensed configurations. We may hope that for a twisted-curve configuration in several dimensions, C will partake of the local one-dimensionality and hence display the condensation.

However, this observation also points up the compelling need to modify C so as to compensate for the shape of the configuration—at least if we are going to compare configurations of different shapes. (Only one of my projected ways of using the index of condensation avoids such comparisons.) For consider two configurations having the same number of points, one strongly clustered in two dimensions, the other diffuse in one dimension. The one-dimensional configuration may well have a larger value of C, simply by virtue of the dimensionality effect, than the two-dimensional configuration has by virtue of the clustering.

To modify C, we develop an approximate formula for $E(m, n)$, the expected value of C for a random normal set of n points subject to the constraint that they have shape exactly equal to m. Here m indicates a finite sequence of descending nonnegative numbers. [The formula for $E(m, n)$, which is interesting in itself, is based on a combination of extensive Monte Carlo results, exact theoretical results using a formula in (Box, 1954), and on approximate theoretical results based on power series. The formula is accurate to about 1% over the fairly extensive regions studied, and it is quite plausible to conjecture that it is almost this accurate everywhere.] For any given configuration Y of n points, let $C(Y)$ be its actual coefficient of variation of the distances, and let $m(Y)$ be its shape. Then

$$C^*(Y) = C(Y)/E(m(Y), n)$$

is the first index of condensation we study.

During the discussion of "internal dimensionality" we saw that the behavior of the cdf of interpoint distances around the medium small values of distance appeared relevant to an index of condensation. Yet here we are using an index C^* which also depends on all the distances, and is in fact sensitive to the behavior of the cdf for large distances. At one stage of this investigation I hoped that C^* might nevertheless be good enough to lead to useful results. Subsequent results, which are presented below, have dispelled this hope.

However, it is possible to improve the index by transforming the distances before calculating the index of variability C. An appropriate transformation should squeeze together the larger distances, so as to deemphasize them, and spread apart the smaller ones. Any pth power transformation with $p < 1$ has this property. Values of $p \leq 0$ lead to difficulties, so the range of interest is $0 < p < 1$. Based strictly on intuition, I have chosen $p = \frac{1}{4}$, and started investigation of $C_{1/4}$, the corresponding coefficient of variation. (J. W. Tukey, personal communication, has suggested using $p = \frac{2}{7}$.) An adequate approximate formula for $E_{1/4}(m, n)$, the expected value $C_{1/4}$, has not yet been developed, but certain evidence presented below suggests that

$$C_{1/4}{}^* = C_{1/4}/E_{1/4}$$

may be substantially better than C^*. This is the second index of condensation studied in this paper.

The Conditional Expected Value and Distribution of $C(Y)$ Given the Shape of Y

Suppose we pick some points $y_1, \ldots, y_n$ in r-dimensional space as random independent points from a normal distribution centered at the origin. Let Y be the matrix whose rows are the y_i. We are interested in the expected value and the distribution of $C(Y)$, *conditioned* on the points y_i having sample mean $\bar{y} \equiv \sum y_i/n$ equal to 0 and having shape $m(Y)$ equal to a fixed, prespecified value m_0. We shall use $E(m_0, n)$ to denote the expected value of $C(Y)$ under these circumstances. It can be proved that $E(m_0, n)$ and the whole conditional distribution of $C = C(Y)$ given $m(Y) = m_0$ are independent of the population covariance matrix from which the y_i were drawn (only supposing that it is nonsingular, so that the conditioning makes sense).

FACT. To a very good degree of approximation (about 1% in the cases tested), the expected value $E(m_0, n)$ (of the sample coefficient of variation of the interpoint distances among n random normal independent points, conditioned on the points having mean 0 and shape $m(Y) = m_0$) is given by the product

$$E(m_0, n) = R(\nu(m_0), n)C_\infty(\nu(m_0))$$

where ν, R, and C_∞ are defined as follows:

Let $m_0 = (m_1, \ldots, m_r)$, let $\| m_0 \| = (\sum m_i{}^2)^{1/2}$ let $\lambda_s = (m_s/\| m_0 \|)^2$, and let the function g be defined by $g(x) = x/(1 + x)$. Then $\nu(m_0)$, which we call the "global dimension" of shape m_0, is defined by

$$\nu(m_0) = [\sum g(\lambda_s)]^2 / \sum g^2(\lambda_s)$$

The global dimension is of course in general not an integer. Note that if m_0 is spherical, then the global dimension equals the ordinary dimension. The global dimension is a modification of the number of degrees of freedom in the Satterthwaite (see Box, 1954) approximation for a linear combination of χ^2 variables as a single scaled χ^2 variable.

The function R is given by

$$R(\nu, n) = \left(1 - \frac{\nu}{n - 1} \right)^{1/2}$$

or with slightly greater accuracy,

$$R(\nu, n) = \left[1 - \frac{\nu - 1/(n - 1)}{n - 1 - 1/(n - 1)} \right]^{1/2}$$

The function $C_\infty(\nu)$ is the coefficient of variation of a χ distribution (not a χ^2 distribution) having ν degrees of freedom, and is given by the power series

$$C_\infty(\nu) = \frac{1}{(2\nu)^{1/2}} \left[1 + \frac{1}{8}\frac{1}{\nu} - \frac{9}{128}\frac{1}{\nu^2} + \cdots \right]$$

It may be thought of as the expected value of $C(Y)$ when $n = \infty$. When only the terms shown are used, the resulting value is about 1.3% too large for $\nu = 1$, .05% too large for $\nu = 2$, and increasingly accurate for larger values of ν.

Let $H_{m_0,n}(\gamma)$ be the cumulative distribution function (cdf) for $C(Y)$, where Y is conditioned as above. Figure 1 presents Monte Carlo curves of $H_{m_0,n}$ for $n = 10$ and spherical shapes of global dimension from $\nu_0 = 1$–7. Note how the curves appear to be horizontal multiples of one another. This suggests that the true cdfs may be representable by a function $H_n(\gamma)$ which is independent of shape m_0, with the abscissa multiplicatively ad-

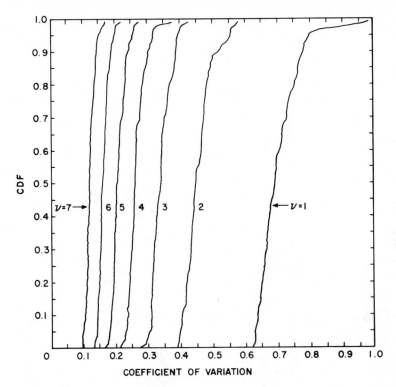

FIG. 1. Cumulative distribution graphs of the coefficient of variation from spherical normal distribution in ν dimensions. 10 points for each sample, 100 samples for each curve.

justed according to $E(m_0, n)$:

CONJECTURE. There is a function $H_n(\gamma)$ such that either exactly, or to a good approximation,

$$H_{m_0,n}(\gamma) = H_n(\gamma/E(m_0, n))$$

Even though this conjecture is not important to the rest of this paper, its correctness would add a certain esthetic appeal. A more sensitive graphical test of this idea is based on a scatter plot (or so-called q–q plot) of each of these seven curves against some composite. Figure 2 displays such a plot. The fact that the curves lie almost on straight lines through the origin gives more accurate substantiation to the conjecture. (The composite was made by averaging "horizontally" across the seven C values for a given p value. If the conjecture were true and the curves contained no

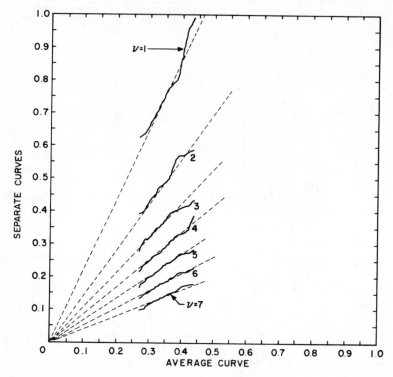

FIG. 2. Scatter diagram (q-q plot) for each curve from Figure 1 against an average curve.

statistical error, this would lead to precisely straight lines through the origin. However, to give equal weight to the fluctuations in the different curves, it would have been better to have taken the geometric average, or alternatively, to have transformed the C scales logarithmically before starting this process.)

Results So Far with Synthetic Data

Unfortunately, Monte Carlo results indicate that C^* is too much affected by the larger distances to be really useful. For example, random points were generated in the plane whose x-coordinates are clustered tightly (precisely equal in groups), but whose y-coordinates are independent random numbers. Then the y-coordinates were multiplied by a number t

which ranged from 0 up, and C^* calculated as a function of t. For 20 points grouped into ten clusters of two points, C^* did decrease as t increased from 0 to .3 (steps of .1) as we would hope, but rather too gently. Two typical examples are given here:

$$
\begin{array}{ccccc}
t = & 0 & .1 & .2 & .3 \\
C^* = & .966 & .946 & .936 & .938 \\
C^* = & 1.396 & 1.369 & 1.347 & 1.337
\end{array}
$$

Such a strong clustering as we have here should show up much more strongly. In particular, we would like the variation of C^* as t changes to be substantially larger than the variation of C^* from one sample to another, so that the large value of C^* for $t = 0$ would reliably indicate the strong clustering which actually occurs there.

Experiments with many similar situations involving five groups of four points each reveal a more rapid decline for t in the same region, which is natural since the clustering is even stronger. However, in these experiments t was continued up to the value 1. It was quite common for the value of C^* to start increasing around $t = .5$ or so, and occasionally C^* at $t = 1$ is larger than C^* at $t = 0$. Since $t = 1$ has no intended clustering and $t = 0$ has strong clustering, this particular behavior of C^* is a serious fault of the index.

Experiments were also done with points on circles, on helices, and on several radial lines. From these experiments, the conclusion clearly emerges that though C^* has tendencies in the right direction, a better index is needed.

At present, work is proceeding based on $C_{1/4}^*$, as explained earlier. A very brief preliminary experiment using five random sets of 20 points on a circle yield five values for the coefficient of variation ranging from .166 to .200. By comparison, five diffuse sets of 20 points in two dimensions yielded coefficients of variation ranging from .133 to .159. The averages of the two sets of values are .1858 and .1434, and the ratio of these averages is 1.30. These figures are a very hopeful sign of the value of the index.

The Problem of Optimizing

Even if a good index of condensation is discovered, its practical value depends in part on the feasibility of optimizing it over a suitable set of linear transformations.

Even though I have not yet arrived at a usable index of condensation, my experience at optimizing the interim indices is relevant to the optimization difficulties.

The first interim index was C itself, the coefficient of variation of the distances. Even though the need for compensation was clear in principle, I did not have the formula for $E(m, n)$ and it seemed worthwhile to see what would happen if C itself was optimized.

Working with me, Mr. Frank Carmone (now at the University of Waterloo) constructed a program to maximize C, which is based on a reasonably general package of programs for optimizing functions by an iterative gradient technique, called OPTPAK, which I had constructed a few years ago. (OPTPAK was originally used to implement a procedure, now called MONANOVA, to find the monotonic transformation which makes data from a factorial design most nearly additive. The theory and use of MONANOVA are fully described in Kruskal, 1965, and Kruskal & Carmone, 1969.)

Carmone experimented with this program on various sets of input data. While it does not seem worthwhile to describe the results in detail, because of the limitations of C (and even C^*) as an index of condensation, it does seem that optimization is practical, though not a routine matter. Thus it is reasonable to guess that it will be possible to find the optimum (or optima— several local optima can all be of interest) of an improved index of condensation. However, the user may have to pay some attention to the question of whether convergence is sufficiently complete and will probably want to start the process from several different starting configurations, since the method of optimizing is not sufficiently powerful to allow the user to drop such precautions.

It is possible to describe briefly in an intuitive way what happens during the iterative gradient optimization of C^*. At each iteration, the derivatives pertaining to C try to make the short distances shorter, and the long distances longer, since this increases C. Likewise, the derivatives pertaining to E (in the denominator of C^*) tend to pull points together along the long principal component directions, and tend to spread the points apart along the short principal component directions, since this increases global dimensionality ν and decreases $E(m, n)$. Of course, every point is subject to many forces in partial conflict from all these tendencies. In order for this process to head directly and "purposefully" toward a maximum value of C^*, it is probably necessary for many short interpoint distances to lie approximately in some linear subspace which needs to be collapsed. However, even if the starting configuration is not close enough to a maximum for this to happen, the process might well "wander around" for a while, until it does get close enough to a maximum to "see" it.

References

Box, G. E. P. Some theorems on quadratic forms applied in the study of analysis of variance problems, I. Effect of inequality of variance in the one-way classification. *Annals of Mathematics Statistics*, 1954, **25**, 290–302.

Forsythe, G., & Moler, C. B. *Computer solution of linear algebraic systems*. Englewood Cliffs, New Jersey: Prentice–Hall, 1967.

Gnanadesikan, R., & Wilk, M. B. Data analytic methods in multivariate analysis. In P. R. Krishnaiah (Ed.), *International symposium of multivariate analysis, Dayton, Ohio, 1968*. New York: Academic Press, 1969. Pp. 593–638.

Kruskal, J. B. Analysis of factorial experiments by estimating monotone transformations of the data. *Journal of the Royal Statistic Society* 1965, (Series B, methodological), **27**, 251–263.

Kruskal, J. B., & Carmone, F. J., Jr. MONANOVA: A FORTRAN IV program for monotone analysis of variance (non-metric analysis of factorial experiments). *Behavioral Science* 1969, **14**, 165–166.

Shepard, R. N. The analysis of proximities: multidimensional scaling with an unknown distance function. I. *Psychometrika*, 1962, **27**, 125–140.

Shepard, R. N., & Carroll, J. D. Parametric representation of nonlinear data structures. In P. R. Krishnaiah (Ed.), *International symposium of multivariate analysis, Dayton, Ohio, 1965*. New York: Academic Press, 1966. Pp. 561–592.

Trunk, G. V. Statistical estimation of intrinsic dimensionality of data collections. *Information and Control* 1968, **12**, 508–525.

THE GEOMETRIC
REPRESENTATION OF SOME
SIMPLE STRUCTURES

Richard L. Degerman

UNIVERSITY OF CALIFORNIA
IRVINE, CALIFORNIA

Investigators have often found it convenient to use geometric representation as a vehicle for understanding and describing certain classes of psychological phenomena. For problems where the restrictions of the metric axioms are tolerable, a multidimensional configuration often appears to convey much of the essential information in the data in a form that can be readily assimilated. The correspondence between the data and the geometrical configuration is usually brought about by assuming that the original data are related in some way to aspects of geometry, such as the angles between vectors, the distances between points, or the projection of one vector on another. Although points may be embedded in Euclidean space by a number of techniques, the fundamental geometric characteristics of the obtained metric spaces remain essentially the same. Such characteristics are generally assumed to exist by virtue of the geometry of the situation rather than by any particular characteristic of the scaling algorithm.

In dealing with experimental data, an interpretation cannot be made solely on the basis of the final solution of points in a configuration. For all types of problems, an investigator attempting to interpret a solution is obliged to admit that his interpretation is based partly on the characteristics of the original data, partly on the structure imposed by the analytical model, and partly on the assumed invariant characteristics of the metric space. (In many cases, the latter two are inextricably combined.) It is a rare occasion on which an interpretation can be restricted to the data itself without reference to a theoretical model. For this reason, it is important to consider some of the aspects of structure which may be characterized in the geometry itself.

It is the purpose of this paper to give an account of a few of the possible Euclidean structures. Some of these are elementary in form and have been in common use as interpretive devices for a number of years. Others, however, have only recently received attention as possible models of structure. It is an assumption in this paper that most of the structures can be discussed in terms of topological structures in Euclidean space without particular reference to idiosyncrasies of particular analytical techniques. Accordingly, the notion of a family of structures can be used to advantage even though any single analytical technique alone may not be appropriate for all structures. Furthermore, the discussion of structure as an abstract construct of spatial geometry is not assumed to demand empirical data in order to be meaningful. From the empirical viewpoint, some of the following structures will prove more plausible than others; however, this fact should not preclude their discussion on formal grounds.

Basic Structures

To begin a discussion of structures in general, it is convenient to start with a description of certain basic structures. From the simple structures, more complex ones may then be derived by the application of specified rules and operations. The choice of which structures to consider basic is a somewhat arbitrary one; so, too, is the choice of the accompanying rules and operations. This account will be based on two operations and three basic structures, where such structures can exist alone or can occur together as a result of being combined by means of one or more of the basic operations.

THE D STRUCTURE—QUANTITATIVE DIMENSIONS

A fundamental notion in multivariate analysis is that of a unidimensional structure, or more simply, a dimension. A rigorous definition is hardly necessary here. But it is worthwhile to note some of the features which have usually been ascribed to this structure. Most commonly, a dimension is taken to be equivalent to a segment of the real line or to a one-dimensional Euclidean subspace. The important characteristics are those relating to continuity and order, by means of which a dimension is assumed to be capable of representing continuous, ordered variation. In addition, certain other relations such as "betweenness" for sets of points (Restle, 1961) and additivity of segments (Beals, Krantz, & Tversky, 1968) are essential concepts.

For obvious reasons, multidimensional techniques have not been used extensively for scaling unidimensional stimuli. It is of interest to note, however, that techniques designed for *multi*dimensional use also appear to perform well in scaling the basic unidimensional structure. For example, Torgerson (1951) found that judgments for sets of gray stimuli varying along the quantitative dimension of brightness yielded a unidimensional solution which agreed favorably with a scale obtained by the traditional method of paired comparisons. Shepard (1962), in reanalyzing some previous data, found that stimulus sets consisting of circles of different sizes were adequately scaled in one quantitative dimension.

Unidimensional scales need not derive from physical dimensions, however. Data reported by Guttman (1961) on ten personality traits, for example, indicated a one-dimensional structure ranging from traits of internal focus (self-rejection, paranoia) on the one hand, to traits of external focus (conservatism, left opinionation) on the other. An additional study, concerning attitudes toward Negroes, showed that the particular attitudes under investigation were arranged according to a linear scale of personal conduct, where one end of the scale concerned face-to-face contact and the other involved only the use of stereotypes (Guttman, 1961). In the above examples, it is important to note that the outcome of unidimensionality occurred in all of the cases despite the fact that different methods were used to collect and scale the data. Thus there seems to be ample evidence in support of the fundamental nature of the unidimensional structure.

Other concepts of unidimensionality are possible but will not be discussed in detail here. One is that of intrinsic or local dimensionality, and another is the related concept of the unidimensionality of the semantic principal components (Guttman, 1954). Furthermore, non-Euclidean unidimensional structures (e.g., Guttman, 1955b) will not be discussed. Cases such as these are mentioned, however, in order to emphasize that the present discussion of unidimensional basic structure does not encompass the entire range of so-called unidimensional variation.

The C Structure—Discrete Classes

The search for clusters in spatial configurations has long been a common practice. Only recently, however, has the class structure itself been given separate formalization in terms of multidimensional scaling. Torgerson (1965, 1968) has remarked that a consideration of n-dimensional geometry leads directly to the idea that discrete classes can be embedded in space in very simple structures. Since members of a single class are usually very similar to each other, they should be found clustered next to each other in space while at the same time separated from members of other distinct classes. The idea of embedding mutually exclusive, independent, nominal classes in space then leads to a structure where the n class prototypes are located at the corners of the geometrical n-simplex in $n-1$ dimensions. Three such classes would be located at the corners of a triangle in two-space, and four such classes would be found at the corners of a three-dimensional tetrahedron, for example. If the classes are equally dissimilar to each other, then the structure will be a regular n-simplex; otherwise it will be irregular to the extent that some pairs of classes are more similar than others. From the framework of the independent, nominal class structure other class structures are also easily visualized. Class mixtures, for example, can be considered as points located on the edges, faces, or interior of the n-simplex, according to the nature of the mixture. For the discrete class structure, therefore, an essential feature is the requirement that certain areas of the space be inherently void of points while other locations allow clusters of points to appear. While the notion of holes in the space may give rise to difficulties in terms of the mathematics of topology, this type of structure will nevertheless prove very useful and will be considered for present purposes as a valid type of structure.

A few experiments have produced data verifying the class structure as a model underlying judgments. For example, Künnapas, Mälhammar, and Svenson (1964) examined similarity judgments on a set of seven different geometric figures. When these judgments were later scaled by the present writer with an iterative multidimensional technique, the configuration was found to form a tetrahedron structure in three dimensions with triangle, circle, square, and cross at the four vertices. Furthermore, mixed figures, such as the diamond and hexagon, occurred at appropriate intermediate locations. In an investigation of taste similarity, Yoshida (1963) found that the resulting structure corresponded reasonably well to the Henning taste tetrahedron, with the majority of the taste solutions clustering about the four vertices, saline, sweet, sour, and bitter. In another area, Green and Rao (1969) investigated the similarity of selected television shows and found a configuration revealing a class structure, with a triangular configuration containing westerns, detective stories, and variety shows clustered at three vertices. When situation comedies were included, a fourth cluster emerged to form a tetrahedron. Thus these examples hint at the wide range of application for which the discrete class structure can facilitate interpretation.

A few comments should be made here concerning the validity and permanence of such class structures. First, these structures arise out of manifest characteristics of the data, and in that sense are real. Although the structures appear to be trivial at times, they are not necessarily degenerate solutions. The fact that some scaling techniques tend to give degenerate solutions in these cases should not obscure the fact that in many cases class structures really underlie the judgments and would still arise even if error-free unbiased data were available for analysis by means of traditional metric methods. Secondly, the existence of clusters depends greatly on the nature of the stimulus set. Clusters may come and go, depending on the particular choice of stimuli, on the context, and on the experimental set or instructions given to the subject. Consequently, it is unwise to expect the class structure always to reflect a stable invariant structure from one context to another. For purposes of analyzing a particular set of data, however, the existence of classes can tentatively be determined, and an interpretation can be made in terms of classes, apart from any discussion of the natural or artificial origin of the classes themselves. It is this sense of an abstract class space which is carried through the rest of this paper.

THE S STRUCTURE—HYPERSPHEROIDAL (CIRCUMPLICIAL) ORGANIZATION

Circular structures have appeared frequently enough in the literature to warrant special treatment here. In some domains, variation appears to be continuous and forms a closed circular structure reflecting qualitative differences. This circular-order effect has been called the *circumplex* by Guttman (1954) and has occurred in several experimental contexts, notably those of the color circle (Shepard, 1962) and the circular tones (Shepard, 1964, personal communication). As Guttman (1954) initially stated, this concept of a closed structure is not confined to that of a circle, but could be extended to the general idea of a hypersphere if and when appropriate data are found. For reasons of generality, therefore, the S structures will be considered here to be those structures which resemble hyperspheroids (with circles being special cases). A more appropriate name for this concept might be that of "generalized circumplex" or hypercircumplex. However, we will often use hyperspheroid to denote this concept, with spheroid and

"S" appearing as abbreviated forms in the figures. An important point is that this structure need not be exactly circular. Any closed, ordered structure similar to a circle or hyperspheroid will be considered to belong to this same general category.

Another interesting example of a circular structure is contained in the theory of emotions outlined by Schlosberg (1952). In this theoretical structure, active emotional expressions are taken to form a circular series going from happiness and love, through surprise, fear, anger, disgust, and contempt, and finally returning back to happiness again. In addition to the natural circumplices described above, numerous examples of *derived* circumplices come from Guttman's facet theory. For certain facet designs, the principle of contiguity maintains that facets may be arranged in a circular order, where adjacent facets differ on only one component (Foa, 1958).

While the status of the circumplex as a basic structure may also be open to question, the advantage of treating it in a fundamental sense will become evident in the context of interpretation of derived structures. Consequently, we will consider the generalized circumplex as one of the basic structures.

Basic Operations

ORTHOGONAL COMPOSITION OF STRUCTURES

According to the operation of Cartesian products, two structures may be combined orthogonally to form a new structure in the product space. When a structure A has r points in m dimensions and B has s points in n dimensions, the Cartesian product, $A \times B$, will consist of rs points in $n + m$ dimensions, thus producing a composite space with the two original structures in disjoint subspaces. Since the composition is accomplished orthogonally, the original (basic) structures may be subsequently revealed by orthogonal projection into the appropriate subspaces. Thus the problem of orthogonal composition may be viewed in reverse: Given an $(n + m)$-dimensional configuration, we may ask whether it is possible to find an orthogonal rotation which will reveal the existence of some basic component structures in the separate projections. In another context, Harris (1955) has already shown the importance of viewing multivariate analysis in terms of a resolution of variation into constituent orthogonal components.

NESTING OF STRUCTURES

It is also convenient to invoke a concept of nesting, or inclusion of structures. In a broad sense, this means that the characteristics of one structure are intrinsically induced in another structure. Above, orthogonal combination was described as one structure being superimposed on another; however, this extrinsic type of relation did not in any way alter the subspace of the original structures. In the present case, however, the nesting operation gives rise to new structures and new subspaces which are somehow qualitatively different from the component parts. The new characteristics arise because one structure becomes an essential, integral part of the other.

An additional concept, that of the origin of a structure, is necessary to facilitate the interpretation of nested structures. When one structure is induced in another, the orientation of the structures with respect to each other becomes important. For the dimensional structure, the origin will be taken in the conventional sense as the (rational) zero point. For a class, the origin will be a prototype or class exemplar; for clusterings, the origin will be taken as the disjoint partition. In the case of generalized circumplices, it is natural to refer to the focal point as the *pole* of the circumplex. This general concept of the origin then allows us to specify the particular orientation of a nested structure with respect to the overall structure and allows us to say that one part of the structure is more central than another.

Derived Structures

With three basic structures, eighteen possible binary composites can be formed when two basic operations are allowed. Figure 1 shows the nine

	D Dimensions	C Classes	S Spheroids
D Dimensions	D x D	D x C	D x S
C Classes	C x D	C x C	C x S
S Spheroids	S x D	S x C	S x S

Fig. 1. Nine possible structures resulting from the Cartesian products of three basic structure types. (Spheroids are to be taken in the sense of generalized circumplices.)

	D Dimensions	**C** Classes	**S** Spheroids
D Dimensions	$D_{(D)}$	$D_{(C)}$	$D_{(S)}$
C Classes	$C_{(D)}$	$C_{(C)}$	$C_{(S)}$
S Spheroids	$S_{(D)}$	$S_{(C)}$	$S_{(S)}$

Fig. 2. Nine possible structures resulting from the nesting of one basic structure type within another.

derived structures obtained from all possible binary Cartesian products, and Figure 2 indicates the nine binary nested structures. Due to the symmetry of Cartesian products, however, structures below the diagonal in Figure 1 are essentially the same as those above the diagonal. Therefore, only six different binary Cartesian product structures remain. The following sections describe each of the 15 different structures included in the three families. Each of these 15 structures will be considered simple since they involve only the binary combination of basic structures. It is clear, however, that greater degrees of complexity could be achieved by concatenating a number of structures with several operations.

CARTESIAN PRODUCT STRUCTURES

D × D—EUCLIDEAN SPACE. When the real line R^1 is crossed with itself an additional $n - 1$ times, the result is R^n, or n-dimensional space with Euclidean properties. Thus, D × D is equivalent to the Euclidean plane. A number of studies have reported results interpretable under this framework. For example, Nurminen (1965) obtained data on nine circles constructed by taking all combinations of three sizes and three shades of gray. A multidimensional scaling solution for her data yields a nearly perfect configuration containing the two expected dimensions, size and grayness. Kingsbury (1968), using butterflies of different sizes and different wing angles obtained two-dimensional configurations with appropriate variation and spacing on each axis. For a more abstract stimulus set, Kuno and Suga

(1966) scaled the similarity between some 30-sec passages of piano music from various composers and obtained two dimensions, one going from Beethoven to Scarlatti and the other going from Liszt to Debussy. Other two-dimensional structures which might be mentioned are those of Morse-code signals (Shepard, 1963), size and brightness, and size and angle of tilt of triangles (Attneave, 1950), and size and bottom-heaviness (shape) of kites (Torgerson, 1965). In addition to these, a number of other examples could be given to demonstrate the pure dimensional structure; however, the examples given here will be taken as representative of the others. In some cases, notably those with salient analyzable dimensions, the non-Euclidean city-block metric is found to give slightly better fits. But the Euclidean fit is close enough in most cases to allow us to consider these examples under the Euclidean framework.

D × C—THE CLASS-QUANTITATIVE STRUCTURE. When classes all vary on orthogonal quantitative dimensions, the clusters in space become elongated in the direction of the orthogonal dimensions. With one orthogonal dimension superimposed on the classes, for example, they become lines in space; with two orthogonal quantitative dimensions, the classes take on the form of planes, etc. This model was proposed by Torgerson (1965, 1968) and has received a fair amount of empirical support from several sources. In a study reported by Torgerson (1965), a group of subjects was found to judge a set of kites on the basis of both a class dimension (sign of asymmetry) and a quantitative dimension (degree of asymmetry), thus resulting in a structure of the class-quantitative type. When an analysis with iterative multidimensional techniques is performed on data on similarity of parallelograms obtained by Künnapas, Mälhammar, and Svenson (1964), the series of figures is found to fall in a configuration with one dimension being continuous (shape variation) and the other being discrete (horizontal versus vertical orientation). In a related area, Degerman (1970) found that classes of geometric figures varying in size and brightness clustered around planes in space. And for the confusion of six English vowels in short-term memory, a reanalysis of Wickelgren's data (1965a) gives a two-dimensional configuration which could be interpreted as the continuous dimension "width of vocal tract" crossed with the binary dimension "front versus back articulation," in accord with the distinctive feature system of conventional phonemic analysis. Thus a body of data is quickly accumulating to bring focus on the importance of the class–quantitative (D × C) structure. Difficulties in interpretation sometimes arise, however, when there is a question about the actual existence of classes. The English vowel configuration is a case in point. Here, the two dimensions could alternatively be labeled as the first and second formants of the vowels, thus giving a reasonable D × D interpretation instead of the D × C distinctive feature interpretation. Thus, the investigator should be warned of the possibility of such indeterminacies when he is attempting to label classes and dimensions in his configuration.

D × S—THE HYPERCYLINDER STRUCTURE. When dimensions are crossed with circles, a type of cylinder is produced in which movement in some directions will be along straight lines, while in other directions it will be along curves. A good example of this structure comes from the color-chip data of Indow and Kanazawa (1960). For selected subsets of stimuli where chroma is held constant, a slightly warped cylinder is revealed. In this case, the circular aspect pertains to hue, and the orthogonal quantitative dimension is represented by Munsell value (brightness). The authors noted that the brighter and darker levels can be projected into a single plane without contradiction, thus indicating that the walls of the cylindrical configuration are roughly perpendicular to the plane of constant value.

C × C—THE PARADIGM STRUCTURE. If an r-simplex class structure in $r - 1$ dimensions is crossed with an s-simplex in $s - 1$ dimensions, the result is a class structure with rs points in $r + s - 2$ dimensions. This structure itself is not a simplex, but can be thought of as a simplicial complex. The components of this structure are related to the *facets* of Guttman's theory (Foa, 1965); and the entire complex itself is similar in spirit to the *cartet* as discussed by Cattell (1966). An important characteristic of the C × C structure is that the dimensionality of the orthogonal combination of class structures is the sum of the dimensionalities of the components. Therefore, a C × C structure is likely to reside in a space of high dimensionality, and for this reason is likely to be difficult to interpret. Furthermore, numerous variations of the overall class structure can occur, depending on the kind of component class structure involved (whether nominal, mixed, nested, etc.), thus making the structure even more complicated. Regardless of the complexity of the component class structures, however, it should always be possible to obtain a rotation of a C × C structure which will project the points down into a rectangular lattice of points, thus revealing the essence of the paradigm (facet) structure in a subspace of low dimensionality.

A good example of a C × C × C structure comes from short term memory data for digrams (Wickelgren, 1965b). Eight syllables (digrams) were formed from combinations of three binary classes: (i) vowel: ā versus ō; (ii) consonant: f versus n; and (iii) vowel-consonant order: VC versus

CV. A priori predictions would place the eight stimuli (āf, ān, ōf, ōn, fā, nā, fō, nō) at the eight corners of a cube in three dimensions (one dimension for each of the binary classes). Subsequent multidimensional scaling analyses of Wickelgren's data in fact reveal a boxlike configuration, thus essentially confirming the expectation of a paradigm structure.

Another interesting structure, coming from linguistic theory is that representing the kernel (K) sentence plus the seven transformations possible with the passive (P), negative (N), and interrogative (Q) transformations: K, P, N, Q, PN, PQ, NQ, PNQ. Miller (1962) displayed these eight transformations in a symbolic sense as the eight corners of a cube. A subsequent test by Clifton and Odom (1966), however, demonstrated that the configuration is more tent shaped than cube shaped. Therefore, the Clifton and Odom analysis called into question the existence of a true C × C × C paradigm structure for this aspect of transformational theory, and a different theory was cited to explain the discrepancy.

C × S—THE CLASS–CIRCUMPLEX STRUCTURE. If all classes vary orthogonally on a circumplicial structure, then the result is a class–circumplex model, where all classes are in the form of a circumplex of one type or another. This structure is rarely found in empirical research, but plausible examples are easily constructed. Geometric figures (triangles, circles, and squares) varying on, say, 14 different hues would form such a structure in four dimensions. Two of the dimensions would contain the three-simplex class structure, and the other two dimensions would contain the circular hue structure. For another example, pictures of the Schlosberg active emotional expressions, for both men and women, would be expected to form a three-dimensional structure, with one dimension revealing the male–female classification, and the other two containing the circular component of Schlosberg's emotion configuration (Schlosberg, 1952; Shepard, 1962).

S × S—THE SPHEREX STRUCTURE. The full Cartesian product of one circle with another is a surface in four dimensions. Such a surface is related to a torus in three dimensions. One study (Foa, 1965) has reported this type of structure, and it involved investigation of components of interpersonal behavior in terms of perceptual and behavioral facets. The eight perceptual types, as well as the eight behavioral types, were found to form circular complexes. The structure resulting from the Cartesian product of such circular structures has been called a *spherex* (Foa, 1965). This term may be somewhat misleading for this general structure, however, since a spherex is not similar to a sphere or hypersphere. In general, the spherex, defined as the Cartesian product of generalized circumplices, is a somewhat circular structure containing holes, analogous to the torus. This type of structure is rather difficult to identify in a configuration of high dimensionality. However, Foa has suggested that the above spherex might be compressed into a three-dimensional torus with little distortion, and Guttman has indicated the possibility of further compression of the spherex into a two-dimensional horseshoe-shaped configuration (Guttman, 1966).

NESTED STRUCTURES

$D_{(D)}$—THE GUTTMAN SIMPLEX STRUCTURE. Observations can almost always be ordered within a variable, but when variables themselves can also be ordered, then another kind of structure is produced. Guttman (1955a) referred to this kind of order effect as the additive simplex (not to be confused with the geometrical n-simplex). In terms of set theory, this structure is described as a series of nested sets. Restle (1961) has pointed out that this type of structure is similar to the prothetic or quantitative dimensions of psychophysics.

Early descriptions of the additive simplex centered around ability tests of increasing complexity, where each test required all that the previous tests required, plus something more. Another example of the additive simplex comes from data on people's interest in news reports as a function of the remoteness of the source. Guttman (1961) reports on a study where subjects were found to be most interested in news about their local neighborhood, next in news about the local city, then nearby towns, and least interested in news from remote locations. This nested-order effect is an example of the $D_{(D)}$ structure. It is worthy to note that the $D_{(D)}$ structure, although unidimensional in a sense, is intrinsically different from the pure D structure. Guttman has remarked that the factor analysis of an n-variable additive simplex generates $n - 1$ common factors (a total of n factors) according to the "law of oscillations," whereas factor analysis of a unit-factor hierarchy gives only one common factor (Guttman, 1954).

$D_{(C)}$—THE INTENSIVE CLASS STRUCTURE. A dimension nested within a class structure produces classes which have an intrinsic dimension in common. The intrinsic or prothetic nature of this dimension implies that the classes themselves exist or vanish as a function of the value of the nested dimension. If a nominal class structure is visualized as a geometrical n-simplex of clusters, then a structure with rays extending from an origin (centroid) to each of the cluster types represents an intensive class structure. The structure of the original Abelson and Sermat (1962) configuration of facial expressions might be interpreted in this sense. The authors reported two main clusters of active expression (as opposed to the continuous circumplex constructed by Schlosberg). If a dimension of "activation" is considered to be nested within the obtained clusters of "actively pleasant" and "actively unpleasant," then this becomes an intensive class structure of two rays extending from the origin. When activation is high, the two classes of emotion are quite distinct; however, when activation is low, the two classes of emotion tend to merge and finally become indistinguishable when activation is zero (i.e., during unconsciousness). Another example might be that of an experiment with only three hues (red, green, and blue) varying in the full range of saturation. Such colors might be considered as classes which become very distinct at high saturations, but vanish as saturation diminishes to zero.

$D_{(S)}$—THE RADEX STRUCTURE. A family of concentric circumplices (hyperspheroids) constitutes a $D_{(S)}$ structure. The structure is that of a generalized circumplex with the addition of a nested quantitative attribute proceeding radially from an origin to the surface of the circumplex. This structure differs from the pure circumplex in that here a definite origin is implied. Guttman has reported on a number of radex structures. The most recent report describes a circular series of ability tests (numerical, figural, verbal) which range over various levels of complexity of required reasoning ability (Schlesinger & Guttman, 1969).

It is interesting to note that from a certain point of view principal component analysis can also be included in this category. The nested variable refers to the length of the test vector and the generalized circumplex is represented by the variation in the hyperspheroid containing the ends of the test vectors. Such a configuration can be subjected to orthogonal rotation and reflection, but cannot be translated from the natural origin without the loss of some of the original information. Ekman's complete vector model for qualitative and quantitative multidimensional scaling would also seem to fit in this category (Ekman, 1965). The quantitative aspect, referring to the potency of stimuli, is represented by the length of the nested radius vector, and the qualitative aspect is contained in the angular variation in the hyperspheroid. As Torgerson has remarked, Ekman's model is no doubt appropriate for some problems where the data conform to this type of structure, but the model often results in an inappropriately large number of dimensions when applied to data outside its domain (Torgerson, 1965).

$C_{(D)}$—THE NESTED ATTRIBUTE STRUCTURE. When clustering occurs along a continuum or in a continuous domain, a nested attribute structure may be present. Information on class membership alone does not fully describe the structure, nor does the quantitative information by itself. As an example, consider a set of sticks, each of a different length. If some of the sticks are very short (like toothpicks) and others are very long (like yardsticks), then the physical structure is one of classes (short versus long) nested within a continuous quantitative dimension (length in inches). Either type of information, when presented alone, would not capture the total impression given by the stimulus set.

Classes may also be nested within several continuous dimensions. An example might be that of clusters of people of high and low socio-economic status nested within two continuous dimensions, "years of education," and "net income." The essential difference between the $C_{(D)}$ nested class structure and the pure class structure (C) is that in the $C_{(D)}$ case the dimensions are assumed to be continuous and interpretable, while in the pure class structure the dimensions reflect only the same–different quality of the judgments and do not necessarily reflect interpretable underlying dimensions.

$C_{(C)}$—THE HIERARCHICAL CLASS STRUCTURE. The embedding of classes within classes yields a hierarchical class structure, or taxonomy. When successive nesting starts with the conjoint partition and continues through to the disjoint partition, a perfect hierarchical class structure is produced. Multidimensional scaling is not particularly useful for capturing the full structure of a *pure* hierarchy, however, because such a hierarchy of n stimuli requires $n - 1$ dimensions for perfect representation. In the first place, such configurations are hard to interpret. And due to metric indeterminacy, there is also great difficulty in obtaining a good solution for so few points in so many dimensions (Young, 1970). However, in many cases compression of such structures into a lower-dimensional space does not seem to have drastic effects on the composition of, and the relations among, the major clusters (Shepard, 1972, in press). Consequently, a great deal of information can be actually obtained from a compressed configuration, although some of the information pertaining to relative distances between classes and the independence of certain features is invariably lost. It is also well known that data appropriate for cluster analysis (as the similarity of word meanings used by Miller, 1969) can also be used to embed points in a Euclidean configuration. Such structures would consist of large clusters representing the major classes, with successively smaller clusters embedded within the larger ones.

$C_{(S)}$—THE CLUSTERED CIRCUMPLEX STRUCTURE. The $C_{(S)}$ structure is simply one where clusters are embedded or nested in regions of the generalized circumplex. Guttman (1954, p. 341) gives an example of this structure, clusters on a circumplex with reference to Thurstone's concept of simple structure. This type of structure is not a common one in multidimensional scaling configurations, however. Nevertheless, it is easy to give examples which would conform to such a structure. Consider, for example, a collection of color stimuli appearing in three general classes (greens, reds, and blues) where each class contains a number of different shades of the particular color. Such a set would yield colors which are treated as classes, but which are at the same time nested within the color circle.

$S_{(D)}$—THE STEREOGRAPHIC MAPPING STRUCTURE. Just as clusters can be nested in continuous dimensions, a circle can be mapped on the real line and a sphere can be mapped on the plane. This nesting of a circumplicial structure on a dimensional framework can be accomplished by stereographic projection. For this operation, the pole or origin of the circumplex must be specified and is identified with the origin of the dimensional structure. The points are then systematically projected from the circumplex down to the dimensional subspace, with the point at infinity being identified with the opposite pole of the circumplicial structure. Thus, the operation results in the mapping of a circumplex with a given intrinsic dimensiqnality onto a subspace of that same dimensionality and may therefore be considered as a type of data reduction. This structure is very similar to the results of the parametric mapping approach taken by Shepard and Carroll (1966). Their procedures were successful in mapping spherical configurations onto a plane and mapping circles onto the real line, for example. The primary importance of this kind of structure comes through the reduction in dimensionality and complexity which can be achieved, and the accompanying simplification of interpretation.

$S_{(C)}$—THE HYPERSPHEROIDAL CLUSTER STRUCTURE. When clusters take on the shape of hyperspheroids and this shape is reflected in the class subspace itself, the $S_{(C)}$ structure exists. It is similar to the S × C structure in the sense that the clusters are shaped like generalized circumplices. However, it differs in that there is no possible rotation which can separate the class component from the circumplicial component, since the two are inextricably nested together. Two circles side by side in a plane, or two spheroids side by side in three-space represent the simplest cases of this structure. To the writer's knowledge, no psychological structures of this general type have been demonstrated.

$S_{(S)}$—THE RINGEX STRUCTURE. The spherex was described above as a Cartesian product of generalized circumplices. In that structure, no part of any circumplex was more central than any other part, and any component circumplex could always be isolated from another by means of orthogonal rotation. When one circumplex is *nested* within another, however, part of the nested circumplex becomes more central than another part. The result, for the case of nesting one circular configuration in another, is a torus-shaped surface in three dimensions. This surface has been called a *ringex* by Foa (1965) and was used by Foa to reinterpret his original set of spherex data, with the additional assumption that some facets in one circumplex are more central than others. In topological terms, the centrality is evidenced by the fact that, for a torus, points on the inner circumference (along the "hole") are closer to the origin than points along the outer circumference. For the general ringex structure, therefore, portions of one circumplex are considered more central than other portions, and the one circumplex is embedded within the other with respect to a certain orientation. Furthermore, the nesting operation precludes a subsequent orthogonal projection for isolating the two component circumplices. These factors serve to distinguish the ringex structure from the spherex structure.

Discussion

A major purpose in seeking a spatial representation for a set of data is that of simplifying the job of data interpretation. A configuration embedded in a space of low dimensionality is more readily interpreted than a large array of numbers, since it places the data in a (spatial) framework, for which we have ready-made intuitions and preconceptions. The concepts outlined in this paper are intended to serve the same end. If we become acquainted with a family of structures, then we may be able to expand our repertoire of intuitive concepts and be more facile in interpreting configurations. Unfortunately, this is not the only possible outcome of an approach like this. The greatest drawback would seem to be the very real danger of reification of the structures. When constructs are outlined in concrete terms and have labels attached to them, there is a tendency for us to reify the constructs to such an extent that we lose perspective. We may be predisposed to "seeing" structures in the data when they are really not there. We may invent an elaborate interpretation when a simpler one would suffice.

It is important for us to try to expand our vocabulary of structural concepts while at the same time attempting to retain a certain amount of perspective. This can be done most effectively by trying different ways of looking at the data and by searching for alternative explanations. It is doubtful whether it is possible, or even desirable, to have a single all-purpose approach to spatial interpretation. What is needed is a flexible approach, including both the structural concepts and the analytical methods, which can be used creatively in treating each set of data in an individualized manner. It would be a mistake, for example, systematically to rotate all configurations by a varimax rotation prior to interpretation. Furthermore, other analytical or interpretive schemes are no doubt valid only in limited circumstances. In a similar sense, we should not feel bound to a certain family of structural concepts when we are attempting to describe the organization in a configuration. Different conceptual approaches will yield different families of structures, and each approach will have its own advantages and disadvantages. A reasonable goal, it seems, would be for us to strive to be versatile in our approach and maintain perspective in the analysis and interpretation of structure.

Acknowledgment

This paper was prepared, in part, while the author was a National Science Foundation predoctoral fellow at Johns Hopkins University.

References

Abelson, R. P., & Sermat, V. Multidimensional scaling of facial expressions. *Journal of Experimental Psychology*, 1962, **63**, 546–554.

Attneave, F. Dimensions of similarity. *American Journal of Psychology*, 1950, **63**, 516–556.

Beals, R., Krantz, D. H., & Tversky, A. Foundations of multidimensional scaling. *Psychological Review*, 1968, **75**, 127–142.

Cattell, R. B. *Handbook of multivariate experimental psychology.* Chicago, Illinois: Rand–McNally, 1966.

Clifton, C., & Odom, P. Similarity relations among certain English sentence constructions. *Psychological Monographs*, 1966, **80** (Whole No. 613).

Degerman, R. L. Multidimensional analysis of complex structure: Mixtures of class and quantitiative variation. *Psychometrika*, 1970, **35**, 475–491.

Ekman, G. Two methods for the analysis of perceptual dimensionality. *Perceptual and Motor Skills*, 1965, **20**, 557–572.

Foa, U. G. The contiguity principle in the analysis of the structure in interpersonal relations. *Human Relations*, 1958, **11**, 229–238.

Foa, U. G. New developments in facet design and analysis. *Psychological Review*, 1965, **72**, 262–274.

Green, P. E., & Rao, V. R. T. V. show perceptions—A note on stimulus invariance in multidimensional scaling. Working paper, University of Pennsylvania, February 1969.

Guttman, L. A new approach to factor analysis: The radex. In P. F. Lazarsfeld (Ed.), *Mathematical thinking in the social sciences.* Glencoe, Illinois: Free Press, 1954. Pp. 258–348.

Guttman, L. A generalized simplex for factor analysis. *Psychometrika,* 1955, **20,** 173–192. (a)

Guttman, L. An additive metric for all the principal components of a perfect scale. *British Journal of Statistical Psychology,* 1955, **8,** 17–24. (b)

Guttman, L. The structuring of sociological spaces. *Transactions of the Fourth World Congress of Sociology,* 1961, **3,** 315–355.

Guttman, L. Order analysis of correlation matrices. In R. B. Cattell (Ed.), *Handbook of multivariate experimental psychology.* Chicago, Illinois: Rand–McNally, 1966. Pp. 438–458.

Harris, C. W. Separation of data as a principle in factor analysis. *Psychometrika,* 1955, **20,** 23–28.

Indow, T., & Kanazawa, K. Multidimensional mapping of Munsell colors varying in hue, chroma, and value. *Journal of Experimental Psychology,* 1960, **59,** 330–336.

Kingsbury, N. R. *The context effect in multidimensional scaling.* (Doctoral Dissertation: Johns Hopkins University) Ann Arbor, Michigan: University Microfilms, 1968, No. 68-16438.

Künnapas, T., Mälhammar, G., & Svenson, O. Multidimensional ratio scaling and multidimensional similarity of simple geometric figures. *Scandinavian Journal of Psychology,* 1964, **5,** 249–256.

Kuno, U., & Suga, Y. Multidimensional mapping of piano pieces. *Japanese Psychological Research,* 1966, **8,** 119–124.

Miller, G. A. Some psychological studies of grammar. *American Psychologist,* 1962, **17,** 748–762.

Miller, G. A. A psychological method to investigate verbal concepts. *Journal of Mathematical Psychology,* 1969, **6,** 169–191.

Nurminen, A. Evaluation of a technique for measuring subjective similarity. *Scandinavian Journal of Psychology,* 1965, **6,** 209–219.

Restle, F. *Psychology of judgment and choice, a theoretical essay.* New York: Wiley, 1961.

Schlesinger, I. M., & Guttman, L. Smallest space analysis of intelligence and achievement tests. *Psychological Bulletin,* 1969, **71,** 95–100.

Schlosberg, H. The description of facial expressions in terms of two dimensions. *Journal of Experimental Psychology,* 1952, **44,** 229–237.

Shepard, R. N. The analysis of proximities: Multidimensional scaling with an unknown distance function. II. *Psychometrika,* 1962, **27,** 219–246.

Shepard, R. N. Analysis of proximities as a technique for the study of information processing in man. *Human Factors,* 1963, **5,** 33–48.

Shepard, R. N. Circularity in judgments of relative pitch. *Journal of the Acoustical Society of America,* 1964, **36,** 2346–2353.

Shepard, R. N. Psychological representation of speech sounds. In E. E. David and P. B. Denes (Eds.), *Human communication: A unified view.* New York: McGraw–Hill, 1972, in press.

Shepard, R. N., & Carroll, J. D. Parametric representation of nonlinear data structures. In P. R. Krishnaiah, (Ed.), *International symposium of multivariate analysis, Dayton, Ohio, 1965.* New York: Academic Press, 1966. Pp. 561–592.

Torgerson, W. S. *A theoretical and empirical investigation of multidimensional scaling.* Unpublished doctoral dissertation, Princeton University, 1951.

Torgerson, W. S. Multidimensional scaling of similarity. *Psychometrika,* 1965, **30,** 379–393.

Torgerson, W. S. Multidimensional representation of similarity structures. In M. M. Katz, J. O. Cole, & W. E. Barton (Eds.), *The role and methodology of classification in psychiatry and psychopathology.* U. S. Department of Health, Education and Welfare. Washington, D.C.: U.S. Government Printing Office, 1968. Pp. 212–220.

Wickelgren, W. A. Distinctive features and errors in short term memory for English vowels. *Journal of the Acoustical Society of America,* 1965, **38,** 583–588. (a)

Wickelgren, W. A. Similarity and intrusions in short-term memory for consonant-vowel digrams. *Quarterly Journal of Experimental Psychology,* 1965, **17,** 241–246. (b)

Yoshida, M. Similarity among different kinds of taste near the threshold concentration. *Japanese Journal of Psychology,* 1963, **34,** 25–35.

Young, F. W. Nonmetric multidimensional scaling: Recovery of metric information. *Psychometrika,* 1970, **35,** 455–473.

INFORMATION DISTANCE
FOR DISCRETE STRUCTURES

John Paul Boyd

UNIVERSITY OF CALIFORNIA
IRVINE, CALIFORNIA

This paper outlines an information-theoretic approach[1] to the problem of using discrete algebraic models on data that have been perturbed by noise. Purely algebraic methods have been used in the past to arrive at interesting results on some domains such as language and kinship. One way to extend these results to other domains is to use more powerful algebraic models. This approach should be pursued, but simultaneously some interesting results may be obtained if some probabilistic slack is introduced into the theory. Information-theoretic measures can then be introduced which describe in a natural way the distances between (a) models and data, (b) different models, or (c) different sets of data.

Euclid as a Social Scientist

Multidimensional scaling, including the nonmetric variety, attempts to embed data points in a Euclidean space. This pursuit is enjoying growing

[1] A basic introduction in information theory is given in Ash (1965).

popularity in many disciplines despite the implausibility of the model in many areas of human behavior. If the model of man in behavioral psychology is characterized as a black box with nothing inside, then the scaling model can be seen as a black box with space inside. Space is not nothing, but it leaves the social scientist with the same empty feeling. In particular, if the explanatory power of the spatial model is compared to some of the major substantive problems of contemporary social science, the shortcomings of spatial models become painfully obvious. For example, what can embedding words in a space really tell us about the meaning and use of these words in sentences? What light does the scaling of role terms shed upon the social structure in which these roles are cast? The only nontrivial answer that comes to mind is that if one did have an interesting (i.e., nonmetric) model of a language or a social structure, then close words should substitute for each other in sentences and close roles should substitute for each other in social relations. That is, if "walk" is close to "run" and "He walks with Mary." is grammatical then so should the sentence "He runs with Mary." Similarly, if "captains" and "majors" are close then many of the social relations, privileges, and obligations should be nearly the same for both roles. Although similar items do tend to substitute for each other, as in these examples, the metric model tells us nothing about which sentences are grammatical or how the social roles operate.

Despite the inadequacy of the metric concept as a model of human behavior, its widespread use requires some explanation. It must be that there is something useful, if not enlightening, about the scaling of data. The key property that makes scaling useful, particularly in applied work, is the relative invariance of distance measures in different contexts. For example, one can scale verbal descriptions of market items with relatively little money. With a considerably greater outlay of cash, one can scale the behaviors toward these items in terms of product substitution effects. What makes the former scaling worthwhile is that, if done correctly, the cheap verbal distances correlate highly with the expensive market data. See Stefflre (this book, Volume II) for more details.

Discrete Systems or Cartesian Social Science

While multidimensional scaling has been prospering, a completely different line of thought that might be called discrete systems theory has been developed by Chomsky (e.g., 1963) and others. Scaling carefully fits objective data with implausible models while the MIT linguists use intuition as data for complex models. That is, the MIT linguists are model oriented rather than data oriented. Their systems are nonprobabilistic and nonmetric in their orientation. Examples of the kind of object to be found in their theories are sets, strings, relations, transformations, and trees. This tradition holds that man is more like a discrete system than a continuous space. The chapters in Volume 2 of *The Handbook of Mathematical Psychology* (1963) by Miller and Chomsky lucidly present this approach to complicated human behavior. It is significant that in some departments of psychology, graduate students are told to read everything *but* these chapters.

One natural way to represent a set Q of points in this tradition is as the Cartesian product of a collection of sets $X_1, X_2, \ldots, X_n$. That is, each q in Q corresponds to one and only one sequence $x_1 x_2 \cdots x_n$ where the x_i are members of X_i. For example, the phonemes of a language are often represented as a sequence of "distinctive features": thus, the English phoneme /b/ might be represented as a voiced, bilabial, plosive consonant—i.e., as the unique member of the intersection of voiced phonemes with bilabial phonemes with plosive phonemes with phonemes that are consonants. The most common number of values on each dimension is two, but any finite or even countably infinite cardinality for the Cartesian factors X_i would still be consistent with such a discrete systems approach.

If the factors X_i are ordered, say, according to their subscripts, then each point in their Cartesian product can be considered as the end point of a complete tree of "depth" equal to the number of factors. Cluster analysis attempts to make an assignment from the data points Q into a tree where no such restrictions are made on uniform depth. These two approaches are readily reconciled, and the only reason for the variation chosen here is to preserve the option of saying that two points are more similar if they agree only on the last factor than if they disagree on all factors. Thus if $X_i = \{a, b\}$, for $i = 1, 2, 3$, then we can choose a distance measure such that the sequence aaa is more similar to bba than it is to bbb. For example, consider the *Hamming* distance measure, which counts the number of factors where two points x, y have different values, i.e.,

$$d_{\mathrm{Ham}}(x, y) = \#\{i \mid x_i \neq y_i\} \quad \text{where } x = x_1 x_2 \cdots x_n \text{ and } y = y_1 y_2 \cdots y_n$$

So $d_{\mathrm{Ham}}(aaa, bbb) = 3$ but $d_{\mathrm{Ham}}(aaa, bba) = 2$. The Hamming distance is, of course, a special case of the "city-block metric." But notice that the Hamming distance takes no account of the ordering of the subscripts. That is, the Hamming distance is invariant under any permutation of the subscripts.

A distance measure that overcomes this difficulty might be called the *arabic* distance since it corresponds to the distance between binary numbers in arabic notation. First, let $x_i \oplus y_i$ be zero or one corresponding to x_i and y_i being the same or different. Then let

$$d_{\text{arab}}(x, y) = \sum_{i=1}^{n} 2^i x_i \oplus y_i$$

More generally still, we can define several finite topologies on trees. For example, the nonterminal nodes of a tree are also considered as points so that the points are all sequences of the form $x_1 x_2 \cdots x_i$ where $1 \leq i \leq n$ and $x_i \in X_i$ together with the empty string which corresponds to the root of the tree. The collection of subsets of points that include with each point $x_1 x_2 \cdots x_i$ all "initial substrings" $x_1 x_2 \cdots x_j$ for $1 \leq j < i$ satisfy the two conditions for a collection $\mathfrak{I}$ of "closed" sets to be a *topology* on X the set of points: The union of any two members of $\mathfrak{I}$ is a member of $\mathfrak{I}$, and the intersection of the members of each (possibly infinite) subfamily of $\mathfrak{I}$ is a member of $\mathfrak{I}$. Notice that single points different from the empty string are not closed. This means that the space is not *metrizable* in the sense that no distance function d exists that generates the same closed sets, starting with closed ϵ-balls around each point x: $\{y \mid d(x, y) \leq \epsilon\}$. This impossibility is a result of the "metrization theorem" in Kelly (1955). In the finite case, it is obvious since ϵ can be chosen smaller than the smallest distance.

An alternative way of looking at finite topologies is to consider instead reflexive, transitive relations, called *preorders*. If $\mathfrak{I}$ is a topology on a set X, then for each x in X, the intersection of all open sets containing x is denoted by N_x. Then the associated preorder $\leq_T$ on X is defined by $x \leq_T y$ if $N_x \subseteq N_y$. Lorrain (1969) has shown that for finite topologies the lattice of all topologies on a set X is isomorphic to the lattice of all preorders on X.

A slight problem with the interpretation of "closed" sets results from the fact that for finite sets any topology of closed sets also satisfies the axioms for open sets (where union and intersection are interchanged since open sets are complements of closed sets). However, even if we interpret the tree sets defined above as open instead of closed, the set of "new" closed sets still does not include all singletons and hence is still not metrizable. The collection $\mathfrak{I}$ that we have defined is sometimes used in linguistics as the domain of "transformations." Thus even metric spaces are not general enough to handle a broad class of topological structures useful to social scientists. The next section, however, represents a retreat from the full generality of topology and instead provides a context that will support reasonable distance functions based on information theory.

Transition Systems

Krohn, Langer, and Rhodes (1967) claim that any experiment can be regarded as a set of transformations on a set of states induced by the action of the stimuli. That is, one may define a set Q of states, a set S of inputs and a function $f: SQ \rightarrow Q$ which assigns to each input s and state q another state $f(s, q)$ which is the "result" of the particular input-state configuration. If one is conditioned by the probabilistic thinking that is distributed throughout social science, this formulation may seem rather unrealistic. Its workability depends heavily on a clever choice of inputs and states, together with an algebraic bag of tricks such as the "subset construction" that turns relations into functions. The fundamental attitude in this approach is that behavior is complicated but discrete and deterministic, and that the probabilistic appearance is a result of poor definitions, inadequate observation, and other noise.

We now consider the relation between a representation φ of the state space Q in a Cartesian product $X_1 X_2 \cdots X_n$ and the transition function $f: SQ \rightarrow Q$. Each input s determines a "partial function" $s: Q \rightarrow Q$ formed by "holding s constant" as follows: $s(q) = f(s, q)$. The action of s is said to be *triangular* if

$$\varphi(q) = x_1 x_2 \cdots x_n \text{ implies } \varphi(s(q)) = (s_1(x_1), s_2(x_1 x_2), \ldots, s_n(x_1 x_2 \cdots x_n))$$

where

$$s_k: X_1 X_2 \cdots X_k \rightarrow X_k, \quad 1 \leq k \leq n$$

Thus the action of s on each coordinate is dependent only upon that coordinate and its predecessors and is independent of its successors. These requirements are sufficiently strong to eliminate most of the permutations

TABLE 1
THE AMBRYM RULES FOR DETERMINING THE CLASS OF ONE'S FATHER, F, AND MOTHER, M

q_i	$F(q_i)$	$M(q_i)$
q_1	q_4	q_2
q_2	q_6	q_3
q_3	q_5	q_1
q_4	q_1	q_5
q_5	q_3	q_6
q_6	q_2	q_4

TABLE 2
THE ASSIGNMENT OF COORDINATES FOR THE AMBRYM STATE SET

q	$\phi(q)$
q_1	$x_1 y_1$
q_2	$x_1 y_2$
q_3	$x_1 y_3$
q_4	$x_2 y_1$
q_5	$x_2 y_3$
q_6	$x_2 y_2$

TABLE 3

THE TRIANGULAR DECOMPOSITION OF THE AMBRYM RULES

x_i	$F_1(x_i)$	$M_1(x_i)$	x_iy_j	$F_2(x_iy_j)$	$M_2(x_iy_j)$
x_1	x_2	x_1	x_1y_1	y_1	y_2
			x_1y_2	y_2	y_3
			x_1y_3	y_3	y_1
x_2	x_1	x_2	x_2y_1	y_1	y_3
			x_2y_2	y_2	y_1
			x_2y_3	y_3	y_2

of any given coordinate assignment. On the other hand, they are weak enough to allow representation of any transition system into coordinates such that the functions on X_i for each s_i and x_j in X_j, $j < i$, that send x_i in X_i onto $s_i(x_1x_2 \cdots x_i)$ are either constant functions or permutations of X_i.

The kinship system of the Ambrym tribe gives a simple example of triangular coding (Boyd, 1969). This society is divided into six classes, which we can denote by $q_1, \ldots, q_6$. There are two cultural rules which tell for a given class q_i the classes $F(q_i)$ and $M(q_i)$ of all the fathers and mothers of members of q_i. The rules are tabulated in Table 1. In Table 2 is tabulated the assignment φ of coordinates for the state set Q. This assignment of coordinates decomposes the two functions M and F into triangular actions given by M_i and F_i shown in Table 3. Formally this triangular decomposition means that $\varphi Fq = (F_1\varphi_1 q, F_2\varphi q)$ where $\varphi_1 q$ is the first coordinate of φq. The analogous formula holds for M. The implication of this decomposition is that the first component of φFq and φMq can be computed knowing only the first coordinates of φq. That is, we can form the quotient system, which approximates the six class system, with the two values x_1 and x_2 on the first coordinate and the rules M_1 and F_1 shown in Table 3. The empirical evidence for the validity of such an approximation is the existence of neighboring tribes which have the appropriate quotient system. See Boyd (1969) for further discussion and examples.

Information Systems

Let us try to build a bridge between the Krohn–Rhodes (see Arbib, 1968) representation of a transition system and the probabilistic data that might be before us. Since no scale assumptions have been made, a very natural statistic is one based on information theory. If P is a probability function on the product set XY, then the marginal distribution on X is defined by $P(x) = \sum_{y \in Y} P(x, y)$ and the conditional probability of y given x is $P(y \mid x) = P(x, y)/P(x)$. $H(Y \mid X)$, the *conditional uncertainty of Y given X* is defined in the usual way

$$H(Y \mid X) = -\sum_{x,y} P(x, y) \log P(y \mid x)$$

The relation R_P *associated* with P is defined to be the set of all pairs (x, y) in XY with nonzero probability. That is, $x R_P y$ if and only if $P(x, y) > 0$. Note that if $P(x) > 0$ for all x, then R_P is a function if and only if $H(Y \mid X) = 0$. A reasonable *function index* for such a probability function P on XY is the expression $1 - (H(Y \mid X)/H(Y))$, where $H(Y) = -\sum_y P(y) \log P(y)$ is the uncertainty of B. If the function index is one, then the associated relation R_P is a function and values of x in X uniquely determine a y in Y. That is, $P(y \mid x)$ is either zero or one for all pairs xy in XY. If the function index is zero, then X and Y are independent with respect to P.

In the case of a probabilistic version of a transition system, we have a probability function on QQS. This can be interpreted as a set of Q by Q matrices, one for each input or stimulus S. If we have defined the correct states and inputs so that $H(Q \mid QS)$ is near zero, then we have a good approximation to a transition system. The discrete analysis task is still to assign coordinates from $X_1 X_2 \cdots X_n$ to the states of Q.

The information-theoretic version of the Krohn–Rhodes representation of transition systems as a Cartesian product $X_1 X_2 \cdots X_n$ with triangular action for each of the input stimuli in S is that $H(X_i \mid X_1 X_2 \cdots X_i S) = 0$ for $1 \leq i \leq n$. If this uncertainty is not zero, the average ratio

$$(1/n) \sum_{i=1}^{n} H(X_i \mid X_1 \cdots X_i S)/H(X_i)$$

is a reasonable index of success which equals zero with perfect success and ones when the coordinates are conditionally independent with respect to the stimulus.

One of the main benefits of the triangular action requirement is that since $H(X_i \mid X_1 X_2 \cdots X_i S) = 0$ we have $H(X_1 \cdots X_i \mid X_1 \cdots X_i S) = 0$ so that the $X_1 \cdots X_i$ is a transition in its own right for each $i \leq n$. Such smaller systems formed from the larger system $X_1 \cdots X_n$ are the *quotient systems* discussed above. For example, the Ambrym system as presented in Table 1 represents an ideal that may not be conformed to completely in reality. That is, there may be a certain number of irregular marriages and hence irregular pairs of people u, v, where u is the mother of v where u and v

TABLE 4

HYPOTHETICAL FREQUENCIES OF FATHER–CHILD PAIRS (F) AND MOTHER–CHILD PAIRS (M) FROM CLASS PAIRS q_i AND q_j

	$P(q_iq_j \mid F)$						$P(q_iq_j \mid M)$					
	q_1	q_2	q_3	q_4	q_5	q_6	q_1	q_2	q_3	q_4	q_5	q_6
q_1	$\frac{1}{16}$	0	0	$\frac{1}{8}$	0	0	$\frac{1}{16}$	$\frac{1}{8}$	0	0	0	0
q_2	0	$\frac{1}{16}$	0	0	0	$\frac{1}{8}$	0	$\frac{1}{16}$	$\frac{1}{8}$	0	0	0
q_3	0	0	0	0	$\frac{1}{8}$	0	$\frac{1}{8}$	0	0	0	0	0
q_4	$\frac{1}{8}$	0	0	$\frac{1}{16}$	0	0	0	0	0	$\frac{1}{16}$	$\frac{1}{8}$	0
q_5	0	0	$\frac{1}{8}$	0	$\frac{1}{16}$	0	0	0	0	0	$\frac{1}{16}$	$\frac{1}{8}$
q_6	0	$\frac{1}{8}$	0	0	0	0	0	0	0	$\frac{1}{8}$	0	0

belong to class q_u and q_v, respectively, but where $Mq_v \neq q_u$. Such irregularities do not invalidate Table 1 as a model of social reality so long as (1) it can be shown that members of the society view such pairs as abnormal in some way and (2) such pairs do not occur too often. Evidence for the first condition could be gathered systematically but in practice has to be limited to quoting a native informant who feels that a child of such a pair is usually feebleminded. The information measures discussed in this paper are designed to measure the second requirement. Consider the hypothetical data shown in Table 4. Such data might be the result of tabulating actual genealogies, as opposed to opinions about ideal types. Table 4 was constructed by substituting $\frac{1}{8}$ for each 1 of the connection matrix corresponding to Table 1. Then the $\frac{1}{16}$'s were distributed in an interesting way. The column entropies $H(Q \mid F)$ and $H(Q \mid M)$ were equal to each other with the value 2.561. The joint uncertainties were $H(QQ \mid F) = H(QQ \mid M) = 3.250$. Thus the conditional uncertainties $H(Q \mid QF) = H(Q \mid QM) = H(QQ \mid M) - H(Q \mid M) = .689$ were equal. The function indices were both $1 - (.689/2.561) = .731$.

Notice, however, that the M matrix seems to correspond better to the coding of Table 2 since all the "errors," indicated by $\frac{1}{16}$'s, are incorrect only on the second coordinates. This better correspondence is reflected in the function indices for the first coordinates which is only .189 for F and is 1.000 for M.

No mention has been made so far of the problem of making unbiased statistical estimates of these information-theoretic measures. The problem is not completely solved although some work has been done. See for example Miller and Madow (1963) and Bašarin (1959).

Triangular Action, Distance, and Learning

The principle of triangular action may appear rather arbitrary at first. The information-theoretic framework, by imposing a natural metric, will help to motivate this notion by showing how systems with triangular coding can be reasonably learned or evolved. It will be shown in this section that the sequence of quotient systems, $X_1,\ X_1X_2,\ldots,\ X_1X_2\cdots X_n$, forms a plausible learning sequence in the sense that (1) each term of the sequence is close to the next term and (2) each system processes more information than its predecessors. The first condition establishes the possibility of learning the sequence, and the second provides the motivation for the individual or group doing the learning.

The standard information-theoretic distance measure between two partitions X, X' on the same probability space is $H(X\mid X') + H(X'\mid X)$, which can be interpreted as the amount of information needed to change from one system to the other. It can easily be verified that this is a true distance measure. It is interesting to note that equality holds in the triangle inequality so that

$$d(X, X'') = d(X, X') + d(X', X'')$$

if and only if either

$$H(X\mid X') = H(X'\mid X'') = 0 \qquad \text{or} \qquad H(X''\mid X') = H(X'\mid X) = 0$$

This can be interpreted to mean that the three points are "on a straight line," in analogy with Euclidean geometry. It can be shown that all the terms in the learning sequence suggested above line on a straight line in this sense.

Of course, the distance between transition systems is dependent upon the set S of stimuli, so the final distance measure is the distance using the conditional uncertainties

$$d(X, X') = H(X\mid X'S) + H(X'\mid XS)$$

Now suppose that X follows X' in the learning sequence. That is, $X = X'X_i$. An easy calculation shows that

$$d(X, X') = H(X\mid X'S) + H(X'\mid XS) = H(X_i\mid X'S)$$

The basic relation used in this calculation is

$$H(X\mid X'S) = H(X'X_i\mid X'S)$$
$$= H(X'\mid X'S) + H(X_i\mid X'S) = H(X_i\mid X'S)$$

where $H(X' \mid X'S) = 0$ by triangularity. This is a "close" distance relative to how far apart they could be, which is $H(X \mid S) + H(X' \mid S)$. In fact, if we let $U_i = X_1 X_2 \cdots X_i$, then the uncertainty can be broken up into the following sum

$$H(U_n \mid S) = H(X_1 \mid S) + H(X_2 \mid U_1 S) + \cdots + H(X_i \mid U_{i-1} S)$$

Thus the triangular action condition gives a straight-line learning sequence of small steps.

Summary and Conclusions

The particular metric used in this paper was based on information theory, but this is only one of several promising approaches and the author makes no claim for its ultimate superiority. The fact, however, that information theory does use probabilistic information, but no other scale assumptions, makes it particularly natural for discrete structures with some kind of frequency information. In addition, facts like the uncertainty measures being additive for direct products is of great theoretical and practical interest.

The main point of this paper is to stress that distance measures are more interesting if they are defined on models or between models and data. That is, a distance function is not of interest as a model but as a way of comparing and evaluating models. The models that seem to be most promising for explaining complicated human behavior are generally of the "discrete" type. The concept of "discreteness" is never defined since it is a scientific tradition rather than a mathematical concept. In general, however, a discrete model does not involve a distance function. Examples of discrete models are grammars, computer models, and kinship systems as illustrated in the Ambrym tribe. A short discussion of the evolutionary and coding implications of the Ambrym model demonstrates that discrete models can describe change and processes, so that the static–dynamic and structural–process distinctions are orthogonal to the opposition between discrete and distance models.

References

Arbib, M. A. (Ed.) *Algebraic theory of machines, languages, and semigroups.* New York: Academic Press, 1968.
Ash, R. *Information theory.* New York: Wiley, 1965.

Bašarin, G. P. On a statistical estimate for the entropy of a sequence of independent random variables. *Teor. Veroyatnoste i Prim.*, 1959, **4**, 361–364.

Boyd, J. P. The algebra of group kinship. *Journal of Mathematical Psychology*, 1969, **6**, 139–167.

Chomsky, N. Formal properties of grammars. In R. D. Luce, R. R. Bush, and E. Galanter (Eds.), *Handbook of mathematical psychology*. Vol. 2. New York: Wiley, 1963. Pp. 323–418.

Chomsky, N., & Miller, G. A. Introduction to the formal analysis of natural languages. In R. D. Luce, R. R. Bush, and E. Galanter (Eds.), *Handbook of mathematical psychology*. Vol. 2. New York: Wiley, 1963. Pp. 269–322.

Kelly, J. *General topology*. Princeton, New Jersey: Van Nostrand–Reinhold, 1955.

Krohn, K., Langer, R., & Rhodes, J. Algebraic principles for the analysis of a biochemical system. *Journal of Computer and System Sciences*, 1967, **1**, 119–136.

Lorrain, F. Notes on topological spaces with minimum neighborhoods. *The American Mathematical Monthly*, 1969, **76**, 616–627.

Miller, G. A., & Chomsky, N. Finitary models of language users. In R. D. Luce, R. R. Bush, and E. Galanter (Eds.), *Handbook of mathematical psychology*. Vol. 2. New York: Wiley, 1963. Pp. 419–492.

Miller, G. A., & Madow, W. G. On the maximum likelihood estimate of the Shannon–Wiener measure of information. In R. D. Luce, R. R. Bush, and E. Galanter (Eds.), *Readings in mathematical psychology*. Vol. 1. New York: Wiley, 1963. Pp. 448–469.

Stefflre, V. *Language and behavior*. Unpublished manuscript.

STRUCTURAL MEASURES
AND THE METHOD OF SORTING

Scott A. Boorman

SOCIETY OF FELLOWS
HARVARD UNIVERSITY
CAMBRIDGE, MASSACHUSETTS

Phipps Arabie

STANFORD UNIVERSITY
STANFORD, CALIFORNIA

The method of sorting is a nominal scaling procedure frequently used by cognitive psychologists and anthropologists in their investigations of semantic and associative structures. The approach has been used, for example, for classifying various syntactic and lexical items, such as grammatical strings (Shipstone, 1960), words (Mandler & Pearlstone, 1966; Miller, 1969), and occupational terms (Burton, this book, Volume II). In the unconstrained method of sorting, a set of labeled objects is partitioned by a subject into a suitable, although arbitrary, number of unlabeled clusters. Subjects typically differ with respect to number, size, and composition of clusters in the way they sort or partition the same set of items. Furthermore, some partitions are apodictically more different than others.

Frequently, we are interested in being able to draw conclusions concerning the *amount* of difference, disagreement, or similarity between partitions. Phrased quantitatively, this may be viewed as the problem of formalizing distances between partitions.

Some progress has been made by experimenters who have dealt with the problem of extracting information from differences between sorts. Miller (1967, 1969) has consistently used the method of hierarchical clustering schemes devised by Johnson (1967), while Burton (this book, Volume II), Shipstone (1960), Rapoport and Fillenbaum (this book, Volume II), and Pavy (personal communication) have used structural measures tailored to fit the particular requirements of their investigations. Our approach is more in the spirit of those experimenters using methods other than hierarchical clustering. However, the focus is not on a particular group of partitions, but rather on the space of all possible partitions.

In contrast to those concerned with a specific application, there have been other investigators who approached the problem with a theoretical emphasis and who were less restricted by the requirements of a particular empirical problem, although these approaches have often been constrained by the theoretical predilections of the investigator (e.g., from an information-theoretic standpoint, Rajski, 1961). We believe that a large number of different approaches may be unified in a common framework subsuming alternative approaches to the concept of structural distance.

In the present article, we propose to set forth some of the basic graph- and lattice-theoretic concepts which are expedient for dealing with partitions, to apply these concepts to the analysis of some simple structural measures, and finally to propose a general classification of partition distance indices. In an analogous context, Shipstone (1960, p. 31) has remarked that "there is no adequate measure of structural similarity." We do not intend to define what an "adequate measure" would be for partitions—much less to supply one, if it could be strictly defined. We do, however, believe that a closer study of such measures may give the experimenter a better basis for deciding which measure is suitable for his particular investigations.

A Graph-Theoretic Approach

When we consider a set of cognitive partitions as a space of relational structures, we are at once operating in an area where our intuitions are often indeterminate. However, if we note that each member of the space (i.e., each partition) possesses internal structure, then one approach is to formalize a concept of an admissible transformation which converts a given partition into a similar partition. Distance between two partitions is then the least (possibly weighted) number of intervening transformations necessary to transform one partition into the other.

Such an approach should be familiar to psychologists acquainted with the Abelson–Rosenberg (1958) thesis that cognitive imbalances are restored by the minimum number of changes in cognitive relations necessary to reach a certain desired (i.e., balanced) cognitive structure. A similar conceptual motivation underlies the rank correlation coefficient τ, which from one viewpoint is "a simple function of the minimum number of interchanges between neighbors required to transform one ranking into the other" (Kendall, 1962, p. 8).

Given this emphasis upon structural transformations and distance-generating sequences based upon them, we may proceed to conceptualize such transformations as segments (or edges) of a network—more specifically, a graph—whose vertices are the actual partitions. In the examples of the following sections, all graphs are considered to be undirected (i.e., the underlying transformations are assumed reversible); this restriction is not theoretically necessary but does simplify computation considerably. We now formalize in graph terminology the idea that distance between partitions, even as Kendall's distance between orderings, is the least number of intervening transformations. Let P and Q be two given partitions and let $\{P_i\}_{i=1}^t$ be any sequence of partitions connected by admissible transformations for which $P_1 = P$ and $P_t = Q$ (this sequence may be thought of as a path from P to Q in our partition space). Assume that the transformations $P_i \rightarrow P_{i+1}$ involved in this path have numerical weights (or "costs") $W_i > 0$. Then we have the following expression for distance d between P and Q

$$d(P, Q) = \min\left(\sum_{i=1}^{t-1} W_i\right) \tag{1}$$

where the minimum is taken over all such paths $\{P_i\}_{i=1}^t$.

The particular concept of a transformation-graph G and weighting structure W used to induce d we term a minimum cost flow (MCF) representation of d. One analogy is the typical problem in operations research, where the vertices of the graph correspond not to partitions but to places, the edges not to transformations but to transportation systems, and the weights not to parameters of structural distance but rather to transportation costs.

In economic theory, cost minimization is both a normative concept and a model of behavior; it is our objective to demonstrate that a large number of concepts of partition distance present in the literature are likewise founded upon some graph-based minimization scheme. These distance concepts can be classified according to the specific type of MCF representation from which they may be derived. The study of MCF representations in turn helps us to determine the behavior of a given distance index, in particular those sequential alterations of structure to which the index is sensitive and those under which it is comparatively invariant. The latter property is a formal correlate to Miller's emphasis (Miller, 1958, p. 485) that "We would like to know what changes, if any, in a set of rules leave performance invariant."

From a purely mathematical viewpoint, we should note that all distances d based upon Equation (1) are *metrics*, and hence are structural measures of a special kind. In particular, *all* distances considered in the present paper are metrics, though frequently the proofs of the triangle inequality are not obvious. In other words, the distances satisfy the following axioms (for all partitions P, Q, and R of a common domain S):

Axiom 1. $d(P, Q) \geq 0$ and $d(P, Q) = 0$ if and only if $P = Q$.

Axiom 2. $d(P, Q) = d(Q, P)$.

Axiom 3. $d(P, R) \leq d(P, Q) + d(Q, R)$.

The first axiom says that distance is a nonnegative quantity which distinguishes nonidentical points; the second says that distance is symmetric; the third, that distance satisfies the triangle inequality. The last axiom may be verified by noting that the shortest distance from P to R ($= d(P, R)$) is less than or equal to the shortest distance from P to R via Q ($= d(P, Q) + d(Q, R)$).

Definitions and Properties of Some Sample Metrics

Underlying all the following structural measures will be a fixed, finite set S of objects which correspond to the stimuli. We define a partition P of a set S to be a collection of subsets $\{c_i\}_{i=1}^{m}$ of S such that (for $i, j = 1, 2, \ldots, m$)

(i) $c_i \neq \emptyset$

(ii) $i \neq j \Rightarrow c_i \cap c_j = \emptyset$

(iii) $\bigcup\limits_{i=1}^{m} c_i = S$

In other words, the c_i (referred to above as clusters) are nonempty, pairwise disjoint, and collectively exhaustive. They will be termed henceforth the *cells* of the partition P. The finiteness of the set of objects S guarantees finiteness of the partition space $P(S)$ (the set of all possible partitions of S); to be more specific, the cardinality $| P(S) |$ of $P(S)$ depends only on the number of elements in S according to the following expression

$$| P(S) | = \sum_{m=1}^{n} \sigma(n, m) \qquad (2)$$

where $\sigma(n, m)$ is the number of ways of partitioning a set of n elements into m nonempty subsets [Stirling number of the second kind: see Riordan (1958) for tables, and Rota (1964) for relevant generating functions]. Here n is just the cardinality (size) of S.

Minimum Element-Moves Measure

Our emphasis upon an admissible transformation which converts a partition into another, similar partition is the motivation for the minimum element-moves measure. This particular measure, introduced in Rubin (1967), is a good starting point for development of an MCF approach because of its readily apparent MCF structure. The following definitions are merely one formalization of the idea that the distance between two partitions should depend upon the number of "steps" needed to transform one into the other:

Definition. An *element-move* transforming one P in $P(S)$ into another is the transfer of a single element $e \in S$ from one cell $c \in P$ either

(i)   to a different cell d already in P;
(ii)   or to form a new, one-member cell.

Given this definition of an element-move, we define the distance A between two partitions P_1 and P_2 as:

Definition. $A(P_1, P_2)$ is the minimum number of element-moves needed to transform P_1 into P_2.

As an example of calculating the minimum element-moves distance, let

$P_1 = \{\{1\}, \{2, 3, 4, 7, 8\}, \{5, 6\}\}$ and $P_2 = \{\{1, 2\}, \{3, 4\}, \{5, 6\}, \{7, 8\}\}$.

Then the following transition sequence is clearly a minimum one, giving

$A(P_1, P_2) = 3$:

$$P_1 = \{\{1\}, \{2, 3, 4, 7, 8\}, \{5, 6\}\} \rightarrow \qquad \text{(via a type (ii) move)}$$
$$\{\{1\}, \{2, 3, 4, 7\}, \{5, 6\}, \{8\}\} \rightarrow \qquad \text{(via a type (i) move)}$$
$$\{\{1\}, \{2, 3, 4\}, \{5, 6\}, \{7, 8\}\} \rightarrow \qquad \text{(via a type (i) move)}$$
$$\{\{1, 2\}, \{3, 4\}, \{5, 6\}, \{7, 8\}\} = P_2$$

For the experimenter who questions the feasibility of computing this distance measure for sets with large values of n, it might be added that the task of determining A in the general case reduces to the optimal assignment problem encountered in linear programming (Ford & Fulkerson, 1962). As we shall presently see, however, this metric does have properties which limit its effectiveness for empirical investigations.

The maximum possible value attained by the distance A between two partitions is equal to $n - 1$, where, as before, n is the number of elements in S. This special case of $A(P_1, P_2) = n - 1$ occurs in particular when (for $n = 8$)

$$P_1 = \{\{1\}, \{2\}, \{3\}, \{4\}, \{5\}, \{6\}, \{7\}, \{8\}\}$$

and

$$P_2 = \{\{1, 2, 3, 4, 5, 6, 7, 8\}\}$$

or vice versa. We shall refer to P_1 as P_{splitter} and to P_2 as P_{lumper}. The partition P_{splitter} corresponds to a subject who segregates all the elements into individual cells, and P_{lumper} refers to a subject who clusters all elements into a single cell.

In order to see that distance A cannot exceed $n - 1$, we note that in a minimum transition sequence no element needs to be moved more than once and at least one element can remain fixed. The upper bound of $n - 1$ for the integer-valued function A means that it can assume only n values, and this discreteness property guarantees a considerable number of ties among inter-partition distances. For example, if $n = 10$, there are 115,975 possible distinct partitions, whereas metric A can assume only ten possible values. If the experimenter is considering the use of Shepard–Kruskal methods for multidimensional scaling of his obtained partitions, the inevitably large number of ties may lead to degenerate solutions.

Minimum Set-Moves Measure

One generalization of the metric A is readily obtained by allowing certain combinations of element-moves to be considered as a single move. That is,

Definition. A *set-move* transforming one P in $P(S)$ into another is the transfer of a subset s of S from one cell $c \in P$ either

(i)   to a different cell d already in P;

(ii)   or to form a new, independent cell.

Define $B(P_1, P_2)$ to be the least length of a set-moves sequence connecting P_1 and P_2. Since all element-moves are set-moves, but not conversely, we have in general $B(P_1, P_2) \leq A(P_1, P_2)$. B is thus a cruder metric than A, since B is not sensitive to quantitative variations in the sizes of the sets being moved as a path is traced. B therefore is at least as vulnerable as A to degenerate Shepard–Kruskal solutions. However, B has the same range as A and, in particular, $\max B = B(P_{\text{splitter}}, P_{\text{lumper}}) = n - 1$. Also, as in the case of A, computation of B reduces to an optimal assignment problem.

As an example of the computation of B in a simple case, let P_1 and P_2 be defined as in the example of A above (p. 229). Then a minimum transformation sequence is

$$P_1 = \{\{1\}, \{2, 3, 4, 7, 8\}, \{5, 6\}\} \rightarrow \quad \text{(via a type (ii) set-move)}$$

$$\{\{1\}, \{2, 3, 4\}, \{5, 6\}, \{7, 8\}\} \rightarrow \quad \text{(via a type (i) set-move)}$$

$$\{\{1, 2\}, \{3, 4\}, \{5, 6\}, \{7, 8\}\} = P_2$$

Thus $B(P_1, P_2) = 2 < A(P_1, P_2)$. Observe that in this particular instance (and more generally, as can be shown by a linear-programming argument) B is well approximated by

$$| P_1 \cap P_2 | - \min(| P_1 |, | P_2 |) \tag{3}$$

where $| P |$ is the number of cells of a given partition P. (Note: In all of the following usage except in Equations (9) and (12) below, $| x |$ refers to the cardinality of the enclosed variable, and not to absolute value.) $P_1 \cap P_2$ refers here to the intersection partition derived from P_1 and P_2 in the following manner: First, enumerate the cells of each partition P_i

P_1	P_2
$c_1 = \{1\}$	$d_1 = \{1, 2\}$
$c_2 = \{2, 3, 4, 7, 8\}$	$d_2 = \{3, 4\}$
$c_3 = \{5, 6\}$	$d_3 = \{5, 6\}$
	$d_4 = \{7, 8\}$

Then the cells of the partition $P_1 \cap P_2$, which we shall subsequently refer to as the $z(i,j)$, are the nonempty entries of the following cross-tabulation ($z(i,j) = c_i \cap d_j$):

	d_1	d_2	d_3	d_4
c_1	$\{1\}$	$\emptyset$	$\emptyset$	$\emptyset$
c_2	$\{2\}$	$\{3,4\}$	$\emptyset$	$\{7,8\}$
c_3	$\emptyset$	$\emptyset$	$\{5,6\}$	$\emptyset$

In this particular case, therefore, $|P_1 \cap P_2| = 5$, the quantity (3) is $5 - 3 = 2$, and the approximation (3) is exact.

MINIMUM LATTICE-MOVES MEASURE

By contrast to measures A and B, the measure we now propose attempts to make use of the mathematical structure of the set of all partitions $P(S)$. One such mathematical structure on $P(S)$ is the partition lattice (Birkhoff, 1967). The lattice is a partial ordering of partitions based on the relation of "fineness" between partitions. Specifically, one partition X is said to be finer than another Y, if X contains more cells than Y and, whenever two elements a and b are clustered together in X, then they are also clustered together in Y. Conversely, we may say that Y is coarser than X. For example, if $X = \{\{1,2\}, \{3,4\}, \{5,6\}, \{7,8\}\}$ and $Y = \{\{1,2\}, \{3,4,5,6\}, \{7,8\}\}$, then X is finer than Y since every cell of X is contained in some cell of Y.

This structural emphasis may be used to derive a new metric C on $P(S)$. The transformation concept on which it is based is that of a lattice-move:

Definition. Two partitions X and Y are connected by a lattice-move if and only if one is *just* finer than the other (i.e., there is no partition Z between X and Y in fineness).

Equivalently, if X is just finer than Y, we must be able to obtain X from Y by the mitosis of the unmatched cell (c_x) of Y into two distinct cells of X whose union is c_x (thus in the last example X may be obtained from Y by splitting the cell $\{3, 4, 5, 6\}$ into the two cells $\{3, 4\}$ and $\{5, 6\}$).

Definition. $C(P_1, P_2)$ is the minimum number of lattice-moves needed to transform P_1 into P_2.

This metric, and certain normalized versions of it, were employed by the late David Pavy to distinguish the sorting behavior of diagnosed schizophrenic and normal subjects (Pavy, personal communication). The resulting partition spaces showed clear differentiation between the two groups of subjects.

Based as it is upon the dimension of fineness along the partition lattice, the metric C is comparatively more sensitive than metrics A and B to transformations of structure which cut across the lattice (i.e., "finer than") ordering. In particular, if $P \rightarrow Q$ is based on a set- or element-move which neither eliminates any cell from P nor adds one to it, then *two* lattice moves are needed to achieve the same transformation. Thus, to go from $P = \{\{1, 2\}, \{3, 4, 7, 8\}, \{5, 6\}\}$ to $Q = \{\{1\}, \{2, 3, 4, 7, 8\}, \{5, 6\}\}$ by lattice-moves, we must first disaggregate

$$P \rightarrow P' = \{\{1\}, \{2\}, \{3, 4, 7, 8\}, \{5, 6\}\}$$

and then reaggregate

$$P' \rightarrow Q = \{\{1\}, \{2, 3, 4, 7, 8\}, \{5, 6\}\}$$

Intuitively, C is a partition analog of the Boolean (set) lattice metrics discussed by Goodman (1951, 1966) and by Restle (1959, 1961). One simple version of the metrics proposed by these authors is

$$m(k_1, k_2) = |k_1| + |k_2| - 2|k_1 \cap k_2|$$

where the k_i are finite sets and $k_1 \cap k_2$ is their set intersection. This metric may also be interpreted (following Flament, 1963) as the least number of moves needed to transform k_1 into k_2, where a move from one set to another is the addition (subtraction) of a single element to (from) it.

We would like a comparable formula for C. In fact, it can be shown that

$$C(P_1, P_2) = |P_1| + |P_2| - 2|P_1 \cup P_2| \tag{4}$$

where $P_1 \cup P_2$ (the union of the P_i) is the finest partition which is coarser than both P_1 and P_2. Comparing Equation (4) and the definition of m just given, we see that $|P|$, a measure of the dispersiveness of P, is an analogue of $|T|$, the cardinality of a set in the Goodman–Restle metric. Equation (4) may be derived by showing that the minimum moves path from P_1 to P_2 always involves first aggregating cells of P_1 to reach the union $P_1 \cup P_2$ and then disaggregating in a new way to form P_2. One corollary is that $C(P_{\text{splitter}}, P_{\text{lumper}}) = n - 1$.

HEIGHT MEASURES

Having introduced the concept of the dispersiveness of a partition—the degree to which it constitutes a division of its universe into many small clusters—it is fruitful to consider the complementary concept of aggregativeness. Together, dispersiveness and aggregativeness form a kind of dimension, and a large number of structural distance concepts may be based upon alternative quantifications along this dimension. The unifying idea in all cases is that the "aggregativeness" (or conversely the "dispersiveness") of a partition can be measured relative to two extreme cases: P_{lumper}, the maximally aggregative partition, and P_{splitter}, the maximally dispersive one. If we consider P_{splitter} as a "south pole" with P_{lumper} as the corresponding "north pole," then we are interested in the projections of the other members of $P(S)$ onto the north–south axis.

C itself is one example of this conceptualization. However, we may also consider distance measures based on a formula similar to Equation (4), where g is some partition function and we have substituted partition intersection for partition union:

$$g(P_1) + g(P_2) - 2g(P_1 \cap P_2) \tag{5}$$

Since there is no particular reason to argue that any particular g is "optimal," we shall suggest various alternative measures of this form, many of which have either appeared in the literature or are formalizations of ideas appearing there. These different measures attempt to take into account the size of the cells being split and merged in the course of sequential transformations.

One intuitively plausible measure of the "height" of a partition is simply the number of nonreflexive pair bonds in a partition P. For example, if $P = \{\{1, 2, 3, 4\}, \{5\}, \{6, 7\}, \{8\}\}$, then the number of pair bonds, as determined graphically below

$$\begin{array}{c}1\text{---}2\\ |\times| \qquad 5 \qquad 6\text{---}7 \qquad 8\\ 3\text{---}4\end{array}$$

is equal to $6 + 0 + 1 + 0 = 7$. More generally, the expression for the number of pair bonds is $\frac{1}{2}\sum_i |c_i| (|c_i| - 1)$, where $|c_i|$ is the number of elements in the ith cell of a partition P, and the summation is over all cells. It is clear that this expression assumes its maximum value for P_{lumper}, and that this value is equal to $\binom{n}{2}$ when the underlying set S has n elements. Hence, if we use $\binom{n}{2}$ as a normalizing factor, then the height will be measured along a discrete subset of the unit interval. Stated formally,

Definition. Define the height of P to be

$$h(P) = \frac{1}{n(n-1)} \sum_i |c_i| (|c_i| - 1)$$

where $P = \{c_1, c_2, \ldots, c_m\} \in P(S)$.

Using these definitions, when we are given two partitions P_1 and P_2, we may calculate their individual distances from the south pole. The task of finding a measure of distance between P_1 and P_2 is then somewhat similar to the elementary trigonometry problem of using the law of cosines to determine the third side of a triangle, given the first two sides and the angle which they form. Hence, the reader should not be surprised to note that our formula is quite similar in appearance to the law of cosines, specifically:

Definition. $D(P_1, P_2) = h(P_1) + h(P_2) - 2h(P_1 \cap P_2)$, where $P_1 \cap P_2$ is again the intersection partition.

This definition is structurally quite similar to the Equation (4) derived for C. In effect, we have taken the expression for C and substituted h, which is a measure of aggregation, in place of the cardinality operator $| \ |$, a measure of dispersion.

If, returning to the pair bonds concept, we now substitute the appropriate expressions for h in the definition of D, then we have

$$\frac{1}{n(n-1)} \left[\sum_i |c_i| (|c_i| - 1) + \sum_j |d_j| (|d_j| - 1) \right.$$

$$\left. -2 \sum_{i,j} |z(i,j)| (|z(i,j)| - 1) \right] \quad (6)$$

where the $z(i,j)$ are the cells of the intersection partition $P_1 \cap P_2$. It is clear from this expansion of D that its range is contained in $[0, 1]$. Without the normalization, the metric defined by Equation (6) is a special case of the distance between graphs defined by Flament (1963) and used by that author and others to formalize a wide variety of structural measures quantifying such concepts as hierarchy, connectivity, transitivity, and balance. The normalized version is discussed in Johnson (1968) and used by Rapoport and Fillenbaum (this book, Volume II). In passing, we may also note that by considering the expression

$$D' = 1 - 2D \quad (7)$$

(where D' thus has the standard range $[-1, 1]$ for correlation coefficients), we then have the "agreement–disagreement ratio" used by Shipstone (1960) in her analysis of sorts of grammatical strings.

In exploring other properties of measure D, it is helpful to consider the incidence matrix $M(P) = [a_{ij}]_{n \times n}$ of a partition P, where

$$a_{ij} = \begin{cases} 0 & \text{if } e_i, e_j \text{ are in different cells of } P \\ \\ 1 & \text{if } e_i, e_j \text{ are in the same cell of } P \end{cases} \quad (8)$$

and the underlying set S being partitioned is $\{e_i\}_{i=1}^{n}$. Given this definition, it can be shown that D is proportional to the city-block or Manhattan metric (Attneave, 1950; Landahl, 1945) on the incidence matrices of partitions. Specifically,

$D(P_1, P_2) =$ the number of pairwise distinct entries in the incidence matrices $M(P_i)$, normalized by division by $n(n-1)$

$$= \frac{1}{n(n-1)} \sum_{i,j} |a_{ij} - b_{ij}| \text{ where } M(P_1) = [a_{ij}] \text{ and}$$

$$M(P_2) = [b_{ij}]$$

$$= \frac{1}{n(n-1)} \times (\text{city-block metric on } n \times n \text{ 0–1 matrices}) \quad (9)$$

The representation Equation (9) of D helps to clarify its structure. In particular, consider the D-distance generated by an element-move from a cell c_y of size $k > 0$ to a cell c_z of size $k' > 0$. This distance is

$$2(k + k' - 1)/[n(n-1)] \approx 2(k + k')/[n(n-1)] \quad (10)$$

(we must first break $k - 1$ bonds and then form k' new ones). Thus the value of measure D depends linearly upon the cardinality of the original cell c_y and the cardinality of the terminal cell c_z. More generally, if we are moving s elements from a cell of size k to one of size k', we have a resulting distance

$$2[(k - s)s + k's]/[n(n-1)] \quad (11)$$

and for s small relative to k we have

$$\partial/\partial s\{2[(k - s)s + k's]/[n(n-1)]\} = 2(k + k' - 2s)/[n(n-1)] > 0$$

Hence, distance depends directly upon the cardinality of the subset being moved.

The implication of this type of analysis is that the particular distance measure we choose entails strong assumptions, a fact which is not always stressed by experimenters and theorists. Thus, for example, the measure D has been employed unexamined in a wide variety of contexts ranging from psycholinguistics to sociometry; it would be worth considering a rival distance model in which the relation between distance produced and the cardinality of the original cell is inverse—the argument being that a single unit can be more readily lost from a large collection (i.e., cell) than from a small one (cf. Weber's Law).

We might also question the structure imposed by D in another direction— namely, the supposition underlying it that all changes in the values of the entries of the incidence matrix have equal weight. A more general formula incorporates differential weightings as follows:

$$\frac{1}{n(n-1)} \sum_{i,j} W_{ij} \, |\, a_{ij} - b_{ij}\,|, \qquad W_{ij} > 0 \tag{12}$$

For example, we might select $W_{ij} = N_{ij}$ = number of times e_i and e_j are lumped together in an obtained group of partitions [see Miller (1969) where $[N_{ij}]$ is used as a basis for an application of hierarchical clustering].

Although D has been used rather extensively by experimenters (e.g., Anglin, 1968; Rapoport & Fillenbaum, this book, Volume II; Shipstone, 1960), there is no apparent reason for its primacy as a height function. Another function, possessing information-theoretic overtones, is given by

$$f(P) = -\log_2 \frac{n!}{\prod_i |\, c_i\,|!} \tag{13}$$

where, as before, $P = \{c_1, c_2, \ldots, c_m\}$. Measure f—originally proposed by Johnson (personal communication)—is the negative of the logarithm to the binary base of the multinomial coefficient of P. Substituting in Equation (5), we obtain

$$\log_2 \prod_i |\, c_i\,|! + \log_2 \prod_j |\, d_j\,|! - 2\log_2 \prod_{i,j} |\, z(i,j)\,|! \tag{14}$$

where all variables are defined as in Equation (6). It can be shown that the resulting measure of distance is a metric. More germane to the present discussion is an analog to the element- and set-move analysis for measure D above. Specifically, if we consider as before the distance generated by moving a subset of size s from one cell of size k to another of size k', then the resulting distance is [eliminating the canceling terms from Equation (14)]

$$(\log_2 k! + \log_2 k'!) + (\log_2(k-s)! + \log_2(k'+s)!)$$

$$- 2[\log_2(k-s)! + \log_2 k'! + \log_2 s!]$$

$$= \log_2 \left[\binom{k}{s}\binom{k'+s}{s} \right] = \log_2 \binom{k}{s} + \log_2 \binom{k'+s}{s} \tag{15}$$

In particular, if $s = 1$ (i.e., the set-move is in fact an element-move), we have Equation (15) reducing to

$$\log_2 k + \log_2(k'+1) \approx \log_2 k + \log_2 k' \tag{16}$$

Hence, in this case the linear growth [Expression (10)] for the pair bonds height metric is replaced by a logarithmic rate of growth, which is of course negatively accelerated.

Still another metric on partitions which behaves similarly to that just considered is the standard distance index of information theory (see Boyd, this book, Volume I). Let us identify a partition with a discrete probability distribution in an obvious way, assigning to the likelihood of inclusion in cell c a probability $|c|/n$ (where n, as before, is the size of S). This identification of probabilities with cells is somewhat inconsistent with our premise that the cells of a partition are unlabeled boxes, and hence intrinsically cannot correspond to attributes in any conventional sense. Still, we feel that the mathematical properties of the measure make it worth considering. We begin by defining the entropy associated with a partition P to be

$$H(P) = - \sum_{c \in P} \frac{|c|}{n} \log_2 \frac{|c|}{n} \tag{17}$$

Next, define the conditional entropy of one partition P given another Q to be

$$H(P \mid Q) = H(P \cap Q) - H(Q) \tag{18}$$

Since $(P \cap Q)$ is a finer partition than Q, and H increases when we move from a given partition to a finer one, we have $H(P \mid Q) \geq 0$. Let us formalize a distance between P and Q to be

$$H(P \mid Q) + H(Q \mid P) \tag{19}$$

This quantity, following a formulation of Boyd (this book, Volume I), may be interpreted as the amount of information needed to transform one partition P into another Q, or vice versa.

Superficially, this information distance has a very different form from the other height measures we have been considering. However, expanding Equation (19) by means of Equation (18) gives the following expression equal to Equation (19):

$$2H(P \cap Q) - H(P) - H(Q) \tag{20}$$

To transform Equation (20) into a form more comparable with the measure D, replace $H(P)$ by $H_{max} - H(P) = \log_2 n - H(P)$ to obtain an alternative form for Equation (19):

$$(\log_2 n - H(P)) + (\log_2 n - H(Q)) - 2(\log_2 n - H(P \cap Q)) \tag{21}$$

Pursuing our earlier method of analysis, let us consider the effect of a set-move of a subset su (where $|su| = s$) from one cell with cardinality k to another with cardinality k'. The analog to Equation (15) is

$$\left(\frac{k}{n}\log_2\frac{k}{n} + \frac{k'}{n}\log_2\frac{k'}{n}\right) + \left(\frac{k-s}{n}\log_2\frac{k-s}{n} + \frac{k'+s}{n}\log_2\frac{k'+s}{n}\right)$$

$$-2\left(\frac{k-s}{n}\log_2\frac{k-s}{n} + \frac{k'}{n}\log_2\frac{k'}{n} + \frac{s}{n}\log_2\frac{s}{n}\right)$$

$$= \frac{1}{n}\left(\log_2\frac{k^k(k'+s)^{k'+s}}{k'^{k'}(k-s)^{k-s}s^{2s}}\right) \tag{22}$$

It can be shown that expression (22) is asymptotic to expression (15) if s is small relative to both k and k'. Therefore, the behavior of the height measures is similar for this particular limiting case.

NORMALIZED HEIGHT MEASURES

One way of obtaining a set of partition distance measures with less of a splitter–lumper orientation is to normalize the previous measures so as to "factor out" the height dimension arising from that particular orientation. Such normalization cannot be achieved by dividing a height measure by a function of n alone (which would merely have the same effect as a similarity transformation in Euclidean space); it is necessary to divide by some nonconstant lattice function. One example is the metric originally proposed by Rajski (1961) and discussed in various subsequent papers (Kotz, 1966; Rajski, 1964). We define the average mutual information associated with two partitions $P_1 = \{c_1, c_2, \ldots, c_m\}$ and $P_2 = \{d_1, d_2, \ldots, d_p\}$ to be

$$I(P_1, P_2) = \sum_{i=1}^{m}\sum_{j=1}^{p} R_{ij}\log_2(R_{ij}/V_iT_j) \tag{23}$$

where

$$V_i = |c_i|/n, \qquad i = 1, 2, \ldots, m \tag{24}$$

$$T_j = |d_j|/n, \qquad j = 1, 2, \ldots, p \tag{25}$$

$$R_{ij} = |z(i,j)|/n, \qquad i, j \text{ as above} \tag{26}$$

(These expressions for V_i, T_j, and R_{ij} may be interpreted as probabilities.) If partitions P_1 and P_2 are orthogonal in the sense that, seen as probability distributions, they are independent (i.e., the c_i meet the d_j randomly), then $R_{ij} = V_i T_j$ (by their probability interpretations), and I in Equation (23) is zero. I achieves its maximum value of

$$- \sum_{i=1}^{m} V_i \log_2 V_i \tag{27}$$

for $P_1 = P_2$. And this is, of course, the entropy of the distribution $P_1 (= P_2)$.

Next, we normalize the expression (23) for I by dividing by the entropy H of the product ensemble

$$H(P_1 \cap P_2) = - \sum_{i=1}^{m} \sum_{j=1}^{p} R_{ij} \log_2 R_{ij} \tag{28}$$

which satisfies the inequality $0 \leq I(P_1, P_2) \leq H(P_1 \cap P_2)$. This normalized quotient can be used as a measure of association which, as Kotz (1966) points out, has some advantages over the coefficient of correlation.

If we consider the ratio of I to H to be a measure of the similarity of two partitions, then we may define an index $E(P_1, P_2)$, where

Definition.

$$E(P_1, P_2) = 1 - \text{similarity}(P_1, P_2) = 1 - I(P_1, P_2)/H(P_1 \cap P_2)$$

E can be shown to be a metric (Rajski, 1961). To see that it is indeed a normalized height measure, recall expression (19), $H(P \mid Q) + H(Q \mid P)$. Next, we expand the formula for I

$$\begin{aligned} I(P_1, P_2) &= \sum_{i,j} R_{ij} \log_2 (R_{ij}/V_i T_j) \\ &= \sum_{i,j} R_{ij} \log_2 R_{ij} - \sum_{i,j} R_{ij} \log_2 V_i - \sum_{i,j} R_{ij} \log_2 T_j \\ &= -H(P_1 \cap P_2) + H(P_1) + H(P_2) \end{aligned} \tag{29}$$

Substituting this expansion of I in the definition of E, the conclusion follows, namely:

$$E(P_1, P_2) = \frac{H(P_1 \mid P_2) + H(P_2 \mid P_1)}{H(P_1 \cap P_2)} = \frac{2H(P_1 \cap P_2) - H(P_1) - H(P_2)}{H(P_1 \cap P_2)} \tag{30}$$

The effect of this normalization by $H(P_1 \cap P_2)$ is to make a measure which is less sensitive to absolute height differences. We might note that this particular normalization is a partition lattice analog of the set metric defined by Galanter (1956) (cited in Restle, 1959) and Marczewski and Steinhaus (1958). This metric is a normalized version of the metric (Goodman, 1951, 1966; Restle, 1959, 1961) defined as

$$m(k_1, k_2) = |\,k_1\,| + |\,k_2\,| - 2\,|\,k_1 \cap k_2\,| \tag{31}$$

and which may be rewritten as

$$m(k_1, k_2) = 2\,|\,k_1 \cup k_2\,| - |\,k_1\,| - |\,k_2\,|$$

since

$$|\,k_1\,| + |\,k_2\,| = |\,k_1 \cup k_2\,| + |\,k_1 \cap k_2\,|$$

Normalizing with $|\,k_1 \cup k_2\,|$ gives

$$\frac{2\,|\,k_1 \cup k_2\,| - |\,k_1\,| - |\,k_2\,|}{|\,k_1 \cup k_2\,|}$$

which is clearly similar to Equation (30) if we place set union in correspondence with partition intersection.

Four MCF Representation Familes

The previous section presented a variety of structural distance concepts for partitions. These concepts were organized around certain central ideas such as a move from one partition to another, the aggregativeness of a partition, and the normalization of a height measure. We now attempt to systematize this conceptual organization by the application of the MCF idea presented earlier.

Concretely, we consider four transformation graphs on $P(S)$, each formalizing an alternative distance geometry whose structure we can at least locally visualize. In the first graph, which we may term G_1, two partitions are edge-connected (i.e., may be transformed into one another) if and only if the one may be obtained from the other by an element-move. The graph G_2 is similarly defined except that in place of element-moves we consider set-moves; since all element-moves are set-moves (but not conversely), G_1 is a subgraph of G_2. A third kind of graph G_3 is defined by connecting two partitions if and only if they may be reached from one another by a lattice-move (or, equivalently, by the joining of two cells to form one). A fourth graph G_4 edge-connects two partitions if and only if they are comparable in the lattice ordering, i.e., one is finer than the other. (Subgraph relations among the G_i are indicated in Figure 1.)

These graphs encompass all the metrics which we have presented; in other words, every metric may be coded by an MCF representation in one of the four graphs. Specifically, metrics A and B are derived directly from G_1 and G_2, respectively, by giving each edge a unit weight; as we have already seen,

	G_1	G_2	G_3	G_4
G_1	X	X		
G_2		X		
G_3		X	X	X
G_4				X

FIG. 1. Subgraph relations among the G_i. An $\times$ in the (i, j)th cell indicates that a graph in the ith row is a subgraph of the graph in the corresponding jth column. The explanation is that: (1) All element-moves are set-moves, and hence G_1 is a subgraph of G_2. (2) All lattice-moves are also set-moves, and therefore G_3 is a subgraph of G_2. (3) If two partitions are connected by a lattice-move then one is finer than the other, and G_3 is a subgraph of G_4.

each involves linear programming for computation in the general case. More complicated weightings W may also be considered, but frequently the induced metrics are difficult to compute. (It is worth noting, in this regard, that because of the rate at which $| P(S) |$ grows as S increases, the shortest-path algorithms of operations research are of little value in computing MCF metrics.)

The graph G_3, by contrast, leads to metrics which possess more interesting fine structure. This structure derives largely from the lattice structure of G_3 (well known in lattice theory as the Hasse diagram of $P(S)$; see Suppes, 1957). The simplest metric on G_3, obtained by assigning each segment a unit weight, is measure C, which was discussed in some detail above. C is thus the analog of A and B for a different underlying graph. The height measures of the general form Equation (5), which we have already identified as being closely related to C, are an important class of metrics possessing informative MCF representations in the graph G_3.

In order to demonstrate this, we begin with a metric having the form

$$r(P_1, P_2) = g(P_1) + g(P_2) - 2g(P_1 \cap P_2) \tag{32}$$

In order to express the metric r in G_3, we define a weighting function on the edges $\overline{PQ}$ of G_3 to be

$$W(\overline{PQ}) = g(Q) - g(P) = r(P, Q) \tag{33}$$

(where P is the *finer* of the two partitions P and Q). For example, in the case of the pair bonds measure D, the quantity in Equation (33) is simply the number of interelement bonds broken in going from Q to P for g as formalized by the definition of h on p. 234. We must now prove that the least-cost metric induced by this particular W on G_3 coincides with the given metric r.

First, it is relevant to make note of two additivity properties of r, namely (where $\leq$ signifies "is at least as fine as")

$$P_1 \leq P_2 \leq P_3 \Rightarrow r(P_1, P_2) + r(P_2, P_3) = r(P_1, P_3) \tag{34}$$

and

$$r(P_1, P_1 \cap P_2) + r(P_1 \cap P_2, P_2) = r(P_1, P_2) \tag{35}$$

Equation (34) says that r is additive along lattice lines, while Equation (35) formalizes a different type of additivity. Together Equations (34) and (35) ensure that $r(P_1, P_2)$ is the sum of the weights along a path from P_1 to P_2 in G_3 which "descends" from P_1 to $(P_1 \cap P_2)$ and then reascends to P_2. Such a path is schematically illustrated in Figure 2. This observation

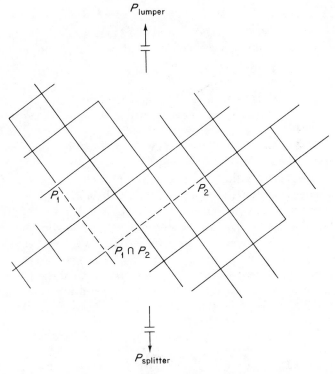

FIG. 2. Least-cost path from one partition to another with a height measure. The path – – – indicates one efficient transformation sequence from P_1 to P_2.

establishes that the W-induced cost distance from P_1 to P_2 in G_3 is bounded above by $r(P_1, P_2)$. Since the distance r is assumed to be a metric, however, the triangle inequality ensures us that the least-cost distance from P_1 to P_2 is bounded from the lower side by Equation (32). Thus, taking these two assertions together:

$$\text{induced cost distance}(P_1, P_2) \leq r(P_1, P_2) \leq \text{induced cost distance}(P_1, P_2)$$

$$(36)$$

and hence the induced cost distance in fact coincides with r.

This result, together with the additivity properties of r employed in its verification, conveys considerable information about the structure imposed by the height measures on $P(S)$. However, the argument depends strongly upon the assumption that the function g with which we started induces a *metric* r; otherwise, the least cost path defined by G_3 and Equation (33) will in general have *smaller* weighted length than the quantity r defined by Equation (32). The following result establishes a test for which g induce metrics r:

Criterion. A given nonnegative g which is monotonically increasing in the lattice ordering induces a metric by Equation (32) if and only if

$$g(P_1) + g(P_2) \leq g(P_1 \cup P_2) + g(P_1 \cap P_2) \tag{37}$$

where $(P_1 \cup P_2)$ is defined as on page 233. If equality holds in the expression for all P_1 and P_2, then g is termed a *valuation* in the nomenclature of lattice theory; a g satisfying the more general inequality is sometimes termed a *supervaluation*. Thus we have an interesting result concerning a certain family of metrics representable in G_3, namely, that g induces a metric by a generalization, Equation (32), of the law of cosines if and only if g is a supervaluation in the sense of lattice theory.

Just as the height measures can be represented in the MCF graph G_3, so normalized height measures can often be represented in the MCF graph G_4. Since G_3 is a subgraph of G_4, we derive less information from MCF representations of metrics in the latter graph. However, we can still employ such representations to derive relevant structural distance information. Thus, for example, in the case of the normalized entropy metric E, we may represent E in G_4 by weighting each segment $\overline{P_1P_2}$ by

$$W(\overline{P_1P_2}) = 1 - H(P_1)/H(P_2), \qquad \text{all } P_2 \text{ finer than } P_1. \tag{38}$$

Proof that the pair (G_4, W) actually induces E by the MCF principle is direct from the Equation (30) for E together with knowledge that E is a metric. The structure of E may be more easily comprehended if we analyze the expression $H(P_1)/H(P_2)$ in Equation (38), a kind of nonstandard relative entropy of P_1 given P_2. As P_2 stays fixed, the weight assigned to a move in the graph G_4 approaches a maximum of unity as $P_1 \rightarrow P_{\text{lumper}}$ in the lattice ordering. Thus "bigger" lattice jumps have greater weight. By further lattice analysis, it can be shown that distances are "expanded" toward the "north" of the partition lattice and "contracted" toward the "south" (i.e., the P_{splitter} region). While such a result reinforces our intuition of entropy-based metrics, it also strengthens the case for demoting such metrics to the status of any other group of partition metrics, embodying a specialized set of (often overlooked) implications which represent only one possible group of options. Various alternative height concepts underlying other measures (e.g., measure D) may also be used as a basis for many of the quantities customarily associated with the entropy-based theory of information. These considerations complement arguments raised by Mandelbrot (1966) and others which challenge the behavioral relevance of the uniqueness proofs for the entropy function. It is therefore conceivable that various alternative measures could serve better than entropy in many contexts.

Discussion

The present authors have written a FORTRAN IV program which, for partitions in numerical form, computes most of the measures described here as well as several others. This program was used by Anglin (1968) in a study of syntagmatic versus paradigmatic organization in word sorts. Different measures were computed from the same set of sorts. Anglin then used the Kruskal (1964) multidimensional scaling program to analyze the values derived from the different measures in order to obtain a separate configuration of subjects for each metric (with spatial locations determined by their sorting styles). These different configurations showed that, in this particular case, the pair bonds height measure was most expedient. One reason was that subjects who used a large number of clusters (cells) tended to use syntagmatic grouping, while those subjects who required a relatively small number of clusters were closer to the paradigmatic style. This means, of course, since all subjects were sorting the same group of words, that the cells for the latter subjects on the whole had higher cardinalities. As we pointed out earlier for the pair bonds measure D, the weighting for elements (i.e., words for Anglin's data) increases linearly with the cardinality of the cell containing a given element. Thus, this measure emphasizes (or magnifies) distances in the configuration between subjects using paradigmatic style and those using syntagmatic style. While some of the other measures considered also give greater weightings to elements in larger cells, the weightings in this case increase at a less rapid rate [e.g., a logarithmic rate for the multinomial measure defined by Equation (14)]. Hence these measures will not offer as great a separation between the two sorting styles as will the pair bonds measure.

While this type of argument has an admittedly post hoc flavor when applied to Anglin's pilot study, it is the first time, to our knowledge, that such comparisons between various metrics have been made. Although we are not attempting to formulate criteria as to which measure(s) should be used in a given study, we do believe that a better understanding of the mechanics of the various measures can help the investigator decide which is most useful in his experimental situation.

While the study of structural measures began in the context of the sorting paradigm, there is no reason why the derived concepts should be associated only with that particular use. For example, one extension of several of the measures to infinite underlying sets is being undertaken by the present authors. Concretely, let us consider a kinship system as based upon certain structural equivalences among a (generally infinite) number of possible kin terms. Viewing such equivalences as generating a partition of this set of terms, we may ask how different are two such partitions (and their underlying semantic systems). It turns out that under certain assumptions most of the height and normalized height measures admit natural and readily computable extensions to partitions of infinite S. These extended measures provide a tentative approach to the problem of metricizing spaces of generative grammars and related systems. Given such a method, it would then be possible to apply multidimensional scaling techniques to project such spaces into low-dimensional Minkowski spaces.

But perhaps all this gives too optimistic a picture. After all, our purpose is to "get closer" to some set of rules governing a semantic space. And it seems that the method of sorting is often used only by default: ". . . since there is no generally accepted method of analysis or established theory against which to validate such measures [of semantic similarity], it is not easy to see why one method of data collection should be preferred over the others" (Miller, 1967, p. 52). While it may well be the case that there is no a priori reason *not* to use sorting, experimenters who have used it provide very little evidence recommending its use. One of the more obvious aspects we should question is the consistency of sorting behavior. Miller (1969) has pointed to the Mandler and Pearlstone (1966) study of conceptual behavior in which subjects showed a considerable degree of consistency under constrained conditions (viz., the "free" subjects were presented sequentially 52 words and were limited to the range of two to seven cells).

Each subject was required to repeat the task until he had replicated his original sort, and 17 out of 40 subjects succeeded on the first trial. However, we still do not have any data obtained from replication of experiments in which the unconstrained method of sorting is used to study semantic similarity. The lack of such data constitutes a serious problem in designing and choosing measures of similarity. Presumably, we are looking for some kind of invariance in sorting behavior and a measure which will preserve that invariance. Since Shepard–Kruskal methods (which are likely to be used for analysis of output from the measures) are invariant up to a monotone transformation of the interpoint distances, there is no apparent reason why we should demand the "absolute invariance" (Stevens, 1959) which would result from perfect replications. But beyond this assertion, any further statement regarding invariance is sheer speculation. Our problem is that the method of sorting is being used to study hypothetical and very much undefined entities—semantic spaces. As a consequence, we can only guess as to the nature of the invariance which should hold for the rules governing a semantic space. In Anglin's particular study, a reasonable expectation would be that a replication of the experiment (using the same subjects) would result in a multidimensional scaling configuration of subjects quite similar to the previous one (at least for some partition measures). But as we stated earlier, such replications for semantic studies are never mentioned. From our orientation, this is a serious oversight, since the question of invariance is particularly relevant as a criterion for determining which structural measure(s) should be used to analyze discrepant sorts.

Another problem encountered in the use of sorting is in comparing and summarizing the results from different experiments. For many psychological studies, this problem is dealt with through the use of statistical distributions and measures of central tendency. But from semantic studies using the method of sorting, questions about "central tendency" cannot at present be asked, much less answered. There simply is no basic quantitative datum derived from sorting which is comparable between experiments, and hence there is no evidence that repetitions of experiments give results which converge on any particular finding. A somewhat similar problem that has often troubled psychophysicists is the large range of exponents in the power law (Stevens, 1957) for a given modality. A solution to this problem has recently been offered by Stevens (1969). Using the extensive data on loudness from Moskowitz (1969), Stevens notes that there is a reassuringly unimodal distribution (which appears to be approximately normal for the Moskowitz data). This solution, of course, involves many replications of the experiment, with emphasis upon holding as many relevant factors constant as is possible from experiment to experiment. The analogous procedure for the sorting paradigm would entail as a minimum the same set of words for each trial. But if the same words were used for many replications, it is questionable whether the payoff is worth the effort. At best, we would have reliable information about a very, very small part of the semantic space.

It is apparent that there are no ready answers for the problems posed by invariance and replicability. Furthermore, there are still many questions unanswered as to which structural measure should be used for the data from a particular experiment. It is perhaps a consequence of the deceptive simplicity of the method of sorting that so many of its problematic aspects have remained unexamined.

Acknowledgments

We are most indebted to Professor David V. Cross of the Harvard Psychology Department for his criticism and suggestions. In addition we would like to thank Dr. François Lorrain, Dr. Stephen Johnson, the late Professor David Pavy, and Professors Donald C. Olivier and A. Kimball Romney.

Preparation of the manuscript was supported in part by National Science Foundation Grant GS–2689, Principal Investigator: Harrison C. White.

References

Abelson, R. P., and Rosenberg, M. J. Symbolic psycho-logic: A model of attitudinal cognition. *Behavioral Science*, 1958, **3**, 1–13.

Anglin, J. M. Notes toward the application section. Unpublished, Harvard University, 1968.

Attneave, F. Dimensions of similarity. *American Journal of Psychology*, 1950, **63**, 516–556.

Birkhoff, G. *Lattice theory*. (Revised ed.) Providence, Rhode Island: American Mathematical Society, 1967.

Boyd, J. P. Information distances for discrete structures. Present volume.

Burton, M. Semantic dimensions of occupation names. This book, Volume II.

Flament, C. *Applications of graph theory to group structure*. Englewood Cliffs, New Jersey: Prentice–Hall, 1963.

Ford, L. R., Jr., & Fulkerson, D. R. *Flows in networks*. Princeton, New Jersey: Princeton University Press, 1962.

Galanter, E. An axiomatic and experimental study of sensory order and measure. *Psychological Review*, 1956, **63**, 16–28.

Goodman, N. *The structure of appearance*. Indianapolis, Indiana: Bobbs–Merrill, 1951.

Goodman, N. *The structure of appearance*. (2nd ed.) Indianapolis, Indiana: Bobbs–Merrill, 1966.

Johnson, S. C. Hierarchical clustering schemes. *Psychometrika*, 1967, **32**, 241–254.

Johnson, S. C. Metric clustering. Unpublished, Bell Laboratories, Incorporated, 1968.

Kendall, M. G. *Rank correlation methods*. New York: Hafner, 1962.

Kotz, S. Recent results in information theory. *Journal of Applied Probability*, 1966, **3**, 1–93.

Kruskal, J. B. Multidimensional scaling by optimizing goodness of fit to a nonmetric hypothesis. *Psychometrika*, 1964, **29**, 1–27.

Landahl, H. D. Neural mechanisms for the concepts of difference and similarity. *Bulletin of Mathematical Biophysics*, 1945, **7**, 83–88.

Mandelbrot, B. Information theory and psycholinguistics: A theory of word frequencies. In P. F. Lazarsfeld and N. W. Henry (Eds.), *Readings in mathematical social science*. Chicago, Illinois: Science Research Associates, 1966. Pp. 350–368.

Mandler, G., & Pearlstone, Z. Free and constrained concept learning and subsequent recall. *Journal of Learning and Verbal Behavior*, 1966, **5**, 126–131.

Marczewski, E., & Steinhaus, H. On a certain distance of sets and the corresponding distance of functions. *Colloquium Mathematicum*, 1958, **6**, 319–327.

Miller, G. A. Free recall of redundant strings of letters. *Journal of Experimental Psychology*, 1958, **56**, 485–491.

Miller, G. A. Psycholinguistic approaches to the study of communication. In D. L. Arm (Ed.), *Journeys in science: Small steps—great strides*. Albuquerque, New Mexico: The University of New Mexico Press, 1967. Pp. 22–73.

Miller, G. A. A psychological method to investigate verbal concepts. *Journal of Mathematical Psychology*, 1969, **6**, 169–191.

Moskowitz, H. R. Scales of intensity for single and compound tastes. Unpublished doctoral dissertation, Harvard University, 1969.

Rajski, C. A metric space of discrete probability distributions. *Information and Control*, 1961, **4**, 371–377.

Rajski, C. On the normed information rate of discrete random variables. *Transactions of the Third Prague Conference on Information Theory, Statistical Decision Functions, and Random Processes*. Prague: Czechoslovak Acad. Sci., 1964. Pp. 583–585.

Rapoport, A., & Fillenbaum, S. An experimental study of semantic structures. This book, Volume II.

Restle, F. A metric and an ordering on sets. *Psychometrika*, 1959, **24**, 207–220.

Restle, F. *Psychology of judgment and choice, a theoretical essay*. New York: Wiley, 1961.

Riordan, J. *An introduction to combinatorial mathematics*. New York: Wiley, 1958.

Rota, G. The number of partitions of a set. *American Mathematical Monthly*, 1964, **71**, 498–504.

Rubin, J. Optimal classification into groups: An approach for solving the taxonomy problem. *Journal of Theoretical Biology*, 1967, **15**, 103–144.

Shipstone, E. I. Some variables affecting pattern conception. *Psychological Monographs*, 1960, **74**, 1–40.

Stevens, S. S. On the psychophysical law. *Psychological Review*, 1957, **64**, 153–181.

Stevens, S. S. Measurement, psychophysics, and utility. In C. W. Churchman and P. Ratoosh (Eds.), *Measurement: Definitions and theories*. New York: Wiley, 1959. Pp. 18–63.

Stevens, S. S. On predicting exponents for cross-modality matches. *Perception & Psychophysics*, 1969, **6**, 251–256.

Suppes, P. *Introduction to logic*. Princeton, New Jersey: Van Nostrand–Reinhold, 1957.

AUTHOR INDEX

Numbers in italics refer to the page on which the complete reference is listed.

Subject Index

Boldface numbers indicate particularly important or extensive treatments of the indicated subjects.

A

Additivity, **7**, 39, 64, 195, 204, 243–244, *see also* Conjoint measurement
Adjacency matrix, 62, 235
Affine transformation, 16, 42, *see also* Linear transformation
Algebraic models, 17, **215**
Analysis of proximities (Shepard), 8, 22, 34, 53, 70
Analysis of variance, **39, 77,** *see also* Variance
Anthropology, applications in, 18, 218
Applications of multidimensional scaling, 15, **18**, 107, 111*ff*., 127–128, 138*ff*., 153, 157*ff*., 194*ff*., 218, 232, 235, 237, 245*ff*.
Arbitrariness of reference axes, **10, 14,** 107, **169**
Association data, *see* Proximity data
Axes, *see* Arbitrariness of reference axes, Interpretation of spatial representations, Nonorthogonal axes, Rotation

B

Bell Telephone Laboratories, **5,** 13, 14, 23, 43
Betweenness, 195
Binary data, 60–61

Boolean lattice metric, 233
Brightness, *see* Perception

C

Canonical decomposition, **109**
Canonical reference frame, *see* Rotation
Cardinality of a set, 233*ff*., 245
Cartesian product, 16, **200,** 217, 219
Categorical data, 39, 50, **60***ff*., 63
Cell, in a partition, 17, **229***ff*.
Characteristic roots and vectors, 34, 36, 126, 133, 181–182.
Choice models, **79,** 101
Circular tones (Shepard), 197
Circumplex (Guttman), 16, 56, **197***ff*., 203
City-block metric, 9, 52, 53, 72, 76, 101, 236
Classical multidimensional scaling (Torgerson), 5, 8, **33,** 165
Clustering, subject-produced, 106, **225***ff*.
Clusters as aid to spatial representation interpretation, 3, 16, **40–42,** 106, 168–169, 172, 179*ff*., 196, 206
Clustering methods, 7, 15, **35, 38,** 40, 62, 106, **164,** 179*ff*., 226, 237, *see also* Hierarchical clustering
Coefficient
   of alienation, 53
   of contiguity, 61

255

T

Taste, *see* Perception of, Tea-tasting data
Taxonomy, *see also* Tree structures
  of methods of analysis, 18, 33*ff.*
  of types of data, 23*ff.*
Teachers' ratings, *see* Education, applications in
Tea-tasting data (Carroll), 111*ff.*, 138*ff.*
Telephone circuits
  judgment of sound quality, 128
Termination of iterative process, **99**, 138
Three-way tables and multiple matrices, **25**, **27**, 29, 35, 106, 109, **113**, **128**
Ties in the data, 53, 97
Time series data, 65
Topological properties, 148, 194, 208, 216
Transformation
  of a configuration, *see* Affine transformation, Linear transformation, Orthogonal transformation or rotation, Similarity transformation, Stereographic projection
  monotone or order preserving, 33, **52***ff.*, **84**, 247
  of two configurations into mutual best fit, 9, **42**, 51, 170
Transition systems (Boyd), **217***ff.*
Transitivity, **26**, 36, 216, 235
Tree structures, **35**, 164, 206, 215
Triads, method of (Torgerson), 26, 165
Triangle inequality, *see* Metric axioms

Triangular decomposition (Boyd), **217***ff.*, 221–222

U

Ultrametric distances, 35
Uncertainty measures, *see* Information-theoretic measures
Unfolding models, **6**, **7**, **29***ff.*, 57, 58, 60, 76, 114, **116***ff.*, 118, **129***ff.*, **148**, 153
Unidimensional scales, 1, 15, 16, **26**, 28, 35, 41, 65, 116, 160–161, **173***ff.*, 176, **195**, 247
Union of partitions, 233
Uniqueness of spatial representations, 6, 14, 15, **42**, 107

V

Variance, 39, 55, 77, 82, 140, 150, 175
Variance–covariance matrix, *see* Covariance matrix
Vector models, **27**, 41, 54, **114***ff.*, 117, **123**, 127, 136, 144, 169, 205
Visualizability of spatial representation, **1**, 9, **10**, 36–37, 42–43, 165, 173, 196, **208**

W

Weber's law, 236
Weighting of dimensions, **14**, 34, **107**, 115, **118***ff.*, **131***ff.*, 136, 150, 173